Comparing Cowboys
and Frontiers

Comparing Cowboys
and Frontiers

By Richard W. Slatta

University of Oklahoma Press : Norman and London

By Richard W. Slatta

Gauchos and the Vanishing Frontier (Lincoln, Nebr., 1983)
Bandidos: The Varieties of Latin American Banditry (Westport, Conn., 1987)
Cowboys of the Americas (New Haven, 1990)
The Cowboy Encyclopedia (Santa Barbara, 1994)
Comparing Cowboys and Frontiers (Norman, 1997)

This book is published with the generous assistance of The McCasland
Foundation, Duncan, Oklahoma.

Library of Congress Cataloging-in-Publication Data

Slatta, Richard W., 1947–
    Comparing cowboys and frontiers / by Richard W. Slatta.
        p.   cm.
    Includes bibliographical references and index.
    ISBN 0-8061-2971-9 (alk. paper)
    1. Frontier and pioneer life—America—Cross-cultural studies. 2.
Frontier and pioneer life—West (U.S.) 3. America—Historiography. 4.
America—History—Methodology. 5. Frontier thesis. I. Title
    E20.S55   1997
    970—dc21   97-1759
                                                                    CIP

Text design by Cathy Carney Imboden. Text set in Berkeley Oldstyle
Medium.

The paper in this book meets the guidelines for permanence and durability
of the Committee on Production Guidelines for Book Longevity of the
Council on Library Resources, Inc. ∞

In loving memory of my aunt,
Eleanor V. Solberg Caswell,
1914–1994

Contents

Illustrations

Maps

Preface

History is full of the unique and the particular. Like snow-flakes, no two individuals or events are identical. Nonetheless we constantly make comparisons—we compare wines, restaurants, beaches, detergents. We also make comparisons in history—and with good reason. Comparative studies do not seek identical, repeated events. Comparisons, rather, illuminate why and how historical similarities and differences arise.

This volume should serve historians of the American West as a guidebook in comparative research and as a text for classes in comparative frontier history. These broad-ranging essays are meant to be suggestive and illustrative, not definitive. They compare geography, American Indian culture, cowboys, frontier institutions, historiography, and sources. Researchers working on Latin American and to a lesser degree Canadian topics will also find avenues of comparison with the western United States.

I am certainly not the first historian in recent memory to urge the comparative study of frontiers. Herbert Eugene Bolton urged comparative frontier study in his 1933 essay "The Epic of Greater America," published in the *American Historical Review*. The 1950s witnessed major contributions to comparative frontier history. In 1951 Walter Prescott Webb published his provocative, sweeping examination of *The Great Frontier*. Dietrich Gerhard and Paul F. Sharp published essays on comparative frontiers. Owen Lattimore, Walker D. Wyman, and Clifton B. Kroeber published collections of comparative essays.[1]

Over the years the University of Oklahoma Press has played the leading role in publishing comparative works. In 1977 Oklahoma published *The Frontier: Comparative Studies, Volume 1*, edited by David Harry Miller and Jerome O. Steffen. Two years later came *The Frontier: Comparative Studies, Volume 2*, edited by William W. Savage, Jr., and Stephen I. Thompson. Essays ranged from early medieval Italy to South Africa to the American West. I strongly recommend the introductory essay by Savage and Thompson, an extensive discussion of the various approaches to comparative frontier history. In 1980 Oklahoma published Jerome O. Steffen's *Comparative Frontiers: A Proposal for Studying the American West*. Steffen limited his comparisons, however, to topics within the American West. He examined the agricultural, fur trade, ranching, and mining frontiers.

In 1981 Howard Lamar and Leonard Thompson edited a collection of essays that provided international comparisons: *The Frontier in History: North America and South Africa Compared*. A year later Donald Denoon examined *Settler Capitalism: The Dynamics of Dependent Development in the Southern Hemisphere*. In 1985 D. C. M. Platt and Guido di Tella edited studies on *Argentina, Australia, and Canada: Studies in Comparative Development, 1870–1965*. In 1991 William G. Robbins and Walter Nugent reiterated the call for comparative analysis of frontiers.[2]

In October 1981 I presented a paper comparing "Argentine Gauchos and Great Plains Cowboys" at the Western History Association conference in San Antonio, Texas. Since that time

I have continued to examine commonalities and differences among the frontier regions of North and South America. *Comparing Cowboys and Frontiers* builds on my previous work in comparative frontier history and on those books noted above.

I take the Western Hemisphere as my unit of analysis. In his 1983 presidential address to the American Historical Association, Philip D. Curtain issued a clear call for the comparative study of the Americas. Walter Nugent and Richard Maxwell Brown have provided stimulating examples of the interpretive power of broad comparative analysis. The promulgation and likely extension of NAFTA (North American Free Trade Agreement) add important political and economic motivations for hemispheric study.[3]

Part One of *Comparing Cowboys and Frontiers* presents several examples of comparative historical study spanning the length of the Americas. These studies are arranged chronologically, taking the reader from precontact and colonial times through the late nineteenth century. Part Two of the volume provides concrete examples of methods, techniques, and historiographical debates that arise in doing comparative frontier history. Broad comparisons necessarily sacrifice some of the detail and nuance important to historical work. One gains, however, a fresh perspective that may illuminate larger issues and ultimately challenge assumptions built on historiographies that may have been too narrow or nationalistic. If these essays inspire other researchers to expand their horizons and to place their own work within a broader, comparative framework, the volume will have achieved its goal.

Acknowledgments

I began work on some of these essays two decades ago, so I have many helpful friends and mentors to thank. At the University of Texas at Austin, the late Thomas F. McGann, the late Joe B. Frantz, Harley C. Browning, and Richard Graham provided solid historical training and strong professional support. More recent discussions with Tom Hall, Tom Sheridan, John David Smith, and other scholars have sparked new questions and ideas.

Michael R. Mitzel merits acknowledgment for making the maps.

I conducted comparative research in the United States, Venezuela, Canada, and Argentina for my book *Cowboys of the Americas* (Yale University Press, 1990). That work helped me greatly in developing this volume. Some of these essays have been published before, as I have noted at the start of each chapter's endnotes. I have updated references in the notes and bibliography to include more recent scholarship. Reid Slaughter, Robert Hartman, and Charlotte Berney at *Cowboys & Indians* magazine merit special praise for providing a high-quality format for popular articles on western culture and history. Finally, thanks to Patricia Nelson Limerick and her colleagues at the University of Colorado for hosting a

xvi \ Acknowledgments

stimulating comparative frontiers conference in April 1995.
Discussions at that Rumours and Borders conference in
Boulder prompted me to publish this book.

Part One

Topics

Chapter 1

Historical Frontier Imagery
in Canada, the United States,
and Latin America

In this chapter I describe the historical development of positive and negative images associated with plains frontier regions throughout the Americas. Examples are drawn principally from cattle frontiers of the American West, northern Mexico, the Canadian province of Alberta, the Venezuelan llanos, Argentine pampas, Brazilian sertão, and southern Chile. Without reducing history to environmental determinism, we can assert that the physical setting of a frontier region plays a major role in shaping the human activities that take place there. Students of the American West may be surprised to find that many Latin American frontiers elicited imagery that is strongly reminiscent of Frederick Jackson Turner's frontier thesis.

The literature about the frontier in the United States is as extensive as it is pervasive. Since Frederick Jackson Turner presented his frontier thesis in 1893, the frontier has become a dominant interpretive theme and political symbol. Over the decades, the definitions and role of the frontier have been debated and revised. Turner's frontier thesis has also been taken out of the North American context for comparative testing elsewhere.[1]

The role of the frontier has preoccupied thinkers in both North and South America. We find important roles and

Branding, southern Alberta (Glenbow Archives, Calgary, Alberta, N

Theodore Roosevelt (shown at his Dakota ranch in 1885) played a role in shaping images of the American West. (Theodore Roosevelt Collection, Harvard College Library)

First Calgary Stampede held in 1912. Frontier imagery remains important in western Canada. (Glenbow Archives, Calgary, Alberta, NA-335-43)

images, often influenced by or consistent with Turner's formulation, assigned to frontiers throughout the Americas.[2]

Frontier definitions are as abundant as they are vague. Is a frontier a place, a process, or both? Do frontier forces modify or override the "germs" of European culture carried across the Atlantic? Do we categorize frontiers by types of economic activity, such as mining, ranching, and farming? In describing Brazilian frontiers, for example, Martin T. Katzman combines geographical and economic categories—the São Paulo coffee frontier and the Amazon rubber frontier. The term as used in Europe, from the Latin *fronteria*, indicated a national boundary. Usage in the United States through most of the nineteenth century followed that definition. By the late nineteenth century, however, one dictionary defined a *frontiersman* as someone living "beyond the limits of a settled or civilized region." Similar definitional differences arise in Latin America.[3]

The Great Plains from Mexico to Canada

Mexico's ranching frontier began during the 1530s in the central valleys and plains of Querétaro, Michoacán, and Guanajuato. Some ranches began with grants of Indian labor (*encomiendas*) or lands given to the conquerors who accompanied Hernán Cortés in his invasion of the Aztec capital in 1521. Livestock became a significant element of conquest against the fierce Chichimec tribes of northern Mexico. Spanish soldiers drove livestock with them. Mission and presidio sites raised livestock for food and transportation. Wild and domesticated cattle thrived in the arid plains of San Luis Potosí, Sinaloa, and Zacatecas, where the craggy Sierra Madre crisscrossed the countryside. From the mid-sixteenth century on, the heavy demand for animals from a silver mining boom fueled northern plains ranching.[4]

Cowboys of South America

Raising cattle in northern Mexico required extensive grazing areas because the native grasses were sparse and less nourishing there than on the bountiful pampas of Argentina, for example. Water could also be scarce, especially during hot summer months when thirsty cattle strayed widely. But aside from the construction of natural fences out of cactus to protect farmlands, the landscape was little changed by humans. The harsh environment, combined with the Spanish cultural values and legal bias, contributed to the growth of large estates in northern New Spain. Great livestock haciendas came to dominate Chihuahua, Coahuila, Durango, and Tamaulipas, and they persisted into the twentieth century[5]

Across the Río Grande, the mountains gradually became the humid, level coastal plain along the Gulf of Mexico to the east and the brush country of south Texas. Traveling north and west of the brush country, one ascended onto the high, dry plains (the Llano Estacado) of west Texas and the Texas and Oklahoma Panhandles. During his explorations in 1541, Francisco Vásquez de Coronado described the lands that became Arizona and New Mexico as "these deserts." Desert imagery would remain associated with much of the Great Plains.[6]

The Rockies were a mighty barrier along the western flank of the Great Plains all the way from Texas to Canada. The American Great Plains, better watered than northern Mexico, provided good grasses and a greater variety of plant life. On the hot southern plains, ranchers learned to use river valleys for precious water and as protection for humans and livestock against occasional freezing "blue northers" that swept down from Canada.[7]

In southern Wyoming the plains change character and climate. The northern plains gave rise to the myth of the "Great American Desert," where early settlers feared that livestock could never winter. But the dry winters cured the grass, and livestock proved capable of surviving all but the harshest winter weather. As the desert myth faded, cattle ranchers and then sheepherders and farmers forged westward across the ninety-eighth meridian. Periodic mineral strikes also spurred bursts of migration westward.[8]

Cattle ranching in western Canada began in the Fraser River valley of British Columbia when Americans trailed herds up the Okanagan Trail from Oregon to the mining areas of the Fraser in the 1860s. Ranching declined thereafter except for brief market spurts fueled by the Canadian Pacific Railway in 1883 and the Klondike gold strike of 1898. The foothills and plains east of the Rockies in Alberta eventually became the great open-range ranching area of Canada.[9]

Crossing the Canadian border in eastern Montana takes one into the Cypress Hills on the Saskatchewa-Alberta boundary. This heavily wooded region offered adequate water, with rainfall of fifteen to nineteen inches a year and such sizable rivers as the White Mud and Strong Current Creek. Coulees, or narrow valleys, gave protection here as they did in the American Southwest. According to John Macoun, writing in 1882, the best prairie pastures were "those near Turtle Mountain, Moose Mountain, Wood Mountain, the Cypress Hills, the valley of the South Saskatchewan and its tributaries, Tail Creek, and along the eastern base of the mountains for forty miles north of Bow River."[10]

Moving west along the forty-ninth parallel, the hills flatten into the famed "short grass country" of northern Montana and southern Alberta. "Prairie wool," a nutritious blend of blue grama, June, spear, bluejoint, and other grasses, provided ample winter feed for cattle. Warm, dry Chinook winds would melt away winter snow and cure the grasses on the stalk. Before their near extermination in the 1870s, buffalo grazed all winter on these grasses. Ranchers assumed that cattle could also forage the plains and survive the winter.[11]

Alberta ranchers also occupied the foothills on the eastern slope of the Canadian Rockies, from the Montana border to the Red Deer River. Mary Ella Inderwick, a rancher's wife, described the countryside near the North Fork Ranch in a letter written in 1884: "We are in the foothills—no plains here—but the most glorious ranges of hills and rolling prairie—which all seems so near that one starts to ride to a certain land mark but finds oneself still no nearer at the end of an hour." She reported being able to see rooftops twenty-two miles away.[12]

Like most frontiers, the Great Plains generated contradictory portrayals. Images of the plains as a Garden of Eden coexist with descriptions of the "Great American Desert." In general, the desert image arose because of the West's sparse population and lack of "civilization." But the term also held climatic significance. Walter Prescott Webb aroused a storm of controversy by asserting that "the heart of the West is a desert, unqualified and absolute." Webb continued, "Once we recognize the desert as the major force in the American West, we are able to understand its history." The dry Southwest had stood as a barrier to Spanish expansion for centuries. The ninety-eighth meridian was for decades an invisible but ominous barrier to the occupation and settlement of the West.[13]

Western Canada also developed a reputation as a desert or wasteland. Henry Youle Hind and John Palliser both mounted expeditions to explore the Canadian West in 1857. Their reports fostered the negative desert images. Hind first applied the name "Great American Desert" to the Canadian prairies, and Palliser's reports later reinforced the image. Because of the lack of rainfall, conventional wisdom held that the prairies of southern Saskatchewan and Alberta could not be farmed. A huge area, called "Palliser's Triangle," was thought to be unsuitable for settlement. The region was bounded on the east by the Souris River in the Turtle Mountains and on the south by the forty-ninth parallel. It extended westward to Calgary and north to Saskatoon. Ironically, both men also stressed the fertility of large areas, but it was the desert imagery that stuck.[14]

In his report of 1882 John Macoun flatly asserted that the Cypress Hills were unsuitable for agriculture. Ranchers with large holdings used the same argument to fend off the subdivision of their lands for farming. Only the great fear of American expansionism from the south pushed the Canadian government to survey its uninviting plains territories.[15] (Chilean migration into Patagonia likewise spurred Argentine concern with populating its far southern frontier.)

But garden myths accompanied these desert images. The boosterism, optimism, and expansionism that pervaded the American West also invaded western Canada. A glowing countermyth to Palliser's Triangle quickly developed. Utopian poetry and prose lauded the richness and opportunity that awaited immigrants to the region. An 1883 pamphlet described the "nice prairie, covered with beautiful grass, and dotted here and there with little poplar forests which gives the whole a very romantic appearance." The settlers, continued the pamphlet, "look forward to a very happy and contented future." Such idealized descriptions convinced many. In the early twentieth century, thousands of American dryland farmers turned their ambitions and energies northward to the "Last Best West"—the Canadian prairies.[16]

Unfortunately for the optimistic new settlers, the image of the Canadian prairie utopia shattered as quickly as it arose. Beset by the harsh realities of chilling winters and inconstant rainfall, prairie farmers faced ruin. By World War I the great dryland farming boom had bust. Thousands of disillusioned homesteaders returned to the United States. Palliser's desert seemed to have gained its revenge. Not until the later development of suitable irrigation technology was the desert finally overcome, in myth and reality. Today wheat farming is big business on these Canadian prairies.[17]

In *Wolf Willow*, Wallace Stegner captures the essence of such frontier regions: "Frontiers are lines where one body of law stops and another body of law begins. Partly by reason of that difference of basic law, and from the moment the boundary is drawn, they also become lines of cultural division as real for many kinds of human activity as the ecological boundaries between woods and plains, plains and mountains, or mountains and deserts. Likewise they have their inevitable corollaries. They create their own varieties of lawbreakers, smugglers particularly, and they provide for the guilty and the hunted the institution of sanctuary."[18] In such plains frontiers, the cowboys of the Americas lived, worked, played, and died.

The Llanos of Venezuela

The llanos are tropical plains crisscrossed by many rivers and shrouded by forests of dense trees and shrubs (*matas*). The prevalence of trees, which are almost always within sight, stands in marked contrast to the vegetation on the Argentine pampas and the American Great Plains. The llanos spill across the Venezuela-Colombia border and are bounded on the north and west by the Andes and on the south by the Amazon jungle. Depending on the definition used, the llanos of Venezuela cover between 237,000 and 300,000 square kilometers, or up to 30 percent of the nation's territory.[19]

Two seasons, a dry summer (*verano*, October–March) and a rainy winter (*invierno*, April–September), divide life in the region. These seasons are extreme and inhospitable. Drought conditions, high temperatures, and no rain alternate with torrential downpours and mass flooding. The llanos of Venezuela average about forty-seven inches of rainfall per year, but it all falls within a six-month period. Some areas, such as Guanare and occasionally Barinas, receive nearly seventy-nine inches of rainfall annually. Subregional variations exist within the llanos, but the livestock industry developed throughout the tropical plains.[20]

The tropical climate of the llanos made infection and disease constant threats to riders and their animals. Travelers found themselves under constant attack by what Karl Sachs, a German physician, termed "monstrous armies of insects." He found that "the feeling of solitude and forlornness that in these desert plains overwhelms the traveler who moves completely alone, is difficult to paint." The many rivers held their own dangers. Voracious piranhas, large crocodiles, and electric eels inhabited the tropical streams.[21]

The foreboding, fascinating plains of Venezuela hold an important position in the nation's economic and political history. They served as the site of the colonial livestock industry and as an important battleground during the war of independence and subsequent civil wars. As birthplace of prominent *caudillos* (regional military chieftains), such as José Antonio Páez, the llanos helped shape Venezuela's political destiny. But despite their historical significance, the tropical plains and their inhabitants remain enigmas in Venezuelan historiography. Few substantial studies exist of the horsemen, the cattle ranches (*hatos*), or the geopolitical and economic development of the llanos.[22]

Images of the llanos, as "garden" and "desert," were contradictory. Despite vastly different climates and natural features, perceptions of the Venezuelan llanos have been very similar to those of the Argentine pampas. Writing in 1875, Manuel Tejera painted a glowing portrait of the llanos, "the immense plains where, without any work by man, livestock multiply, grazing on the abundant grass." He waxed eloquent over the region's "picturesque variety of plants," the "majestic silence of the forests," and the "prodigious vegetation." Some believed that the natural bounty of the llanos, as on the pampas of Argentina, killed initiative by permitting a comfortable life without toil.[23]

Many observers held fast to the vision of the under-populated llanos as the key to Venezuela's future greatness. Agustín Codazzi, a French geographer, estimated in 1841 that the llanos, with only 390,000 people, could support a population of six million. About three decades later, Luis Alfonso (an apologist for Antonio Guzmán Blanco, who ruled intermittently as dictator of Venezuela from 1870 to 1888) stressed that because of "the fertility of the land, its vast extension, varied climates" and other advantages, Venezuela needed only capital, roads, and labor to prosper.[24]

The plains frontier of Venezuela gave rise to an important novel about civilization and barbarism, *Doña Bárbara*. Rómulo Gallegos makes the battle between these forces the central motif of this powerful work, in which a handsome young gentleman from the city, Santos Luzardo, confronts the powerful, bewitching mistress of the Venezuelan llanos, Doña Bárbara. Civilization triumphs over barbarism, but at the cost of revealing the close ties between the two. Like most other Latin American writers, Gallegos presents a frontier of wild, dangerous, powerful forces that must ultimately succumb to civilizing influences.[25]

The role of the llanos in Venezuela's political and military history constitutes yet another element of the region's negative image. Fierce llanero cavalrymen turned the tide of battle against the royalists during the savage independence wars. Thereafter, the llanos continued to serve as the theater of countless military engagements as ambitious caudillos erupted from the llanos to keep Venezuela in turmoil. To Venezuelans, the llanos came to represent political disruption and anarchy. As the writer and geographer Antonio Arraiz mused cryptically, "the llano is the enemy and the explanation of Venezuela."[26]

In contrast, other politicians and thinkers conceived of the llanos as bleak, backward, unchanging, and unchangeable. They emphasized the vile, extreme climate, unhealthy for humans and beasts. The region suffered from repeated, devastating epidemics. Periodically, wet-season rains exceeded the norm and flooded vast stretches of the llanos. Gallegos, whose writings strongly molded Venezuelan perceptions of the llanos, found many negative elements in the plains. But in his romantic optimism, he hoped that the obstacles could be overcome. In *Cantaclaro*, his novel published in 1934, he has a dying man utter the following lament: "But we're in a completely savage desert! The desert! The enemy against which we should first fight! The cause of all our problems."[27]

The closing of plains frontiers in Latin America came for widely different reasons. Ranching declined precipitously on the llanos of Colombia and Venezuela during the independence and civil wars lasting from 1810 through the 1850s. Generalized political violence decimated herds, drained the labor pool, and interrupted market routes. Shorter-lived disruptions hit Chile and Uruguay. Similarly, northern Mexico's ranching frontier was shattered by the violent revolution that swept the nation from 1910 to 1920.[28]

The llanos of Colombia and Venezuela had begun experiencing Spanish exploration by the mid-sixteenth century. Cattle raising and the expansion of missions to convert the Indians quickly followed. For a variety of reasons, the llanos remained a "static, permanent" frontier into the twentieth century. The region experienced little of the modernizing changes that altered the livestock industries of Argentina, Canada, and the United States. But despite the persistence of a traditional cattle frontier over centuries, llanos imagery has less significance in Venezuelan and Colombian national life than the western cowboy does in the United States.[29]

Chile's Far Southern Frontier

Chile, wedged tightly between the towering Andes to the east and the vast Pacific Ocean to the west, did not enjoy the wide expanses of open range available in the Río de la Plata. Suitable grasslands for livestock existed in the central valley of Chile, near Santiago. Agricultural food production and grazing developed side by side in the fertile central valley. Chile's frontier extended to the south, encompassing some 40,000 square kilometers between the Bío Bío and Tolten Rivers. Today the area includes the provinces of Arauco, Bío Bío, Malleco, and Cautín. But the Spanish military faced stiff, successful opposition from Araucanian Indians. The southern frontier in Chile could not be opened to European settlement until nearly the twentieth century. This long period required to subdue the Indians generated a frontier ambience of violence, brutal repression, coercion, and disrespect for law.[30]

The independence wars that swept Chile in 1817 and 1818 had similar negative effects. Livestock and agricultural production suffered particularly in the southern part of the nation. Livestock production during the 1820s fell to less than half of what it had been during the first decade of the century. Taking advantage of the turmoil, Indians in the south pushed the frontier of European settlement back toward the north. Like llaneros, Chile's cowboys (*huasos*) found themselves fighting as cavalrymen rather than working on ranches.[31]

As in Argentina, elites in Chile viewed their land as perhaps overly abundant. Landowners complained that the benign climate and fertile land permitted the shiftless rural population to subsist with little or no labor. To the jaundiced elite eye, the rural poor enjoyed a secure life of fiestas and merriment. Supposedly they worked only long enough to earn a few coins to be squandered at the next celebration.[32]

Little rancher-farmer conflict occurred in Chile. Agriculture had always coexisted with ranching in the fertile central valley around the capital because a few wealthy landowners controlled both grazing and farmlands. Sharecroppers worked the land, supplemented by migrant labor during the harvest and roundup seasons.[33]

The history and imagery of Chile's southern frontier are much like those of the Argentine pampas. Both Argentines and Chileans faced indigenous populations too strong militarily to be defeated and dislodged until the late nineteenth century. The white perception of the frontier as a savage, barbarous region derived in part from the continued presence of these so-called savages. The Araucanians held fast to the lands south of the Bío Bío River. They launched devastating attacks on white and mestizo settlements well into the nineteenth century; Chilean officials conceded the south to them until nearly the twentieth century. Official policy encouraged Chile's growing landless labor surplus to cross the Andes and settle in the vacant lands of Argentina's Patagonia.[34]

In Chile, European immigration is closely tied to the expansion of agriculture. Chilean elites looked down on the native rural population, which leaders worked assiduously to replace with "superior" immigrant blood. Chilean officials even evicted Chilean squatters in order to give the land over to immigrants. As a result of such policies, rural landless Chileans ended up working for foreigners in the countryside. Southern Chile became a virtual German colony during the late nineteenth century. Marginalized ranch workers and other landless Chileans migrated to Patagonia. Ironically, Chile's discrimination against its rural poor spurred Chilean settlement of this southern Argentine frontier.[35]

Chile's landed elite nurtured great hopes that European immigrants would improve the nation racially and culturally. The nation's elite deprecated the abilities of natives (*criollos*). Chile succeeded in attracting substantial numbers of German immigrants to the southern frontier, where they prospered as farmers and sheep ranchers, although immigration did not insure national greatness on either side of the Andes.[36]

Pampas of Argentina

The pampas of the Río de la Plata are probably the world's richest natural grazing lands. A temperate climate and adequate, but not excessive, rainfall contribute to a near ideal environment for livestock. Ranging from flat to gently rolling, the pampas stretch nearly unbroken by hills for several hundreds of miles from the Atlantic Ocean inland. Only two ranges of hills, one in southern Buenos Aires Province and another in Córdoba Province, interrupt the vast grasslands. These rich prairies continue northward across the Río de la Plata into Uruguay and on into the *campanha* of Rio Grande do Sul, Brazil's southernmost state.

Unlike the llanos, the pampas were nearly treeless, a condition that may have been natural or was created by the indigenous Indian tribes. Upon their arrival, Spaniards found only occasional, twisted *ombú* trees. Tall, coarse grasses, thistles, wildflowers, and, in swampy areas (called *pajonales*), low shrubs covered the plains. The spongy ombú is worthless as lumber or firewood. Europeans planted fruit, eucalyptus, and other usable trees that gradually changed the physiography of the pampas. But the rich, natural pastures remained the mainstay of ranching until the advent of alfalfa, wheat, and corn farming in the latter half of the nineteenth century.[37]

The Argentine thinker Ezequiel Martínez Estrada believed in the tellurical power of the pampas. He expresses the mystical forces of the plains in his brooding, masterful, existential *X-Ray of the Pampa*:

> The vastness of the horizon, which always looks the same as we advance, as if the whole plain moved along with us, gives one the impression of something illusory in this rude reality of open country. Here prairie is expanse, and expanse seems to be nothing more than the unfolding of the infinite within, a colloquy of the traveler with God. Only the knowledge that one is traveling, fatigue, and the longing to arrive gives scale to this expanse seemingly without measure. It is the pampa, the land where man is alone, like an abstract being, that will begin anew the story of the species—or conclude it.[38]

The pampas of the Río de la Plata stood as a hostile, forbidding barrier to European settlement. Spaniards made two determined attempts before they established the backwater settlement of Buenos Aires in Argentina. Compared with the human and mineral riches of Upper Peru and Mexico, the Río de la Plata seemed singularly unappealing for conquistadors bent on New World glory and wealth. Furthermore, once the many Indian tribes of the plains acquired horses, they became even more formidable opponents to Spanish expansion.[39]

The image of a desert persisted long after the vast plains had been explored and become better known to Europeans.

In reality, the humid pampa, radiating out in a semicircle from the Atlantic coast had nothing in common with a true desert except for the flatness and sparse population. The dry pampa bridged the humid coastal plain, the western Andean foothills, and the stony Patagonian plains south of the Río Negro. It constituted a geographical and ideological desert. Argentines refer to the incorporation of the dry pampa into the national patrimony as the "conquest of the desert."[40]

Argentine intellectuals and politicians developed views of the pampas similar to those expressed in Venezuela toward the llanos. Domingo F. Sarmiento best expressed Argentina's perceived struggle between "civilization and barbarism." He viewed the plains as the bastion of barbarism. The pampas sheltered disruptive caudillos who stifled progress. Yet he found the strength and skill of the gaucho strangely compelling. Argentine political development was the struggle between caudillos and gauchos of the backward pampa and civilizing, Europeanizing leaders of Buenos Aires. Only by pacifying the pampas and repopulating them with "civilized" European immigrants would Argentina enjoy progress and prosperity. Some Argentines today continue to view their society through a similar lens, substituting Juan Perón for Juan Manuel de Rosas and the "shirtless" masses of Peronism for yesterday's gaucho.[41]

The concepts of "civilized" and "barbaric" have usually included a racial component. In general, white people have pronounced nonwhites to be barbarians. But this means of conceptualizing the frontier involves more than white racism. It can carry a religious component that divides people into heathens and believers. Recall that the unchurched gauchos of the Argentine plains referred to themselves as "Christians" to distinguish themselves from Indians whom they called "savages." Europeanized elites in Argentina in turn defined themselves as civilized and the lowly gaucho as the barbarian. The construct can involve multiple levels of definition.[42]

But we find another aspect to the history of dominance and racism. Frontiersmen, those labeled "barbarians," frequently hold outsiders, even their conquerors, in contempt. One unlettered gaucho of the nineteenth century complimented a European visitor to the Argentine plains: "He is a foreigner, true, but very civilized." To the gaucho, this meant that the man could ride a horse well—the gaucho's hallmark of civilization. It is the views of frontiersmen, including indigenous peoples, that are needed to round out our social description of these regions.[43]

Juxtaposed with disparaging views, positive images of the pampa also developed. Observers expressed amazement at the prodigious livestock wealth of the plains. Ironically, some considered the Argentine plains to be too rich. The natural bounty of the region was seen as the root cause of the gaucho's perceived indolence. On the pampa, abundance made it possible to live without labor. Henry Marie Brackenridge noted that in Uruguay in 1817, "horses are so cheap and abundant, that the best can be had for only a few dollars." Cattle remained so plentiful in Buenos Aires Province through midcentury that meat was not even sold in some areas. Anyone with a lasso could find dinner. After consuming a few delicacies, the gaucho left the remainder of the carcass for scavengers.[44]

The modernizing liberal elites of the nineteenth century viewed the pampa as an area of great potential because of its natural abundance. But the rich land needed better people— white people—they thought. The backward mestizo population of the plains held back progress according to the urbanites. Several administrations hatched a variety of colonization schemes to populate and cultivate the frontier.

Argentine leaders, including Juan Bautista Alberdi, Sarmiento, and Julio A. Roca, all believed that large numbers of European immigrants could almost magically turn the desert into a garden. According to liberal dogma, sturdy European yeomen would push aside the racially and culturally inferior Argentine rural natives and regenerate the nation economically and socially. Alas, for the immigrants and for the nation, very few success stories emerged from these quixotic dreams of agricultural paradise.[45]

The Argentine pampas showed little evidence of the freedom and democracy that Turner imputed to the frontier. From the 1820s on, elites ruling from the port city of Buenos Aires waged military and political war against the frontier gaucho population. They passed a plethora of restrictive laws—internal passports, working papers, military conscription, and vagrancy ordinances—that curtailed the movements of gauchos. Elite policy used the gaucho to fight against another "barbarian" threat: Indians of the pampas. Governmental oppression, coupled with massive immigration, new technology, and rural economic changes ended the open range of the gaucho.[46]

The demands of ranch work as well as powerful, negative pressures from the landed elite condemned most gauchos to enforced bachelorhood or, at best, serial concubinage. Some ranchers discouraged or even prohibited women from living on their land. Women were thought to arouse jealousy and fighting among the men. The requirements of ranch work and the desire to escape military conscription forced gauchos to live nomadic lives. With little hope of owning land, gauchos had few opportunities for a stable home life.[47]

Observers have often found frontiers to be violent places. For example, cowboys and the expanding livestock industry came into conflict with Indians throughout the Americas.

Argentina's lengthy confrontation with various Indian groups of the pampas extended from the sixteenth century to nearly the end of the nineteenth. Only a massive military mobilization and superior technology applied by Julio A. Roca in the "conquest of the desert" finally defeated the Indians. Bandit gangs operated with impunity and even controlled many rural areas of Latin America well into the twentieth century. Pillage, extortion, rape, rustling, theft, murder, and kidnaping victimized inhabitants of such bandit-infested areas.[48]

Gauchos of the Río de la Plata engaged in ritualized, but nevertheless bloody, knife duels. The traditional goal of gaucho duels was simply to mark an opponent's face. But drunken fights often went far beyond simple marking. One Argentine rancher suggested (with some exaggeration) that 99 percent of homicides, injuries, and disorders occurred at *pulperías*—combination general stores and taverns frequented by gauchos. (See chapter 6). Police and judicial records are full of cases in which knife duels ended in wounding or death. The perpetrator usually fled to other, more remote areas of the frontier. Some passed through the cultural membrane of the frontier and took up a new outcast life among Indian raiders.[49]

Officials and gauchos took very different views of such frontier violence. Gauchos considered the killing of someone in a drunken duel to be a *desgracia*—an unfortunate accident. In the eyes of his peers, the killer deserved sympathy, not blame. Police viewed the incident as murder. In many other instances, the perspective of the frontiersman and those seeking to extend their domination over the frontier diverged widely.[50]

The landed elite controlled the expansion of agriculture in the late nineteenth century by maintaining ownership of the land. Spanish and Italian immigrant farmers worked the land as sharecroppers on three- to six-year contracts. Farming only became established where it complemented or did not compete directly for land with livestock raising.[51]

Faced with a growing foreign population on its soil, Argentina took belated interest in developing the southern Patagonia frontier. In 1895 only 300 of 24,000 inhabitants of the border territory of Neuquén were Argentine. Argentines remembered that earlier Chilean emigration to Bolivia and Peru fueled Chilean expansionism. Argentina did not wish to see Chile's victory in the War of the Pacific (1879) repeated in Patagonia.[52]

Like its Brazilian neighbor, Argentina continues to view its vast hinterland as the key to future national greatness. In 1964 Brazil made such faith a matter of public policy by moving its national capital from coastal Rio de Janeiro to the new city of Brasilia in the backlands. Likewise in the late 1980s Argentina contemplated moving its national capital from the megalopolis of Buenos Aires south to the Patagonian "desert." In both nations future progress has been equated with frontier expansion.

Brazilian Frontiers

Topographically, southern Brazil is a slightly more tropical and rolling extension of the pampas of the Río de la Plata. Summer temperatures in January and February are a mild seventy-two degrees Fahrenheit at night but soar to the midnineties during the day. Fresh breezes moderate the climate and blow early morning fog from the hills during the less oppressive autumn months. The rich, rolling hills of the campanha region of Rio Grande do Sul proved well suited to livestock grazing. As a result the area that later became the counties of Alegrete, Bage, Dom Pedrito, Livramento, Quarahy,

Rosario, and Uruguayana developed a robust livestock economy. The southern mountains (serra) and coastal plain (littoral) bound the campanha on the north and east.[53]

Brazil's southern plains served as an important military buffer against Spanish expansion in the Río de la Plata. Spain and Portugal both sought to expand and control the lush grazing lands of the Banda Oriental, modern-day Uruguay. Seesaw battling over the area persisted for decades. Brazil invaded and occupied the territory in 1817. Brazilians stole large herds of Uruguayan cattle and drove them over the border to Rio Grande do Sul. Ranchers in Rio Grande do Sul, covetous of the fertile grasslands to the south, vigorously supported the Brazilian cause. Eight years later Uruguayan exiles supported by Argentina launched an attack to oust Brazil. To preserve the regional balance of power and the profits of trade, the British intervened and denied the lands to both contenders. They insisted on a new, weak independent country as a buffer between Argentina and Brazil. Thus, the small nation of Uruguay was born in 1828. Like Buenos Aires in Argentina, Montevideo developed as a large, dominating city that profited from and dominated the surrounding plains.[54]

But the rich lands alone of southern Brazil did not guarantee prosperity. In its political and economic development, the southern Brazilian plains area has more in common with the llanos than with the pampas of nearby Argentina. Ranching areas in Argentina, the United States, and Canada modernized in the late nineteenth century, but the Colombian and Venezuelan llanos and the campanha of southern Brazil remained technologically backward. A few Colombian ranchers did bring fencing, hybrid cattle, and improved pasture to their estates; they produced beef for a local meat market and exported a few hides. Neither the llanos nor the campanha participated in the profitable cereals and chilled beef export booms that boosted other livestock economies.[55]

Part of the diminished significance of the frontier in Brazil is attributable to its coastal settlement pattern. Exploration and settlement began in 1550 on the northeastern "hump" and crept slowly southward to Rio de Janeiro, São Paulo, and Rio Grande do Sul. The sharp escarpment that rises from the coastal plain, a dearth of navigable rivers outside the Amazon basin, and hostile, nomadic Indians inhibited Portuguese expansion inland. Thus Brazil developed a "hollow frontier." The inland sertão and the Amazon remained largely unpopulated by Europeans. Despite the difference in frontier development between the United States and Brazil, imagery not unlike that employed by Frederick Jackson Turner also developed in Brazil.[56]

The campanha of Rio Grande do Sul with its *gaúchos*, would seem an ideal place for the growth of strong frontier imagery. In addition to being a traditional cattle-raising region, southern Rio Grande also constitutes a frontier in the European sense—a boundary between the nations of Brazil and Uruguay. To be sure, the gaúcho became an important regional symbol. In terms of popular values and material life, the gauchos of Uruguay and the gaúchos of southern Brazil share a common, equestrian folk culture (see chapters 5 and 8). But the national boundary did create two different political climates.[57]

Brazil's frontier seems to fit midway between the ready abundance of Spanish America and the scarcity of North America. In the early sixteenth century, Portuguese explorers encountered only hostile Indians and stands of wood suitable for making red dye. No major mineral deposits were found until the very end of the seventeenth century. Sporadic gold and diamond strikes have occurred since, but for the colonial period, "the mining industry in Brazil never went beyond a fleeting venture." Neither did Brazilian planters subdue large numbers of Indian laborers. They had to import black slaves from Africa instead. Most Indians avoided direct conquest except for those enslaved by the marauding *bandeirantes* (see below). Plentiful herds of cattle did develop in Minas Gerais and Rio Grande do Sul. But Brazilian ranches mostly produced beef for local markets and did not develop the large export capacity that characterized ranching in Argentina.[58]

Although not as prevalent as in the United States, frontier images have played a role in Brazilian historiography. A number of Brazilian scholars, including Caio Prado, Jr., Gilberto Freyre, and J. F. Normano, have pondered the nature of frontier characteristics and influences. In Brazil the frontier region is generally defined as the sertão, the rugged interior plains or "backlands" of the country lying between the narrow coastal plain and the Amazonian basin. The Portuguese word *fronteira* is employed like the customary European usage of "frontier" to mean a national boundary.[59]

Unlike the cowboy in the popular culture of the United States, the Brazilian cowboy remained a regional, not a national type. Neither the gaúcho of southern Brazil nor the *vaqueiro* of the northeastern sertão became the archetypical frontiersman. It is, rather, the *bandeirante* of São Paulo—a mestizo who trekked into the interior in search of natives to enslave—who was mythologized. These slave-hunting expeditions, sometimes involving thousands of men and lasting for years, depopulated many Jesuit Indian missions of Brazil and Paraguay. But Brazilian mythology created a figure very different from that of history. Throughout the Americas, frontier expansion is accompanied by myth making.[60]

In 1902 Euclides da Cunha cast Brazilian history in terms similar to Sarmiento in another classic of Latin American literature, *Rebellion in the Backlands (Os Sertões)*. The author based his work on conflict between frontiersmen and government forces at Canudos in 1896–1897. Followers of the messianic figure Antonio Conselheiro lost the fight against central control. But, like Sarmiento, da Cunha found much to admire in the frontiersman. Nevertheless, both concluded, in da Cunha's words, that "we are condemned to civilization. Either we shall progress or we shall perish." Admirable traits of a "noble savage" are sometimes attributed to "barbaric" frontiersmen. But ultimately, the frontier savage, whether Indian or mestizo, must yield to the press of civilization.[61]

In Brazilian mythology, the sertão or frontier is a place of racial and social democracy. João Capistrano de Abreu (1853–1927) is one of the first Brazilians to take up the frontier theme. His nationalism and "New Worldism" invite comparison with Turner. Inspired by the writings of de Abreu, Cassiano Ricardo, Freyre, da Cunha, and other Brazilians came to believe that the miscegenation characteristic of the nation gave rise to more democratic race relations. The mestizo bandeirantes, residents of colonial São Paulo, became the heroes of this myth. Ricardo depicted the slavers as explorers who successfully bridged the cultural and racial gap between the Portuguese and indigenous cultures. The mythical bandeirante became the moral equivalent of Turner's hardy frontiersman, an archetype of Brazilian national identity, and a force in cementing Brazilian national unity. The bandeirantes explored and expanded the national territory (at the expense of the Spanish) and stimulated the economic development and settlement of the frontier. The reality of the rapacious, brutal, plundering bandeirante raids was quite different from this mythology.[62]

Comparing Plains Frontiers

Turnerian frontier mythology in the United States emphasizes the frontier as a place of opportunity—a social safety valve for oppressed urban workers. But on the cattle frontier cowboys for the most part had only the opportunity to work long hours for low pay. Few enjoyed upward mobility into the ranks of landholders. Laws in several Latin American nations imposed sharp restrictions on the rural population. Insofar as military and legal powers permitted, Latin American governments attempted to curtail and control their unruly rural populations. The burden of restrictions fell with special force on horsemen, who might form an impromptu cavalry for a threatening political strongman.[63]

Turner's critics have especially questioned whether the frontier experience stimulated American democracy. Others have expressed doubt that the frontier offered a "safety valve" of enhanced opportunity for the common citizen. Frontiers of Latin America offered neither greater democracy nor more opportunity than more settled regions.[64] To be sure, a small rancher and his one or two hired hands might develop a familial, egalitarian relationship, but in general the livestock industry replicated and sometimes magnified class distinctions in the society at large. Race, wealth, and culture determined one's standing. Whites looked down on people of color on the frontier as in society at large. And whites controlled frontier resources, just as they controlled opportunity and assets elsewhere in society.[65]

The advent of the farming frontier is generally associated with the decline of the ranching frontier. But the relationship between farming and ranching frontiers varies widely across the Americas. In general, the wealthy landed elites of Latin America preserved special prerogatives for cattle ranching.

Under Spanish law and custom, it fell to agriculturalists, often Indian peasants, to protect crops from marauding livestock. This bias coupled with labor shortages retarded agricultural development in some plains areas of Latin America for centuries. Most often, Indian agriculture suffered as Spanish livestock raising expanded.[66]

Economic significance is often related to historical visibility. Regions, frontier or other, that lacked economic importance rarely loom large in a nation's historiography. But this argument only partially explains the relative significance attached to cattle frontiers of the Americas. Ranching played a secondary role in the economic development of Brazil, Venezuela, and Chile. Agricultural or mineral development overshadowed the livestock economy. And in those three nations, the cowboy figure remains of only regional, not national, significance. In contrast, the cattle industry played a central economic role in Argentina and Uruguay until the late nineteenth century, and the gaucho is a prominent topic for intellectuals in both countries.

But this economic argument breaks down for the United States. There the ranching industry was ephemeral (circa 1865 to 1885) and far overshadowed by the rise of industry during the same period. Yet the cowboy and the frontier loom large in the nation's written history. Clearly, forces beyond economic development worked to shape the significance of frontier imagery in the nation's history.

Taking inspiration from Turner, Walter Prescott Webb and David Potter focused on frontier abundance as a key historical force. According to Webb, the silver, gold, and new lands of the Americas fueled a four-century economic boom for Europe. New World natural riches created Old World wealth. In Potter's variant of the frontier riches thesis, resources and open lands in the American West helped shape the national character. The frontier remained an important historical force until industrialization and urbanization opened other avenues to abundance.[67]

By drawing from Turner, Webb, and Potter, we might argue that differential abundance accounts for some differences between Spanish and Anglo frontiers. Spaniards found numerous, readily accessible sources of wealth in Latin America. As Webb emphasized, precious metals in Mexico and upper Peru fueled fortunes for some. More importantly, some Spanish conquerors harnessed massive numbers of Indians to labor for them in a wide range of enterprises. "Red Gold" in the form of Indian labor began the economic boom of Latin America. Black slaves, imported from Africa, quickly augmented the labor pool.

Spaniards "seeded," often inadvertently, several plains regions with livestock. Without effort, a few decades after initial Spanish exploration, herds of wild cattle and horses flourished in plains regions from the Río de la Plata to the Spanish Border-lands. In terms of gold, silver, labor, and livestock, Spaniards enjoyed tremendous riches in their frontier regions.[68]

The Anglo-American frontiers of the United States and Canada lacked easily extracted sources of wealth. British North America did not include large concentrations of Indian tribes suitable for impressed labor. The Aztec and Inca empires in Spanish America had already organized and concentrated the work force. Spanish conquistadors simply took over governance from indigenous rulers. Nothing comparable to these vast Native American empires of Latin America existed in the British colonies. In British North America, this slower, more difficult path to riches gave rise to a society of settlers, not conquistadors.

Seeing Both Sides of the Frontier

As we have seen, frontier imagery has been rife with mythology and stereotypes. In addition, our vision of the frontier has been dominated by one side, that of the conquering white society. Ethnohistorians have rightly criticized Turner for an insensitivity to indigenous populations in frontier regions. Researchers today have extended their vision to both sides of the frontier experience by including indigenous societies.[69]

Indian-white race relations and the Indian policies of various nations have also come under examination. John Hemming has criticized Brazilian governmental policy toward Amazonian Indians. Equally critical of Argentina's "final solution" against the Indians of the pampa are Julio Aníbal Portas and Kristine L. Jones. Ricardo Ferrando Keun provides an important study of Indian pacification on Chile's southern frontier. He argues that long years of Indian-Spanish conflict had a strong formative impact on the Chilean frontier population.[70]

If we extend this corrective ethnographic vision, frontiers might well be viewed as membranes separating indigenous and European cultures. Influences pass in both directions, but the dominant pressure on the membrane is from the European side. White, European values meet and mix with indigenous cultures on plains frontiers. The two societies compete for and fight over the natural resources of the frontier. Frontiersmen often blended the language, equipment, and values of both European and Native American cultures.[71]

Spanish cultural values penetrated to frontier regions in Latin America. The medieval Spanish Catholic culture carried a stigma against manual labor. White elites in the New World avoided manual labor, thus much work was left entirely to mestizos, blacks, and Indians. As in the antebellum American South, slaves tended cattle in most ranching areas of Latin America. Spanish colonies languished where labor was in short supply. Sharp lines of class, culture, and race stratified Spanish colonial society. Spaniards carried over these prejudices to frontier society where virtually no social leveling took place.[72]

Marvin Mikesell has shown that British settlers in North America created frontiers of exclusion that sharply divided whites and native peoples. Despite their racial biases, Spanish and Portuguese men mixed with indigenous women to create a new mestizo race. In Latin America, much more so than in Anglo-America, Indian influence complemented and modified Hispanic tradition. The gaucho, for example, acquired his most formidable weapon, the bolas, and his favorite beverage, *mate*, from indigenous cultures. The vocabulary of the gaucho and the llanero is heavily peppered with indigenous terms. There is, however, virtually no indigenous element detectable in Anglo-American cowboy life because the Anglo-American frontier of exclusion and the reservation system isolated North American Indians from Anglo settlements.[73]

Despite a large body of criticism, the frontier concept, embellished by many Turnerian images, retains much of its compelling power. Clearly the idea will not die, nor should it—but further refinement is necessary (see chapter 7). William Norton, a Canadian geographer, has suggested a number of options, including viewing the frontier as "a zone of land competition, ecological imperialism, recent settlement, contact, transfer, acculturation, or a cultural region." Further comparative questioning, such as that done nearly thirty years ago by Dietrich Gerhard, is also needed. Comparative studies in agricultural history, like those of Donald Denoon and John Fogarty, offer useful research models.[74]

A wide range of frontier attributes, real and imagined, has developed in the Americas. The imagery and history of frontiers is still relevant, because the frontier remains a potent political symbol. President John F. Kennedy invited Americans to support his "New Frontier." We speak of the remaining frontiers of undersea and space exploration. Argentina's contemplated Patagonian march to the south and Brazil's march inland to Brasilia and the Amazon remind us that frontiers still symbolize hope for a better future.

Chapter 2

Indian
Equestrian Economies

A Hemispheric Perspective

This chapter identifies some of the similarities and differences between North and South American Indian tribes in their acquisition and use of the horse. The arrival of horses and cattle with the Spanish conquistadors wrought tremendous changes. Although economic and military utilization of horses differed among Indians on the plains of the American West and Argentina, Native Americans on both frontiers developed complex hunting, trading, and raiding systems involving many different tribes spread across vast distances. Thanks to the horse, many plains groups resisted white domination until the end of the nineteenth century.

My goal in this chapter is a modest one: to offer a comparative perspective to readers who are probably more familiar with the North American than the South American cases. For convenience, I refer to North America as the northern frontier and to Argentina as the southern.

Plains Environments: Climate, Terrain, and Fauna

Differences in climate, terrain, and fauna between what we now call the Spanish Borderlands and the pampas strongly influenced native societies and economies in the two regions. Despite these differences, however, Indians on both the northern and southern plains effectively exploited animal resources and built extensive, integrated trading and raiding systems.[1]

Some early descriptions of the Borderlands portrayed the region as one of lush, "stirrup-high" grasses. These grasslands, never plentiful, quickly disappeared as human actions permanently altered the landscape. Water diversion and heavy use, overgrazing, chopping firewood, and other human-induced changes permitted mesquite, sage, and other scrub brush to expand at the expense of grass. On the short- and tall-grass prairies of the Great Plains, immense bison herds antedated cattle and made formidable grazing competitors. Feral livestock roamed, but not in the immense numbers found on the pampas of the Río de la Plata.[2]

The northern frontier of New Spain included some fertile, well-watered "oasis areas," particularly valleys, capable of sustaining agriculture and livestock. Many Indian groups, especially in Sonora, cultivated maize and other crops; some even created novel economies based on mobile agriculture. But fertile riverine lowlands made up only about 1 percent of New Mexico's territory. The so-called Little Ice Age (circa 1450–1850) kept growing seasons short. As historian Elizabeth A. H. John observed pointedly: "Spaniards found the arid north sorely disappointing."[3]

The journal of the Domínguez-Escalante expedition through the northern Borderlands in 1776 discloses a continuous preoccupation with finding adequate water and grass for their mounts. An August entry is revealing: "On the 16th we discovered more than half of the horses missing, since, having had no water, they strayed away looking for it and found it near the trail halfway back on yesterday's march."[4]

Drought occasionally struck the pampas, but most areas enjoyed an abundance of water sources, and unlike the fauna of the northern plains, relatively few large predators roamed the well-watered pampas. Perhaps the world's richest natural grasslands, these humid plains have very deep, fertile topsoil. Even the drier western and southern fringes of the pampas receive more rainfall on average than the Borderlands. Well into the nineteenth century, visitors marveled at the natural abundance of the pampas and their wealth of livestock.[5] Furthermore, Argentina's coastline and navigable rivers provided cost-effective outlets to market livestock and agricultural produce. Such fluvial transportation and ready access to external markets did not exist in the Spanish Borderlands of the northern frontier.

Introduction of Horses to the Pampas

Indians of the pampas generally lived in *toldos* (hide tepees) gathered in mobile villages called *tolderías*, not unlike the villages of the Shoshone, Cheyenne, and other Great Plains tribes that followed the buffalo herds. This mobile culture antedated the arrival of the horse, just as buffalo hunting did on the northern plains. In place of bison-hunting, pre-Columbian Indians of the pampas hunted the guanaco (*lama guanacoe*). Indians prized these small llama-like mammals as food and for their soft pelts. They also hunted the *avestruz* (rhea) for feathers and meat.[6]

Alfred J. Tapson well summarized the major indigenous groups of the Río de la Plata.

At the time of the conquest, the Querandí occupied an area between the mouth of the Plata and Córdoba. Between this area and the Río Negro lived the Puelches, while south of this river the Tehuelches wandered over the plains of northern Patagonia, occasionally spilling over into the Colorado River area. The Pehuenches, of historical importance because they controlled the passes through which the Araucanians of Chile entered the

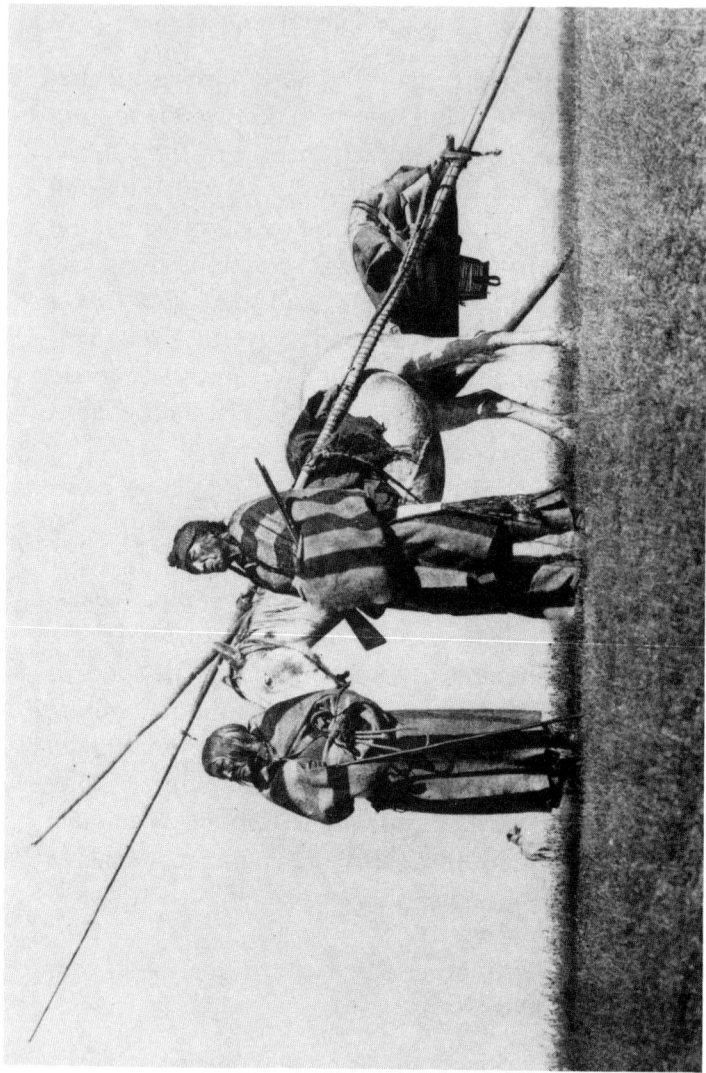

Blackfoot travois. Photograph by Edward S. Curtis. (Prints and Photographs Division, Library of Congress)

Elk Tongue, Kiowa, 1891. (Prints and Photographs Division, Library of Congress)

"Sioux Indian Rider Making Good Medicine before the Race." 1905 photograph by Ingersoll View Company. (Prints and Photographs Division, Library of Congress)

plains, occupied a small zone in the Andean foothills. All these inhabitants of the Pampa were nomadic hunters who existed on the meat of the guanaco, the rhea, the deer, and the otter. They practiced no agriculture.[7]

According to the Scottish writer Robert B. Cunninghame Graham, Portuguese brothers named Goes brought cattle to the region by introducing eight cows and a bull into Uruguay in 1555. Official documents of the Río de la Plata first mention wild cattle in 1589. The first horses to reach the pampas probably arrived from Tucumán and Paraguay in the north or over the Andes from Chile to the west. A document of 1610 refers to Indians in possession of horses.[8]

As Tapson has noted, "the horse provided the greatest single social and military transformation of the Indian character." Appropriation of horses and cattle transformed pampas bands into able cavalrymen and equestrian nomads. Well armed with bow and arrow, lance, and, in some cases, slingshot, Indians made formidable enemies. The versatile *bolas* (*boleadoras*), two or three balls attached to long rawhide thongs, entangled the feet of game animals and enemy mounts.[9]

With the arrival of the horse, hunting and gathering tribes of the pampas quickly evolved into nomadic, pastoral societies. Mare's meat replaced other animal protein sources. Many groups became highly proficient equestrians. In 1599 Governor Diego Rodríguez Valdez of the Banda Oriental (modern-day Uruguay) complained that Indians traded horses for knives and other goods with British ships.[10]

By the early eighteenth century, Araucanians from Chile had migrated over the Andes Mountains eastward to the pampas. Originally an agricultural people, this Chilean tribe developed highly effective resistance to Spanish rule. The Italian commentator J. Ignatius Molina, writing in the 1780s, noted their quick acceptance of the horse: "In their first battles with the Spaniards, perceiving the great advantage which their enemies derived from cavalry, they soon began to discipline themselves in the same manner. Their first care was to procure a good breed of horses, which in a short time became so numerous that in the year 1568, seventeen years after first opposing the Spanish arms, they were able to furnish several squadrons [of cavalry]."[11]

Despite their rapid incorporation of the horse into warfare, Araucanians continued to rely primarily on infantry tactics. They used horses to move quickly into striking position against the Spanish invaders. During the actual engagement, however, they fought mostly on foot, utilizing a wide range of inventive, effective weaponry.[12]

Having breached the Andes in the eighteenth century, Araucanians competed with other Indians and with the Spanish for the wild livestock on the pampas. They spread across the plains and permanently altered indigenous cultures there. Most Indians of the pampas, the Querandí excepted, adopted Araucanian language and culture.[13]

According to Fray Reginaldo de Lizárraga, a Dominican who visited Argentina in the late sixteenth century, horses were so plentiful that Spaniards "hunted them like deer." In 1729 Cayetano Cattaneo, an Italian Jesuit priest, remarked on the superb horsemanship of "almost all these tribes." They rode "without saddle, nor stirrups, nor spurs, nor even a quirt."[14]

Graham, drawing upon Pierre François de Charlevoix, described Chaco Indian equestrian skills in similar terms: "They use no stirrups, and with a simple halter manage their horses as they like, in such a way that the best-mounted Spaniard cannot follow them." The minimal bridle and lack of stirrups parallel equipment used by many northern Plains tribes.[15]

Thomas Falkner, a Jesuit missionary, remarked on the vast herds of wild horses on the plains:

In an inland expedition which I made in 1744, being in these plains for a space of three weeks, they [horses] were in such vast numbers, that, during a fortnight, they continually surrounded me. Sometimes they passed by me, in thick troops, on full speed, for two or three hours together.

This great plenty of horses and horned cattle is supposed to be the reason why the Spaniards and the Indians do not cultivate their land with the care and industry which they require, and that idleness prevails so much among them.[16]

Spanish scientist Félix de Azara, writing in 1802, warned that large herds of wild horses (*baguales*) could pose a danger to riders crossing the pampas.

They [wild horses] charge at full gallop on the herds of tame horses and mares as soon as they see them; and passing amongst them, or near to them, they call to them and caress them with low neighings; they startle them, and without difficulty they (the tame horses) join with them and go off with them.

Thus it often happens that travelers are charged by the Baguales and they are left on foot, the wild horses taking away not only their mounts, but the spare horses that they always drive in front of them.[17]

The profusion of feral livestock provided most essentials of life—food, clothing, building materials, and transportation. Graham described the impact of the livestock bounty:

The wild cattle were in such abundance in the time of [Félix de] Azara and of [Thomas] Falkner [i.e., mid- to late-eighteenth century] that travelers on the Pampa often used to kill them in order to have something to which they could fasten up their horses at night on the treeless plains.

All these wild horse and cattle existed at the same time with an enormous quantity of semi-domesticated animals, so that life on the Pampa for the first two centuries after the conquest was easy, and the settlers naturally were not disposed to cultivate the land.[18]

Introduction of Horses to the Great Plains

Perhaps a millenium ago Athapascan-speaking hunters arrived in the Southwest, having migrated southward through the Great Plains. They raided Pueblo villages for food and (after Spaniards had established slave markets) for captives to sell. From the Pueblos, they learned to farm. Later they would also learn to raise sheep and horses. Today these peoples are the Navajo and the several tribes of Apache (Inde or Nde, "the people"). Trading as well as raiding became important parts of their economic activities.[19]

Early Spanish colonial law forbade providing horses or firearms to Indians. As early as the Mixtón War in 1542, however, military exigencies forced Spaniards to permit Indian allies to use horses. Horses quickly spread northward. Strayed or stolen from Spanish settlements, they came into the hands of Indians in increasing numbers. The expansion of the mining frontier rapidly pushed horses and mules northward during the latter half of the sixteenth century. The Pueblo uprising of 1680 left thousands of head of livestock ownerless and thus available to Indians. By the 1590s, Indians as far north as El Paso, Texas, prized Spanish horses enough to steal them.[20]

During the seventeenth century, many Athapascan-speaking bands, notably the Apache and Navajo, became highly skilled equestrian raiders, attacking Pueblo and Spanish *rancherías* and larger settlements. Both groups stole or traded to acquire silver-embellished Spanish riding tack. The Navajo kept strings of horses and regarded them as a measure of wealth and status. In contrast, the Apache used the horse as a work and war tool and as food. As anthropologist Edward Spicer noted, Apache "promptly killed and cured most of their booty from a raid, whether horses, burros, or cattle and used the meat. They became, in other words, more completely parasitic on the Spanish sources of supply and failed to develop a livestock economy of their own."[21]

Livestock Trading and Raiding Economies: Southern Frontier

Millions of head of livestock grazed the pampas by the mid-seventeenth century. By the 1670s enterprising Indians on the pampas had developed a significant livestock trade with the Araucanians in Chile. Traders traveled from the pampas up the Río Neuquen and over the Andes to Chile. They exchanged livestock, salt, ostrich feathers, guanaco, and horsehides for blankets, seashells, and beans (see also chapter 3).[22]

Because of the great abundance of feral cattle and horses, Indians of the pampas did not engage in livestock herding and breeding. Instead, wild cattle and horses played a role analogous to that of bison on the northern plains. Horses enhanced success in hunts, raids, and warfare. Horses served as meat and as a valuable, highly mobile trade commodity.

Molina noted that even the war-like Araucanians in Chile engaged in trade with Spaniards:

> The trade is conducted altogether by the way of barter, as it is not possible to persuade the Araucanians to open the gold mines, nor to produce any of that metal. Their returns therefore are in *ponchi* [ponchos], or Indian cloaks . . . , in horned cattle, horses, ostrich feathers, curiously wrought baskets, and other trifles of a similar kind. This commerce, although generally prohibited, is carried on in the Indian country, whither the traders go with their merchandize by bye-roads, and deposit it

in the cabins of the natives, to whom they readily trust whatever they wish to sell, certain of being punctually paid at the time agreed upon, which is always the case, these Indians observing the greatest faith in their contracts.[23]

Livestock Trading and Raiding Economies: Northern Frontier

On the northern plains, Indians had engaged in extensive trade during the precontact period. Archeological evidence, such as marine shells from the Pacific or Gulf Coast, have been unearthed along the Missouri River in the Dakotas. Through trade the Comanche turned the Kiowa from enemy to ally. In the eighteenth century, the Kiowa fought the Comanche, but beginning about 1790 the two tribes agreed to share territory and to cooperate on raids against settlements in Texas and New Mexico. They traded horses, mules, captives, and other booty to various plains tribes, including the Wichita. Nomads and sedentary groups cooperated in an extensive network of integrated trade relations.[24]

The arrival of the horse on the northern plains in the eighteenth century radically changed the way of life for the Cheyenne, Arapaho, and other plains groups. Francis Haines charted the chronology of horses moving northward across the Great Plains: "Plains Indians began acquiring horses some time after 1600, the center of distribution being Santa Fe. This development proceeded rather slowly; none of the [Plains] tribes becoming horse Indians before 1630, and probably not until 1650."[25]

The Cheyenne were using horses by 1760. A decade later horses had become common among tribes north and east of the Missouri River. In later years the Cheyenne would acquire horses by capturing them from their enemies. The Cheyenne became famous as mounted hunters and warriors, battling the Kiowa, Apache, and Comanche until 1840 when they joined their former antagonists in an alliance against encroaching whites. They had always been hunters, but the horse allowed them to follow the migratory buffalo and other big game. They could kill enough food in one day to last for months.[26]

Spanish introduction of livestock, however, was certainly a mixed blessing. Spanish animals trampled Indian crops. The *alcalde* (mayor) of Ostimuri (Sinaloa) blamed a Pima uprising in 1690 on "Spaniards who took away their land and populated it with horses and cattle. . . . The Indians could no longer cultivate their land because the beasts damaged it and ate the crops." Yuma Indians likewise protested crop destruction by Spanish livestock about 1780. Relations worsened to the point that on July 17, 1781, the Yuma went on a several-day rampage, killing more than 100 Spaniards. The Indians beat four priests to death and beheaded two of them. Father Diego Miguel Bringas de Manzaneda y Encinas complained in his report of 1796 that at Tucson, "the Indians' crops are also badly damaged by the cattle and other animals belonging to the inhabitants of our presidio."[27]

The acquisition of the horse altered and enhanced the way of life for buffalo hunters. It also changed the life of tribes that had practiced agriculture. When the Blackfoot acquired the horse, the tribe's traditional way of life vanished as an entirely new method of survival emerged. They abandoned their crops and supported themselves primarily with the spoils of the buffalo hunt. The horse replaced both the canoe and the dog as their primary transport. Wealth and honor were measured by the number and health of one's horses. Children played on hobby horses and molded miniature horses from clay. Boys began tending family herds at age ten and by their early teens could break horses. Horses became an essential, valued element of trade.[28]

In contrast, nearby Plains Cree acquired fewer horses than did the Blackfeet and used them mainly for transporting household goods. Only a few Cree owned mounts swift enough for hunting buffalo. Consequently, owners of buffalo-hunting horses enjoyed great prestige and power. As with most other Indian cultures, the Cree preferred to acquire horses by raiding other tribes—generally their Algonquian-speaking neighbors, the Blackfoot (Siksika), Piegan (Pikuni), and Blood (Kainah). Although women could own horses, men took charge of the care and feeding of the animals.[29]

Economic Cooperation and Conflict

The Crow, Arapaho, Cheyenne, and many other tribes underwent the vast cultural transformation from semisedentary horticultural life to nomadic hunting and gathering. As Plains Indians tossed aside old ways for new, the horse became the symbol of wealth and social status. Plains Indians used horses to gamble, arrange marriages, and pay for shaman services.[30]

The Cheyenne abandoned permanent earthen lodges for transportable buffalo-hide tepees. They gave up farming for buffalo hunting and trading. The Cheyenne served as intermediaries between fur traders and their Indian allies. They also bartered British and American goods to southern tribes, such as the Arapaho and Kiowa, for horses and Spanish goods.[31]

While Great Plains tribes remained hunters and raiders, the Pueblos added pastoralism (cattle and sheep) to their agricultural pursuits. They traded corn, textiles, and pottery with plains nomads in exchange for salt, buffalo, and deer products. Vicente de Zaldívar remarked on the extensive trading done by the Apaches in New Mexico in 1598. A year later Alonso Sánchez complimented the Pueblos on their skill at agriculture and trade. In 1601 Marcos Leandro noted that

Pueblo Indians traded with "a nation of Indians outside the
law who are called Apaches. . . . These said Indians bring to
the settlements hides of the buffalo which they kill, meat, and
fat and they trade it with the settled people for maize."[32]

In his report of 1803 Governor Fernando de Chacón
(1794–1805) described the extensive trade between Spaniards
and nomads (*naciones gentiles*) in New Mexico.[33]

> The products traded by the Spaniards to said nomad Indians
> are horses, saddlebags, *anqueras* (leather skirt covering the
> horse's rump), bits, hatchets, war axes, lances, knives, scissors,
> scarlet cloth, serapes, cloaks, woolens, indigo, vermilion,
> mirrors, [illegible interlinear word], loaf sugar, native tobacco,
> corn in flour and on the ear, bread, and green or dried fruit. In
> exchange, the nomads give Indian captives of both sexes, mules,
> moccasins, colts, mustangs, all kinds of hides and buffalo meat.
> The result is that the balance of the trade between the two
> parties always comes out in favor of the Spaniards.

Spaniards sometimes showed intermittent sparks of interest
in working within preexisting Indian economic relations.
Some profit-minded officials, such as New Mexico Governor
Bernardo López de Mendizábal (1659–1661), used Pueblo
intermediaries to establish extensive trade relations with the
Apache. But, regrettably, the avaricious governor poisoned
Spanish-Apache relations by launching massive slave raids
and selling the captives in Sonora.[34]

Deceitful practices of Spanish merchants and traders also
undercut budding frontier economic relations. In 1778 Juan
Agustín de Morfí, a Franciscan friar, complained of debt
peonage, "tyranny and fraud," and "the insidious way trade is
carried on." He concluded that "it is not surprising that
disorder grows out of this usury." In 1803 Governor Chacón
likewise castigated the "malicious and deceitful behavior and
bad faith" that characterized New Mexico's traders.[35]

Conclusions

Horses brought a better quality of life, a "golden age" to Indians in both the northern and southern frontiers. Improved hunting, expanded trading, additional protein, and more rapid transportation stimulated population growth. Indian populations rose with the advantages brought by the horse. Francis Haines estimated that the number of Indians on the Great Plains rose from 50,000 in 1650 to 100,000 by 1780. Thomas E. Mails cited a total of about 200,000 by 1800.[36]

Regardless of the precise figure, by 1781 periodic epidemics quickly reduced Indian populations and devastated economic production. Obviously, Spaniards had little control over the impact of the diseases that they had brought to the New World. But Spanish colonial policies that concentrated Indians in villages or reservations fueled epidemics, worsened famines, and thereby increased the rate of population decline. Forced relocation touched off the great Tepehuan rebellion of 1616. Even with the use of force, Spanish conquerors failed to force most Indian villages into their cultural model. Within a century of Spanish contact, the Pueblo had been reduced from about 150 villages to only forty-three. Recurrent epidemics deterred Indians from seeking contact with Spaniards and they came to call smallpox the "Spanish disease."[37]

With a few notable exceptions (Navajo, Tarahumara, Opata, Papago, and Pima), European-style pastoralism did not take root among indigenous societies. Relatively few northern and no southern tribes developed true ranching economies during the colonial era. Julian Steward and Louis Faron summarized the situation on the pampas. No Indians "became stock breeders until they were thoroughly assimilated into the cash economy of the republics, and it is doubtful whether they practiced horse breeding, important as horses were to them." The tremendous bounty of wild horses on the pampas made breeding less important.[38]

A few groups on the northern frontier did take up horse breeding. The Nez Percé (French for "pierced nose") raised their famed Appaloosas. As white immigrants reached the Pacific Northwest via the Oregon Trail in the 1840s, Umatilla and Yakima Indians eagerly provided them with horses. Because of the importance of this trade, these tribes cared for their horses, successfully bred animals, and created a surplus for trading. The Blackfeet also bred horses, but most tribes relied on raiding to increase their herds. Indians often used pregnant mares as pack animals and thereby reduced the number of foals. They gelded stallions to control them, thereby further reducing the horse gene pool.[39]

Differences in climate and terrain certainly influenced economic activities (see also chapter 3). It would appear, however, that climate played a secondary role in determining the size of horse herds accumulated on the northern plains. Correcting the analysis of Alan J. Osborn, Jerrod Levy argues convincingly that proximity to raidable horse herds played a more important role in determining tribal horse wealth than did harsh winter weather. Winter losses occurred, because most tribes left their horses to paw through snow to find grass for themselves (rustle). Epidemics of mange and other diseases also reduced herd size.[40]

Equestrian-based plains trading and raiding systems permitted effective resistance to Spanish domination. Thanks to the horse, Indians competed successfully with Spaniards for access to plains resources and resisted Spanish attempts to incorporate them politically, economically, and culturally. Spain established and defended pockets of incorporation by means of missions, forts, and towns. Outside these areas, however, equestrian-based indigenous populations effectively contested for control over the land, their labor, and the natural resources, including cattle, horses, bison, minerals, and salt.[41]

Large-scale ranching economies, defined as herding and domesticating cattle and/or horses, did not arise until relatively late in many regions of the Western Hemisphere. Wild-cattle hunting occupied gauchos, cowboys, and Indians in Argentina, Uruguay, southern Brazil, Spanish California, and on the Texas Gulf Coast through the first half of the nineteenth century.[42]

The spread of open-range ranching claimed as a victim the long-standing Indian raiding, trading, and hunting systems of both the Great Plains and the pampas. On the northern plains, vast bison herds gave way to longhorns during the 1870s. About the same time on the southern plains, Argentina's military "conquest of the desert" pushed Indians of the pampas onto reservations or into Chile. Ironically, some Great Plains tribes forced onto reservations took up cattle ranching in the late nineteenth century. Bereft of their traditional equestrian pursuits, they, like whites around them, became cowboys and ranchers.[43]

Chapter 3

Extremes of Empire

Spanish Colonial Military Policy
in the Pampas of Argentina
and the Internal Provinces of New Spain

For more than three centuries Spain ruled a vast expansive New World empire stretching from Chile and Argentina in the south to what is now the American Southwest. This chapter compares Spanish military policy at these extremes of empire—the pampas of southern South America and the Internal Provinces of New Spain, what is today Arizona, New Mexico, and portions of northern Mexico. I examine Spanish military responses to Indian threats and sources of conflict between the Indians and the Spanish conquerers. Despite considerable differences between the two regions—the American Southwest and the Argentine pampas— the Spanish tried to pursue similar, mostly defensive, military strategies and policies.

Indians in the northern and southern extremes of the Spanish colonial empire proved extremely difficult to subdue. Many had no wish to subject themselves to Spanish rule or religion and very effectively resisted outside domination. In this chapter I focus on New Spain's northwestern frontier lying between the Sierra Madre Oriental and Sierra Madre Occidental, primarily Nueva Vizcaya (established in 1562) and New Mexico (established in 1598). Some data are drawn from the broader, general area of what the Spaniards termed the Internal Provinces. The area encompasses what is today Sonora, Chihuahua, northern Sinaloa, Arizona, New Mexico, and far west Texas. For the Río de la Plata, I draw evidence mainly from the pampas to the west and south of Buenos Aires. Both areas remained frontier regions at the end of the colonial period and well into the nineteenth century.[1]

Defining a Frontier

Frontier regions have long been subject to conflicting definitions and images. Political, economic, and cultural differences have been used to identify regions as frontiers. For this chapter I define a frontier as a region in conflict where native populations and encroaching Spaniards met and contested for control of land and resources. Goods and cultural influences passed in both directions through the frontier cultural membrane. Conflict persisted for centuries at the extremes of empire, because neither colonizers nor natives held a decisive edge in applying violent force.[2]

In such a frontier the colonizing power, Spain, sought to establish and defend "pockets" of incorporation with missions, ranches, forts, and towns. Spain sought to incorporate frontier Indians politically, economically, and culturally. A region remained a frontier as long as natives provided significant resistance to attempts at political incorporation (that is, becoming tax-paying citizens). Some Indians, however, showed a willingness to accept economic incorporation through trade with outsiders. Others fought against Spaniards for access to the frontier's resources: cattle, horses, bison, salt, and other minerals.[3]

Conflict and weak incorporation characterized large areas of both the northern and southern frontiers until the late nineteenth century. Indians who adopted the horse proved most resistant to conquest and conversion. As Alfred Tapson has noted, "the horse provided the greatest single social and

"Start of the War Party." 1907 photograph by Edward S. Curtis. (Prints and Photographs Division, Library of Congress)

"Mounted Indians Preparing to Attack." 1889 photograph by Underwood and Underwood. (Prints and Photographs Division, Library of Congress)

military transformation of the Indian character" (see chapter 2). As early as the Mixtón War in 1542, Spaniards were forced to permit Indian allies to use horses. The power of the horse quickly spread northward and—strayed or stolen from Spanish settlements—horses came into the hands of Indians. The expansion of the mining frontier rapidly pushed horses and mules northward during the latter half of the sixteenth century. By the 1590s Indians as far north as El Paso, Texas, prized Spanish horses enough to steal them. During the seventeenth century, the horse became a central component of many Native American cultures, such as the Apache and the Navajo.[4]

Pampas of Buenos Aires Province

Spanish military forces of the colonial period and later nineteenth-century national armies in Mexico, the United States, Argentina, and Chile found it difficult to hold, much less expand, the frontier line. Given the quick conquest of the huge, well-organized Aztec and Inca empires, the successful long-term frontier resistance is all the more striking. Native resistance forced Spanish strategists to devote considerable time, energy, and money to subdue relatively small frontier populations.

North-South Frontier Differences

Missions

The very different role of missions is among the most striking differences between the northern and southern frontiers. The familiar dual thrust of presidio and mission appeared in many areas of the Spanish empire. But only the military element, not the religious component, materialized on the southern Argentine pampa. In the lower Río de la Plata, including most of present-day Argentina and Uruguay, missions played virtually no role as frontier institutions. The few sporadic attempts to establish missions failed quickly and completely. To the north in Paraguay and southern Brazil, priests, principally Jesuits, did establish sizable mission settlements. But the southern pampas frontier remained largely devoid of significant religious activity. In 1675 Governor Andrés Robles convinced some 8,000 Indians to settle into three villages and grow maize twenty-five to thirty miles from Buenos Aires. After eight months a smallpox epidemic wiped out most of this population.[5]

Jesuit attempts to establish missions on the pampa failed quickly. In 1740 some 300 peaceful Indians requested that a mission be built southeast of Buenos Aires. Later that year Jesuits founded Concepción, near where the Río Salado empties into the Río de la Plata.

Some Spanish officials distrusted the missions. On June 28, 1752, Florencio de Escurra, the town clerk (*procurador*) of

Buenos Aires, petitioned the governor to close all missions. Escurra charged that mission Indians served as spies for hostile Indians forewarning them of government military actions. The Concepción mission stood abandoned by early 1753.[6]

Two missions farther south on the coast at Pilar (1746) and Desamparados (1750) also disappeared quickly. Lack of zeal by Spanish officials and indifference or hostility by Indians doomed the proselytizing efforts. Thomas Falkner, an English Jesuit missionary, labored on the pampa to the south of Buenos Aires in the 1740s. The expulsion order of 1767 halted the activities of that order. Falkner and his coreligionaries boarded a Swedish ship in January 1768 and returned to Europe.[7]

The Indians of the pampa—nomadic, hostile, and self-sufficient—seemingly had little interest in the Spanish God. Sánchez Labrador, an Indian who refused conversion, explained the matter simply: "I want to live and die as a good pampa, not as a bad Christian." Recurrent smallpox epidemics also deterred Indians from seeking contact with Spaniards. Blessed with bountiful herds of wild cattle and horses, Indians had little incentive to submit to or compromise with the white invaders.[8]

Spain established a much stronger mission presence in New Spain than on the pampa. Scholars, however, differ in their appraisals of mission effectiveness. Herbert Eugene Bolton maintains that, in spite of setbacks, missionary activity on the northern frontier of New Spain remained strong and sustained. Missionaries from various orders served as "frontier agents," "explorers and diplomatic agents," and "peace emissaries to hostile tribes."[9]

According to Elizabeth A. H. John, "Both Franciscans and the Crown could take just pride in much of the missionary program." Missions and presidios served in tandem as defensive institutions on the frontier. Expenses for both came from the "war fund," a royal account called the *Ramo de Guerra*.[10]

Other scholars find such appraisals of the mission presence too optimistic. Jack Forbes criticizes the Franciscan failure to learn Indian languages in New Mexico. He uses the terms "tyranny," "forced Indian labor," and "control" in describing their activities. Odie B. Faulk acknowledges some missionary inroads with sedentary tribes, like the Pima, Opata, Papago, and Pueblo. The western Apache and the Comanche, however, steadfastly refused to submit to the "civilizing" efforts of mission life. Periodic uprisings—1680 in New Mexico, 1693 in Texas, 1751 in Arizona and Sonora—interrupted frontier life. In Faulk's view, "for the most part the mission system was a failure." The presidio, "both fortress and farce," functioned somewhat more effectively than did the missions.[11]

Native Populations

The very different role of missions in the north and south of the Spanish empire is doubtless linked to the different types of native populations. Given the variety and complexity of pre-Columbian societies, generalization is difficult. It would seem, however, that the northern frontier held greater numbers of sedentary, agricultural Indian communities. These groups proved more adaptable to the socialization and political control exerted by the missions. Others, notably the Apache and Comanche, resisted mission life as did most native groups on the pampa.[12]

Natives of the pampa generally lived in mobile villages (*tolderías*), not unlike the Sioux and other Great Plains tribes that followed the buffalo herds. The rapid profusion of feral livestock provided most essentials of life, including food, clothing, and transportation. Large-scale livestock trading gave Indians in Argentina access to regional trade goods, such as ponchos and other textiles, *mate*, and tobacco. Incorporation of cattle and horses transformed these groups into able horsemen and equestrian nomads. Indians seemingly found little reason to accept imposed cultural change, including a foreign religion.[13]

Terrain and Availability of Livestock

"Aridity in varying degrees dominates the physical environment of the Borderlands," wrote geographer Alvar W. Carlson. Walter Prescott Webb put it even more starkly: "The heart of the West is a desert, unqualified and absolute." To be sure, many Indian tribes cultivated maize and other crops. Human actions quickly and permanently altered the landscape. Water diversion and heavy use, overgrazing, and other changes permitted mesquite, sage, and other scrub brush to expand at the expense of grass. Broken, arid terrain and natural predators kept the wild livestock population small.[14]

Inhospitable frontier conditions made life difficult for human and beast. For example, the Governor of Nueva Vizcaya, Gaspar de Alvear, led an attack against the Tepehuan in 1617. A Jesuit, Alonso de Valencia, described their travails in a report of May 1618.

> Many great misfortunes beset us there. Both snow and rain fell in abundance, and we suffered from cold and hunger. Because we had left the main camp with the intention of attacking the Tepehuanes the next morning, we brought supplies for only one day. The maize and beans the Humes gave us lasted only two or three days; because we were away so long, the soldiers were obliged to kill horses for meat in order not to perish.

The force suffered without supplies for ten days.[15]

In contrast, the pampas featured rich, well-watered grasslands and a relative scarcity of large predators or grazing competitors, such as the North American bison. Feral horses and cattle multiplied rapidly and became the region's main resource. Perhaps the world's richest natural grasslands, most of the pampa enjoyed ample water and very deep, rich topsoil. Even the drier western and southern fringes of the plains enjoyed more rainfall on average than the Borderlands. Well into the nineteenth century visitors marveled at the natural abundance of the pampa and its wealth of livestock.[16]

According to Fray Reginaldo de Lizárraga, a Dominican who visited Argentina in the late sixteenth century, horses were so plentiful that Spaniards "hunted them like deer." In 1729 an Italian Jesuit priest named Cayetano Cattaneo remarked on the superb equestrian skill of "almost all these tribes." They rode "without saddle, nor stirrups, nor spurs, nor even a quirt." The great, ready supply of livestock kept prices low. Thomas Falkner recorded the cost of bullocks or horses as only two dollars a head during the 1740s. The missionary watched wild herds pass, "in thick troops, on full speed, for two or three hours together."[17]

Millions of head of livestock grazed the southern plains by the mid-seventeenth century. Livestock gave Indians mobility, meat, and an all-purpose building material, leather. Enterprising Indians on the pampa developed a significant livestock trade with Chilean Araucanians (Aucas). With the arrival of the horse, hunting and gathering tribes of the pampa quickly transformed into nomadic, pastoral societies. In 1599, Governor Diego Rodríguez Váldez of the Banda Oriental (modern-day Uruguay) complained that Indians traded horses for knives and other goods with British ships. The Pehuenche controlled crucial Andean mountain passes that regulated livestock trade with Chile. By the early eighteenth century, Araucanians from Chile crossed the Andes eastward and began competing with Indians and Spaniards for the livestock bounty of the plains. Araucanians spread their culture to the tribes on the pampa and permanently altered native plains culture.[18]

Sources of Conflict

The Spanish urge to incorporate the indigenous tribes into their political system and to exploit frontier resources generated fierce native resistance. Furthermore, from the beginning of the conquest, soldiers and freelancing explorers considered slave sales a legitimate means of profit. By the 1530s, Indians as far north as Sonora and New Mexico already exhibited hostility to Spaniards because of their slave raids. Spanish rape of Indian women also touched off intense conflict. Coronado and many others after him summarily demanded cloth, food, and other goods from Indians and punished those who resisted.[19]

In 1567 New Spain's fourth viceroy, Martín Enríquez, sought to make official a previously de facto policy of total war (*guerra a fuego y a sangre*). Soldiers could enslave Indians, an added incentive for frontier service. Viceroy Manrique de Zúñiga (1585–1590) later banned official Indian slavery, but the practice persisted at least through the late seventeenth century.[20]

Atrocities designed to terrorize Indians into submission often stiffened resistance. Spaniards sometimes beheaded Indians killed in battle. Alonso de Valencia described the governor of Nueva Vizcaya's actions taken against the Tepehuan in 1617. An old Indian named Antonio would not answer the governor's questions: "When his lordship saw that

Antonio was lying, he had the Indian submitted to the most rigorous torture. Blood ran from the Indian's fingertips and his legs were covered with blisters left by the hot coals applied to his feet. Yet he lay so still and silent that he could have been made of stone. . . . The governor finally believed the old Indian."[21]

Many Spaniards and Portuguese practiced Indian slave-hunting well into the colonial era. For residents of Buenos Aires, slave-hunting expeditions (*malocas*) helped reduce their chronic labor shortage. Likewise, slave hunting explorers, called *bandeirantes*, of São Paulo, Brazil, launched huge expeditions into the South American interior. Slave raiding worsened Spanish-Indian relations from one extreme of the empire to the other. Despite official denunciations, Indian slavery remained in northern New Spain and in northern Argentina until at least the 1680s. Slaves often fled or succumbed to disease. As early as 1608, the *cabildo* (town council) of Buenos Aires expressed alarm at "the great mortality among Indians of service" and asked permission to import African slaves. As elsewhere in the Americas, European conquerors imported Africans to augment the work force.[22]

Even after the end of Indian slavery, Spaniards employed other forms of coercion. Such actions drove many Indians away from Spanish settlements and aroused others to fight. The Río de la Plata suffered from labor shortages throughout its history. In December 1718, for example, the cabildo of Buenos Aires ordered "Indians, mulattos and mestizo shoemakers, tailors and carpenters" to work at the wheat harvest.[23]

On the pampas, eighteenth-century Spanish expansion in search of wild livestock and essential salt spurred Indian-white conflict. Wild cattle hunts (*vaquerías*) spearheaded the Spanish drives into the plains. As early as 1714 the town council of Buenos Aires worried about diminishing livestock numbers. Spaniards came into competition and conflict with Araucanians, Serranos, and other Indian groups for wild livestock. In 1722 the cabildo requested that the governor field a force of 300 to evaluate the livestock supply. As *estancieros* pushed their herds across the Río Salado, their cattle reduced wild herds and displaced game animals used by the Indians for food. Indians responded with raids on ranches. In a dawn raid on Magdalena on November 26, 1740, Indians killed more than 100 people and took an equal number of captives. The raiders also drove off large herds of livestock. These actions occurred a mere thirty miles from Buenos Aires.[24]

Likewise, the search for salt generated conflict on both the northern and southern frontiers. Indians had long used salt for food preservation; Spaniards used it for the same purpose and for their mining enterprises. Navajo and possibly other groups undertook ritualized salt pilgrimages to gather the mineral for ceremonial use. Sources for salt remained scarce through the late seventeenth century.[25]

Writing to the viceroy from New Mexico in 1599 Juan de Oñate described the importance of salt to native trade. He remarked on "the wealth of the abundant salines, and of the mountains of brimstone, of which there is a greater quantity than in any other province. Salt is the universal article of traffic of all these barbarians and their regular food, for they even eat or suck it alone as we do sugar."[26]

High demand for salt pushed Spaniards into conflict with Indians to the south of Buenos Aires. By the 1730s and 1740s, Spaniards began mounting large expeditions from Buenos Aires to the salt beds at Salinas Grandes. They traveled, wrote Falker, "with a guard of soldiers, to defend them and their cattle from the attacks of the Indians, and load two or three hundred carts with this necessary commodity." A 1778 expedition reportedly included sixty-five dragoons, 400 soldiers, 600 horsebreakers, 300 cartwrights with 580 carts, 1,200 workers, and 2,600 horses.[27]

Native Technology and Tactics

Spanish soldiers faced formidable military foes among frontier Indians. Many tribes used the bow and arrow, which had a surprisingly long range. The Araucanians in Chile quickly learned that Spanish firearms could be devastating against bow-and-arrow attacks, and they adjusted by turning to lances, some up to twelve feet long. Athapascans of the high plains also wielded long lances.[28]

Well armed with bow and arrow, lance, *bolas*, and, in some cases, slingshot, Indians on the pampa also made formidable enemies. The bolas, or *boleadoras*, two or three balls attached to long rawhide thongs, entangled the feet of game animals and enemy mounts. Everywhere on the pampa Indians used the bolas or *bola perdida*, a single ball on a rawhide thong, to strike potentially fatal head and body blows. Given the deadliness of these native weapons, gaucho cavalrymen adopted them. Small pointed cudgels, knives, and leather armor completed the stock of Indian weapons.[29]

Thomas Falkner described the Indian's leather armor: "Their defensive arms consist of a helmet, made like a broad-brimmed hat, of a bull's hide sewed double, and of a coat of mail; which is a wide tunic, shaped and put on like a shirt, with narrow short sleeves, made of three or four folds of the *anta*'s [antelope] skin. It is very heavy, strong enough to resist either arrows or lances; and some say it is bullet-proof."[30]

Indians used ambush, sneak attack, and extraordinary equestrian skill to wage war effectively. A Jesuit, Ignacio

Chomé, recorded that in 1729 Guaycurúes, "who had made themselves master of the entire country," launched a surprise attack on the city of Santa Fe, Argentina. With great agility, they changed positions on horseback very quickly, even riding below the animal's belly. They beheaded many men and escaped with horses and other booty.[31]

Skilled tacticians, pampa Indians could move under cover of darkness to wage surprise attacks. According to Falkner, "a few hours after midnight they make the assault, kill all the men who resist, and carry away the women and children as slaves." In attacking ranches or Spanish units, Indians often separated into several small strike forces to multiply the points of attack and overwhelm the enemy.[32]

Spaniards also faced formidable native opposition on the northern frontier. Diego Pérez de Luxán described the weapons of the Tanpachoa near El Paso in 1582: "Turkish [sinew-backed] bows and arrows and bludgeons half a yard in length made of Tornillo [mesquite] wood, which is very strong and flexible." In 1602 Juan de León described the Apache along the Canadian River: "All carried bows and arrows, leather shields, and war clubs with a stone at the end like a hatchet, and a strap for the wrist."[33]

In 1590 Captain General Gaspar Castaño de Sosa reported on a difficult encounter with native resistance at a New Mexico pueblo:

> We attacked it with a large number of guns; and the Indians, realizing the strength of our onslaught, replied in kind. None of them abandoned his section or trench; on the contrary, each one defended the post entrusted to him, without faltering in the least. Such intelligence among barbarians seemed incredible.[34]

Miguel Costansó described native weapons he observed on a 1769 expedition to California:

Their quivers, which they bind in between the girdle and the body, are of skins of wild cat, coyote, wolf or male deer, and their bows are two varas long. Besides these arms, they use a kind of war club of very hard wood [*macana*], whose shape is like that of a short and curved cutlass, which they fling edgewise and it cleaves the air with much violence. They hurl it a greater distance than a stone. Without it they never go forth to the field, and if they see a rattlesnake or other noxious animal, they throw the *macana* at it and commonly sever it in half.[35]

Buying Frontier Peace

Outnumbered and in some cases at a disadvantage in tactics and weapons, Spanish frontier military men had to adapt their policies to local conditions. From the earliest days of the conquest, Spaniards sought to bribe and buy off any natives whom they could not defeat militarily. Officials used a special fund, variously called the *fondo de aliados*, *fondo de paz y guerra*, or *fundo extraordinario*, to purchase gifts and food for Indians. From the beginning Spanish policy sought to reduce the Indians to dependency and to set one group against another. In 1786 Viceroy Bernardo de Gálvez made explicit the motives guiding Spanish frontier policy: "They should be made accustomed to the use of our foods, drinks, arms, and clothing, and they should become greedy for the possession of land."[36]

Friendly chiefs received various gifts, including livestock, tobacco, jerked meat, salt, clothing, sugar, and gunpowder. The gifts brought the Ute, Comanche, and Navajo into alliance against the Apache, some of whom sued for peace. But the demands of countering movements for independence disrupted this payment system. When Spain had to move its troops and supplies elsewhere to counter the independence threat, Indians returned to their raiding activities.[37]

Officials during both the colonial and national periods also bribed Indians on the pampa to remain peaceful. Under the Bourbons, officials during the 1790s offered Indian chiefs (caciques) gifts and access to local trade goods. During the 1820s ranchers on the plains encouraged the government to pay Indians annual subsidies. Historian Kristine L. Jones explains why: "By removing the Indians from commercial networks with the annuity agreement, ranchers were able to protect, control, and take over the trade. While commerce in Buenos Aires Province continued to expand, the Indians were now locked out of participating in it."[38]

Félix de Azara, a Spanish scientist, explored the pampa in 1796. He noted with disgust that the frontier boundaries, "because of a few annoying barbarians, are approximately the same as those which [Juan de] Garay took with sixty men 216 years ago." He urged populating the plains by granting land for frontier service, a policy that would give soldiers a stake in defending their own lands against attack. Azara revived the idea of itinerant "early-warning" patrols based at small frontier installations.[39]

In May 1804 Captain Sebastián Undiano y Gastelú seconded Azara's goal of populating the frontier. He reemphasized the importance of utilizing natural barriers against the Indians and urged Viceroy Sobremonte to push settlements and forts to the Río Negro. Then "the peaceful conquest of 17,000 square leagues of land, with the best soil in the Universe" could be achieved. Most Spaniards, however, had little interest in broadening landownership.[40]

Relative calm prevailed on the frontier toward the end of the colonial era (until the disruptions of the independence wars). Indians came to "corrals" in many cities to trade hides and skins. Feliciano Antonio Chiclana suggested in 1804 that Indians be given a monopoly on the salt trade to end conflict over that critical resource. In an interesting role reversal, Spaniards now paid tribute or protection money to friendly Indians in exchange for peace and intelligence on the movements of hostile tribes.[41]

David J. Weber well summarized the character of the postindependence northern frontier: "From Texas to California, then, the so-called indios bárbaros effectively checked the expansion of many portions of the frontier. The decades following independence saw relations between Mexicans and Indians worsen throughout the young nation, but the persistent attacks by the indios bárbaros in the north constituted one of the country's most serious problems."[42]

The Failure of Spanish Frontier Policies

Problems of many types beset Spanish policy on the far northern and southern frontiers. Both regions suffered relative neglect and insufficient support from the Hapsburg Crown throughout the colonial era. Despite prolific rumors, no great mountain of silver or concentration of Indian laborers greeted Spaniards in the Río de la Plata (a misnomer) or on the northern frontier. As religious wars and imperialist competition drained the Spanish treasury, the dynasty sunk into ineffective decay during the seventeenth century. To the Crown, the meager potential benefits of expanding remote frontiers did not justify increased expenditures.[43]

The failure of frontier military strategy stemmed more from faulty conceptualization and official priorities than from problems in technology, tactics, or military intelligence. Elizabeth A. H. John's conclusion for Spanish failure with the Pueblos explains part of the problem. Cultural prejudices led the "Spanish to miscalculate the complexity and difficulty of Hispanicizing them. . . ; nothing in the Spaniards' experience prepared them to understand the Pueblo world." This explanation of cultural ignorance, however, does not account for the Spanish failure to learn from their own mistakes. Slaving, exploitation, and rapaciousness continued, indeed heightened, as Spanish knowledge of the New World increased. Conflict increased.[44]

On the northern frontier, Spain attempted to develop a policy of inclusion. But nomadic tribes, like the Apache, refused to adapt and some settled groups, like the Pueblo, rebelled against Spanish attempts at deculturation. On the southern frontier, Spanish policy sought to exterminate and subjugate—but never to integrate—the nomadic Indians of the pampa.[45]

According to Thomas Falkner, Spanish actions bore primary blame for spurring major uprisings on the pampas. In 1738 "the Spanish, very injudiciously, and indeed ungratefully, drove Mayu Pilqui-Ya [Mayulpilqui], the only Taluhet Cacique who was their friend, to his destruction, by forcing him to retire to a distance, exposed to the enemies which he had gained by defending their territories." Angered by his death, other caciques attacked Spanish ranches on the southern plains. In retaliation *maestre del campo* Juan de San Martín slaughtered peaceful Indians led by Calelián the elder. The slain cacique's son and 300 warriors took revenge with a bloody raid on the town of Luján. San Martín and a militia troop of 500 responded with yet another slaughter of unarmed Huiliches. He then turned on Tolmichi, a friendly Tehuel cacique. "This Cacique, with the Governor's letter in his hand, and shewing his license, was shot through the head by the Maestre del Campo; all the Indian men were killed, and the women and children made captives."[46]

When Spaniards arrived in Texas and the Interior Provinces various Indian nations had long-established trade relations with each other. The early explorer Alvar Núñez Cabeza de Vaca traded with natives in order to survive. After being shipwrecked in the late 1520s, Cabeza de Vaca traveled and traded among Texas Gulf Coast natives for six years. In the late 1530s Fray Marcos de Niza noted the richness of available goods in New Mexico: "They brought to me a quantity of game—venison, rabbits and quail—also maize and meal, all in great abundance. They offered me many turquoises, cowhides [probably buffalo skins], very pretty cups, and other things, of which I accepted none, for such was my custom since entering the country where we were not known."[47]

Pueblos traded corn, textiles, and pottery to plains nomads in exchange for salt, buffalo, and deer products. Even the rapacious Vicente de Zaldívar observed in 1598 that the Apache in New Mexico "sell meat, hides, tallow, suet, and salt in exchange for cotton, blankets, pottery, maize, and some small green stones which they use [likely turquoise]." The variety and quality of clothing—cotton, wool, and buffalo hides—greatly impressed Oñate. In 1599 Alonso Sánchez termed the Pueblos "excellent and intelligent farmers; they are much given to commerce, taking from one province to another the fruits of their lands." The Apache seemingly would have preferred trade to war. They became implacable enemies, however, after suffering eighty years of Spanish slaving and other provocations.[48]

Indians of the pampas developed a cattle-trading network spanning the Andes into Chile. Indians traded ponchos for weapons, liquor, and others goods in Buenos Aires and other towns on the pampa. In the mid-eighteenth century, Falkner suggested that "a commerce might also be established with the Indians; who for sky-coloured glass beads, cascabells of cast brass, broad swords, heads of lances, and hatchets, would exchange cattle for the use of the colony, and fine furs to send to Europe."[49]

More enlightened Spanish policy might have sought to work with and expand existing Indian trade patterns: Spain might have built a peaceful multicultural economic trade network. Is the idea of such cultural and economic exchange anachronistic? I do not think so. Spaniards did not reject and attack all elements of Indian culture. They quickly came to appreciate the utility of buffalo hides. The porous membrane of the frontier permitted cultural transmission in both directions. By the 1580s, Athapascan deerskin clothing had passed to Pueblo tribes. According to Juan de Ortega, in 1601 Spanish women in New Mexico wore deerskin clothing as well.[50]

Even the resistant Apache reached an accommodation with the Spaniards on one occasion. Following a series of military defeats in the late 1780s, a number of Mescalero and Warm Springs Apache made peace with New Mexico Governor Fernando de la Concha. In the 1790s the Indians settled with permission in the valley of the Rio Grande at Sabinal between Belén and Socorro. Spaniards furnished tools and seed, taught the Apache to irrigate, and provided rations while the crops were growing. Unfortunately, Concha became ill and left New Mexico. His successor, Governor Chacón, abandoned the Sabinal Apache who in turn abandoned the settlement and returned to nomadism.[51]

We might turn to other empires of the ancient world for cases of imperial expansion into frontier regions. On the eastern Roman frontier in Transjordan, sedentary populations traded with Bedouin desert nomads. Such cooperation lasted "as long as a strong government policed the frontier." The line of Roman frontier forts, however, "was not an iron barrier to movement of goods and peoples, but was rather a regulator of traffic between the desert and the cultivated zone to the west." The Chinese, Mongol, and Ottoman empires likewise negotiated trade agreements with threatening nomads.[52]

Despite several centuries of military effort, the far frontiers of New Spain and the Río de la Plata remained perilous places for Spaniards and Creoles well into the nineteenth century. Not until Julio A. Roca's "conquest of the desert" in the 1880s did Argentina achieve a "final solution" to its frontier Indian threat. In the United States, the cavalry fought the last Indian wars in the Southwest at about the same time.

Significant differences existed between the southern and northern extremes of Spain's New World empire. Nevertheless Spanish policy in both regions aspired to the same end: forced subjugation of native populations and uncontested control of frontier resources. The mission system proved much more important on the northern frontier. Spanish military force failed to subdue either region; native groups remained outside white political control until late in the nineteenth century.

Asking "what if" of history is perhaps a futile endeavor. Given the extensive, successful preexisting native trade networks, however, one cannot resist asking "What if the Spanish had worked to cooperate with, not to obliterate, what had existed before?"

Chapter 4

Vaqueros and Charros

Mexico's Horsemen

Mexico developed two important equestrian cultures. Vaqueros—poor, working cowhands on the great haciendas of Mexico—represent figures comparable to the American cowboy or the Argentine gaucho. Charros, on the other hand, represent a middle- and upper-class tradition linked to stylized riding exercises dating to medieval Spain. These exercises form the basis of what later became Mexican rodeo (charreada or charrería). This chapter compares the two historical figures and reminds us that significant class differences arose in frontier regions just as they did elsewhere in society.

The vaquero is the working cowboy of Mexico's missions and ranches. Spaniards, ever fearful of attacks from their Indian subjects, initially forbade Indians to ride horses. But ranch labor demands, coupled with the upper-class Spanish aversion to manual labor, gradually opened riding to Indians, blacks, and mestizos.

Colonial Spanish law had to be amended to permit mission neophytes to tend cattle on horseback. Mission Indians quickly became skilled at all aspects of ranch work. They made and threw lariats, herded, and branded. Unfortunately for Spanish settlers, hostile Indians, such as the Apache and the Comanche of the North American Southwest, also became excellent horsemen and formidable enemies.

Missionaries played a leading role in establishing ranching in Arizona, New Mexico, Texas, and California. From 1687 until his death in 1711 Father Eusebio Francisco Kino (an Italian Jesuit) established many missions that raised livestock in what is today southern Arizona and northern Sonora, Mexico.

Beginning with the establishment of San Diego in 1769 Father Junipero Serra built a string of Franciscan missions that spread northward along the California coast. As in Mexico, Indian vaqueros tended the livestock. Spanish California developed a major trade in cattle hides. Visiting the coast in the 1830s, Richard Henry Dana noted that "the men in Monterey appeared to me to be always on horseback. . . . There are probably no better riders in the world."

Jo Mora, author of several books on the *californio*, the vaquero of Spanish California, described this colorful figure:

A kerchief was bound about his head, atop which, at a very rakish, arrogant angle, sat a trail-worn weather-beaten hat, wide of brim, low of crown, held in place by a *barbiquejo* (chin strap) that extended just below the lower lip. His unkempt black beard scraggled over his jowls, and his long black hair dangled down his back to a little below the line of his shoulders. His ample colonial shirt was soiled and torn, and a flash of brown shoulder could usually be seen through a recent tear. The typical wide, red Spanish sash encircled his lean midriff. His short pants, reaching to his knees, buttoned up the sides, and were open for six inches or so at the bottom. Long drawers (which were once white) showed wrinkles at the knees and were folded into wrapped leather *botas* (leggings). He wore a rough pair of buckskin shoes with leather soles and low heels, to which were strapped a pair of large and rusty iron spurs. This costume was finished off by a *tirador* (a heavy, wide-at-the-hips belt) that helped him to snub with the *reata* (rawhide rope) when lassoing on foot. The ever-present long knife in its scabbard was thrust inside the garter on his right leg.

Mexican charro in Pawnee Bill Lillie's Wild West Show. (Prints and Photographs Division, Library of Congress)

The charro represents a second equestrian tradition of colonial Mexico. The charro tradition perpetuates the upper-class equestrian heritage of the Spanish gentlemen rider or *caballero* (this Spanish term for *gentleman* literally means *horseman*).

The first charros were the Spanish elite who received *encomiendas*, royal grants of Indian labor bestowed upon conquistadors and court favorites. These *hacendados*, or gentlemen ranchers, became New Spain's landed elite.

The charro tradition retained *jinetea*, a short-stirrup riding style earlier adopted by Spanish riders from the Moors. The style evolved as a military tactic. By riding with short stirrups, cavalrymen could stand high above an enemy and slash downward with a sword or lance. Charros favored this style over the long-stirrup *la brida*, used by heavily armored medieval knights.

Riding exhibitions in Mexico began during the early days of the conquistadors. To impress their Indian subjects and hone cavalry skills, Spanish gentlemen gathered periodically for mounted drills called *alardes*. Gradually these military parades evolved into pleasure rides and exhibitions. Spaniards performed a number of riding contests from the sixteenth century on, including the popular ring race and jousts with cane poles.

Charro dress evolved from the rich silks, velvets, and silver trim favored by landowners as they performed or rode out to survey their estates. Their stylized riding and costumes evolved over time into the distinctive Mexican rodeo, called *charrería* or *charreada*.

The vaquero's much humbler dress varied with the terrain. Many wore a poncho, called a *serape* in Mexico. They wore a broad-brimmed *sombrero* whose design influenced early cowboy hats in the United States. F. Warner Robinson described the vaquero of northern Mexico (*Scribner's Magazine*, February 1912):

> [His dress] consists of a short jacket made of some cheap coarse material, usually in colors, and tight-fitting pantaloons belled out at the bottom just enough to permit easy foot action. Down the outside seam of his trousers runs a broad strip of brilliant cloth. Instead of a belt he wears a *faja* (sash) which is wrapped around his body several times with the ends tucked in. It is always of some bright color, usually red or blue. His sombrero, of course, is an object of almost universal conjecture, often having a three-foot expanse of brim, which is dipped at a rakish angle, with a conical-shaped crown. It is made of braided straw and is invariably decorated with bands of brilliant colors.
>
> On the range he always has about him somewhere his beloved *serape*, which seems indestructible. He wears it thrown over his shoulder like a shawl, and how he keeps it on, in the thick of a round-up, always puzzles the American cowboy. He also uses it as his bed at night; and when it rains, one will see him stoically sitting his horse (he rides a horse on the plain but not in the mountains), enjoying the full glory of it like an Indian chief on dress parade. His foot-gear is almost laughable, for instead of the high-heeled graceful boot worn by American cowboys, he wears the *charro* shoe, which is low-heeled, thin-soled, and very pointed at the toe, resembling, in every respect but the toe, the old-style congress shoe. It is usually of russett leather of very soft texture. As a rule, he wears no kerchief round his neck, and his chaps fit tight and flare at the bottom like his trousers.

Spanish colonial ranchers faced many difficulties. During the eighteenth century ranches and missions in Spanish Texas suffered from drought and Indian raids. Ranchers lacked legal market outlets so herders smuggled cattle into French Louisiana. By the late eighteenth century, some 15,000 to 20,000 head moved eastward to Louisiana each year.

By the early 1800s illegal horse and mule trade joined the contraband cattle drives. The movement of Anglo settlers into the Mississippi valley opened another market for livestock. Meanwhile, problems plagued the economic and religious activities at the missions. Unable to convert the indifferent Indians, priests abandoned the missions in east Texas; but livestock remained.

In Baja California and northwestern Mexico, vaqueros faced an especially hostile desert environment. They rigged their saddles with *armas*—large, stiff leather skirts hanging off the saddle. The leather protected riders from thorns and cacti. Later riders attached smaller skirts (called *armitas* or *polainas*) to their legs. These leather protectors were of course the forerunners of the vaquero's *chaparreras* and the chaps used by American cowboys. Leather made up practically the entire outfit and equipment of the rider in Baja California. He wore a leather hat (*vaqueteada*) and a long, leather wrap-around coat (*cuera*). He also made his stirrup coverings (*tapaderas*), saddle bags (*cojinillos*), and lariat (*reata*) from leather.

While vaqueros worked the range, charros played. During the 1880s Mexico City hosted the nation's first public exhibition of charro riding. In 1894 charros exhibited their riding and roping skills to audiences in the United States. The group, led by Vicente Oropez, performed with Buffalo Bill's Wild West show in New York. A richly dressed Mexican rider named Magdaleno Ramos rode in the first Calgary Stampede in 1912.

Texas folklorist J. Frank Dobie penned a memorable description of the vaquero (*Survey*, May 1, 1931):

He is full of stories about buried treasures, which priests and *gachupínes* [Spaniards] are usually somehow connected with and which are guarded by white *bultos* [ghosts], clanking chains, eerie lights and other mysteries. If he does not know a witch, he knows of one. If he does not fear the evil eye, he respects it.

Either despite or because of his nearness to nature, he is as insensible to the sufferings of nature's progeny as nature is herself. He will run his horse into thorns and then have no thought of pulling the thorns out; he will ride a thirsty horse within fifty yards of a water hole and unless he himself is thirsty will not turn aside. He will rub sand into the eyes of a wild cow that he has roped, though in this he is no more cruel than the average old-time cowpuncher. He will sit all day in the shade of his *jacal* [hut] and never offer to carry a bucket of water for his over-worked wife.

For all that, the *vaquero* is kind to his family, sets no limit to his hospitality, and probably goes beyond the average human being in faithfulness. He will divide his last *tortilla* with any stranger who happens by. He will take the side of his *amo* [master], if he likes him, against any Mexican that tries to do his *amo* an injustice.

Folk songs and tales reveal the vaquero's pride and machismo. "The Ballad of Manuel Rodríguez," supposedly based on a true incident at the King Ranch in Texas, depicts these characteristics. An especially bad horse threw Rodríguez in front of his fellow riders. An excellent broncobuster, the humiliated Rodríguez quit the ranch and vowed to go pick cotton, a particularly demeaning type of footwork. Like his equestrian fellows elsewhere, the vaquero looked upon the lowly farmer (as well as goat- and sheepherders) with mixed pity and contempt.

Vaqueros admired riders who were long-suffering, patient, uncomplaining, and persevering. Like Anglo cowboys they esteemed men who worked in bad weather or with pain, went without food, and tracked down stray animals at all costs. Vaqueros valued courage, riding into the midst of a milling herd. Virtuous actions would not bring praise, but failing to measure up to the vaquero standard could bring criticism, censure, or ridicule.

Mexican vaqueros worked hard but often found themselves in debt. In New Mexico, for example, debt peonage was already common by 1800. It persisted through the nineteenth century in Mexico. Frederic Remington noted that vaqueros "are mostly *peoned*, or in hopeless debt to their *patrons*, who go after any man who deserts the range and bring him back by force."

Vaqueros also had their own favorite pleasures and foods. A writer described a vaquero feast after branding (*Lippincott's Magazine*, January 1880): "We shudderingly watched several of the Mexicans tear out the small intestines from the carcass of the heifer, and, smoking as they were from the heat of the newly killed animal, throw them into the coals to roast, and greedily devour them. This dish is highly regarded among the Mexicans and is known by the relishing name of 'marrow guts.'"

Political violence repeatedly disrupted the Mexican ranching industry. Civil wars and the great Mexican revolution decimated herds and turned vaqueros into cavalrymen. During the revolution, armies proliferated under Emiliano Zapata, Francisco "Pancho" Villa, Alvaro Obregón, Pascual Orozco, Venustiano Carranza, and other revolutionary chieftains. All the armies needed mounts, draft animals, and meat. They also needed vaqueros to tend the animals and to fight.

The revolution largely destroyed Mexico's livestock industry. In 1902 an estimated 396,000 cattle roamed the state of Chihuahua. In 1923 pillage and disruption had cut the number by about 75 percent. Other northern states suffered similar declines. Overall the number of cattle in Mexico dropped 67 percent between 1902 and 1923.

A new revolutionary elite emerged during the 1920s. The vaquero and other poor rural Mexicans found that they had gained little from the revolution. The livestock industry gradually recovered, but vaqueros remained exploited, poorly paid, and landless.

Because vaqueros were illiterate, they left few personal records. Some vaquero folklore, however, passed into Mexican *corridos* (folk songs). The Huasteca variant often includes cowboy yells (*gritos de vaquero*). Many corridos celebrate famous horses and horse races and deal with the realities of ranch work, important elements of vaquero life and culture. Vaqueros of the King Ranch in Texas sang "El Toro Moro" in honor of a particularly fierce bull, and "Gallo de Cielo" celebrated a famous fighting cock.

In 1883 a Cheyenne, Wyoming, newspaper printed a poem called "The Jolly Vaquero."

> The jolly vaquero is up with the sun,
> And quick in the saddle, you see,
> He swings his quirt and jingles his spurs—
> A dashing vaquero is he.
> He "Hangs and rattles" and "Hits the high places,"
> That bound the lone prairie;
> And woe to the steer, when he draws near,
> For a bold bad roper is he.

Like the cowboy in the United States, the vaquero's numbers have diminished. His skills remain important on the rugged terrain of north Mexican ranches. The charro's legacy is carried forth in Mexican rodeo. Both the vaquero and charro remain important parts of Mexican culture and major contributors to the western ranching culture of the United States.

Chapter 5

Cowboys, Gauchos,
and Llaneros

In this chapter I compare three leading cowboy types of the Western Hemisphere: Argentina's gaucho, the llanero of Colombia and Venezuela, and the western American cowboy. I examine dress, work techniques, the political fortunes of these historical figures, and their virtues and vices. Strong similarities exist between the three social groups, since all were strongly shaped by their Hispanic legacy. Furthermore, these equestrian heroes all exerted an important historical and cultural impact on their respective countries.

Horses and horsemen played a leading role in the Spanish conquest of Indians of the Americas and remained a central part of Latin America's history for centuries to come. As the Spanish conquerors and explorers moved northward out of Mexico into what is today the United States' Southwest, they brought their equestrian values, practices, and terminology with them. Considering these intrepid horsemen who had spread themselves across the length and breadth of the Americas, Edward Larocque Tinker wrote that "there are on this continent large bodies of men that have become a tradition in their various countries and, in spite of language barriers and differences in blood, are as alike as Model T Ford cars. All endured the same hardships, solved the same problems . . . and became symbols of daring, virility, patriotism, and fanatical independence; each inspired a picturesque literature."[1] Tinker overstated the similarities between the various horsemen, but their commonalities and differences make a fascinating contribution to New World history.

Gauchos of the Río de la Plata region (modern-day Argentina, Uruguay, and southern Brazil) and llaneros of Colombia and Venezuela represent two of the leading equestrian subcultures of South America. By the seventeenth and eighteenth centuries, millions of wild cattle and horses grazed in the grasslands of the llanos in northern South America and the pampas to the distant south. Spanish officials in Buenos Aires, seat of government for the Río de la Plata, made determined efforts to limit access to the abundance of livestock to the very few who held royal monopolies. But freelance wild cattle hunters, termed *changadores*, *gauderios*, and finally gauchos by the officials, persisted in slaying some of the seemingly unlimited herds of animals for their hides and tallow. During the eighteenth century, these wild cattle hunters became vagrants and thieves in the eyes of Spanish officialdom. In their own eyes, however, gauchos were merely living the traditional life of the pampa and enjoying the fruits of the plains that God had given for the use of all.[2] Over time, gauchos developed a unique culture and a set of values that were increasingly at odds with the desire of officials and the ruling elite to monopolize the land and its wealth.

Theodore Bland, a special commissioner sent to Argentina by the United States government in 1818, reported back on the singular inhabitants of the region:

The herdsmen or peasantry of the pampas plains form a very considerable proportion of the population of the country. Thinly strewed over the great pastures, those residing at a

Llaneros of Venezuela. From Ramón Páez, *Wild Scenes in South America* (New York, 1862).

Llanero family of Colombia. Anonymous nineteenth-century watercolor. (Prints and Photographs Division, Library of Congress)

Roundup and branding. (Prints and Photographs Division, Library of Congress)

CA camp eating dinner. (Rio Grande Historical Collections, New Mexico State University Library)

"O'Donnell on Whirlwind." Photograph taken at the Cheyenne Frontier Days, 1911. (Prints and Photographs Division, Library of Congress)

Colombian llanero clothed in poncho. Anonymous mid-nineteenth-century watercolor. (Prints and Photographs Division, Library of Congress)

distance from the cities have, most commonly, each one the charge of an estancia, many leagues in extent. They have little society, are totally illiterate, lead an indolent life, and dwell on an immense waste, in continual solitude. Their habitations are constructed in the simplest form; in general, they consist of low mud walls, thatched with the long grass of the plains, tied on a layer of reeds, with raw hide thongs, or stuck on with mud. . . . The bedding and clothing of the family, and the whole household furniture, exhibit a scene of laziness and dirt, yet mingled with apparent cheerfulness, great kindness, much natural intelligence, and an evident independence of character.

Bland also reported on the equestrian and martial skills of the gauchos:

They may be considered as the most formidable guerrilla or partisan soldiery that ever existed. In courage they are inferior to none; and the exploits that are related of their adroit and rapid horsemanship exceed what has been told of the Parthian, the Scythian, or the Cossack of the Don. Such are the herdsmen of the pampas and plains, who are usually called gauchos; an epithet, like that of yankee, originally cast on them in derision, but one which has now ripened into a distinctive and common appellation that is no longer offensive.[3]

Bland accurately described the gaucho of the early nineteenth century and pointed up some central characteristics. The wars for independence from Spain, fought in the Río de la Plata from 1810 to 1816, provided a perfect theater for the gaucho's cavalry skills. Armed with long lances and swordlike knives called *facones*, gauchos won fame and a better reputation among Argentinians. Their role in the independence wars helped gauchos partially to escape their unsavory reputation among the new Argentine nation's leadership. But throughout the nineteenth century officials persisted in ultimately successful attempts to coerce, tame, and finally totally subdue the fiercely independent riders of the pampa.[4]

The llaneros of the swampy plains of Colombia and Venezuela played a similar role in their societies. Considered social outcasts, llaneros also enjoyed a rise in their stock for the part they played in the independence wars. Behind the leadership of a chieftain, or *caudillo*, named José Antonio Páez, llaneros made themselves a cavalry and thus a political force to be reckoned with. Their lives, housing, and material goods remained at a primitive level just as did those of the gaucho. The German geographer Alexander von Humboldt visited the wild llanos during a trip through Latin America from 1799 to 1804. He described the rustic ranch house of the llanos, surrounded by a few small huts, covered with reeds and skins. The cattle, oxen, horses, and mules are not penned, but wander freely over an extent of several square leagues. There is nowhere any enclosure; men naked to the waist, and armed with a lance, ride over the savannahs to inspect the animals, bring back those that wander too far from the pastures of the farm, and mark with a hot iron all that do not already bear the mark of the proprietor. These Mulattoes, who are known by the name of *Peones Llaneros*, are partly free men and partly slaves. There does not exist a race more constantly exposed to the devouring heat of the tropical sun. Their food is meat dried in the air and a little salted; and of this even their horses sometimes eat. Always in the saddle, they fancy they cannot make the slightest excursion on foot.[5]

Civil wars plagued Venezuela and Colombia during the nineteenth century, disrupting the livestock industry, often uprooting the llanero from pastoral pursuits, and putting him at the service of one political faction or another. Like the gaucho, the llanero found his lot in life increasingly worse as the century progressed.

The western American cowboy's many similarities to his Latin American cousins naturally stem from their common Spanish legacy. Edward Tinker pointed up a few of the cowboy's debts owed to the vaquero: "They had to learn how to ride herd from the Mexican vaquero, how to break a bronco, and to use riatas and branding irons. They adopted his entire equipment—the ring bit, that was copied by the Spaniards from the Moors and is still in use in parts of the Southwest, and the stock saddle. . . . Even the cowboy's work-a-day vocabulary is still generously peppered, in the Southwest, with Spanish words."[6]

Perhaps the clearest attribute shared by the gaucho, llanero, and cowboy was their powerful preference—indeed their demand—for a life in the saddle. These horsemen would mount up to cross the street and considered footwork beneath them. In fact, on both the Argentine pampas and the United States plains, the unusual appearance of a pedestrian might cause a stampede among cattle (not recognizing such a figure). Sir Woodbine Parish, a British diplomat serving in Argentina, remarked that "everything in this country is done on horseback: if a bucket of water is to be drawn from a well, there must be a man and a horse to haul it up. . . . One might fancy oneself in the land of centaurs, amidst a population half men, half horses: even the beggars ride on horseback."[7]

Although work methods varied among these horsemen, the work calendar appeared very similar. Daily rides across the range in search of strays, treating sick or injured animals, and a miscellany of never-ending chores occupied dawn-to-dusk hours. The annual roundup and branding season stood out in all three regions as the busiest and most important time. In his vivid 1862 recollections, *Wild Scenes in South America; or, Life in the Llanos of Venezuela*, Ramón Páez described a roundup:

> The hunters, in squads of six or eight, proceeded on the afternoon of the day before the hunt to their stations at various points of the savanna, having instructions to start at early dawn for the appointed center. . . . The cattle being so unexpectedly roused from their slumbers, naturally endeavored to fly from their pursuers. Soon, however, meeting those from opposite directions, they whirled in mad despair, vainly endeavoring to break through the extended line of horsemen, who were constantly galloping about the struggling mass with shouts and thrusts from their steel-pointed *garrochas* [long prods][8]

South American cattle remained largely wild until the mid-nineteenth century, so they, like the fierce longhorns of the old Texas brush country, made dangerous adversaries during roundup.

After a rough day in the saddle, the horsemen enjoyed similar but not identical pleasures. All three groups were addicted to strong tobacco—many cowboys and llaneros chewed, while gauchos preferred to smoke black cigars. The former groups downed huge drafts of thick, black coffee, whereas the gaucho favored a caffeine-rich herbal tea called *mate*. Gauchos sipped *mate* through a communal metal straw from a hollowed-out gourd, which was passed around a circle. Gambling and horse races proved immensely popular for after-hours diversion. Card games often separated ranch hands from their wages, and gauchos developed a unique practice called *taba*. In this game of chance, contestants threw the knuckle bone of a cow and bet on whether the result would come up heads or tails. Gauchos, cowboys, and Mexican vaqueros enjoyed the ring race (*la sortija*) in which galloping riders tried to skewer with a short lance a small gold ring dangling by a thread.[9]

To the often unsympathetic outsider, gauchos, llaneros, and cowboys seemed to share another trait—they were more superstitious than religious in their beliefs. In 1869 Richard A. Seymour noted that "the gauchos make a perfect jest of everything connected with religion, and are scarcely ever seen inside a church."[10] Ramón Páez described the beliefs of the llaneros: "Being of a rather superstitious turn of mind, these people believe that by decorating their deadly weapons with some insignia of their religion, they are rendered more effectual. . . . Christianity, like the Spanish language, exists among them, it is true; but corrupted and enveloped in dark superstition, almost bordering on idolatry."[11] A cattle dealer, quoted in the Fort Worth *Texas Live Stock Journal* of January

21, 1888, summarized the role of religion in cowboy life: "The average cowboy does not bother himself about religion. The creeds and isms that worry civilization are a sealed book to the ranger, who is distinctively a fatalist."

All three of these equestrian types wore clothing well adapted to their local environments. On the temperate pampa, the gaucho clothed himself in woolens and cottons. His large poncho kept out cold winds and rains that swept down from the high Andes Mountains to the west. Initially, Indian and mestizo women of the interior provinces of Argentina hand wove these versatile garments. By the 1830s machine-loomed textiles from Great Britain began to displace handmade ponchos. When finances permitted, a gaucho decorated his broad leather belt, the haft of his long knife, and his riding gear with silver coins and tooled designs.[12]

In the last half of the nineteenth century, gauchos adopted other items of European clothing, including baggy trousers and machine-made boots. The latter replaced his traditional *botas de potro*, crude leggings that the gaucho fashioned from the hide of a colt's legs. He stripped the hide off a freshly killed horse and molded the still wet skin to his own legs, leaving the toes open to clutch the stirrups. A short-brimmed straw hat and bright kerchief topped the gaucho's head and kept his long, shaggy hair out of his eyes.[13]

Llaneros, working on a humid, tropical plain, wore scant clothing. Loose, light-colored cotton garments generally sufficed. Lraneros worked barefooted or with only light sandals on their feet. The flashy ornamentation that graced the gaucho (when he could afford it) appears to have been largely absent from the llanero's wardrobe.[14]

The cowboy had access to a much wider range of factory-made clothing and equipment. His broad-brimmed hat, wool or cotton shirt and trousers, belt, and boots came from growing centers of manufacturing in the cities. A cowhand might splurge and spend most or all of his meager wage on a fancy outfit to wear to town. Individual touches of color and unique design helped to differentiate one cowboy "uniform" from another.[15] Thus the varied clothing of these three groups reflects both the different climates in which they worked and the varying levels of industrial activity in their respective countries.

The literary and symbolic evocations of these three groups of horsemen, even more than their actual historical development, show strong similarities. All three remain important in their respective nations as symbols of rugged individualism, unbending principle, and frontier spirit and courage. All three inspired major works of literature, although the gaucho and llanero genres hold a much higher place in Latin American letters than cowboy writings do in the United States.[16]

The gaucho came to be immortalized in a host of writings in Argentina, Brazil, and Uruguay. Most importantly, José Hernández recorded the injustices and persecution visited upon the gaucho by unscrupulous officials in his two-part poem titled *Martín Fierro*. This work, published in 1872 and 1879, became the national epic of the Argentine pampas. In 1926 Ricardo Güiraldes added his classic novel, *Don Segundo Sombra*, to Argentina's gaucho literature. And *Doña Bárbara*, a heroic tale of civilization coming into conflict with the barbarism of the llanos, became one of Venezuela's literary treasures. Rómulo Gallegos, the author of this 1929 novel, later became president of his nation.

Although U.S. cowboy memoirs and novels are numerous, none is as treasured in North American letters. On the other hand, because many cowboys could read and write (unlike the always illiterate gaucho and llanero), we have quite a few firsthand accounts of their lives that add immeasurably to our understanding of cowboy culture.[17]

The many similarities between these three equestrian types should not blind us to major differences. In both working and fighting, the three chose different tools and weapons. According to Ramón Páez, llaneros in battle utilized "a lance, a blunderbuss, and a fine sword."[18] The gaucho became deadly with lance and knife (*facón*). They frequently engaged in knife duels, wielding their long deadly *facones* and wrapping a poncho around one arm as a shield.[19]

Gauchos also twirled the *bolas*. William MacCann, a British visitor to Argentina in the late 1840s, described the weapon: "The bolas consists of three stout thongs, each five feet from the centre, with a ball at the end of each. When flung at an animal's hind legs, the bolas entwines round them. . . . It may be thrown fifty to sixty yards with some certainty."[20] The six-shooter and repeating rifle, available in the technologically more advanced United States, never found a place among gauchos.

Jane M. Loy Rausch, a leading scholar of the llanos, has identified other significant differences between llaneros and gauchos. The strictly equestrian gaucho spent so much time in the saddle that his legs became bowed and his big toe was curved and deformed from gripping the stirrup barefooted. Some gauchos could barely walk. The llanero, faced with the varied habitat of a tropical plain, also had to be a skilled swimmer and boatman. The tropics provided a varied diet of yucca, bananas, rice, and corn as well as dried meat and coffee. The gaucho lived almost strictly on fresh beef (never dried) and *mate*. Finally, the economic modernization of the Argentine pampas, with new railroads, barbed wire, hybrid livestock, and agriculture, helped doom the gaucho to obsolescence. No comparable modernizing changes swept the llano, which remained an isolated, static frontier well into the twentieth century.[21]

A major difference between these three groups is the time spans that they occupied in their nation's histories. The wild cattle hunters of the pampa plied their trade as early as the seventeenth century, and gauchos as a social group continued in existence until the 1870s. Thereafter, only scattered individuals continued to live the traditional gaucho life. The llanero of Colombia likewise spanned centuries of his nation's history. The great U.S. cattle drives northward from Texas began in 1866 and ended by 1890. Fencing and farming quickly altered traditional open-range ranching, and the free-riding days of the cowboy were numbered. Of course, cowboys did not disappear from the American West, but the classic era of cowboy life was gone.[22]

Cowboys lived in less remote and primitive circumstances than their Latin American counterparts. The fast-growing industrial base of the United States provided the cowboy with a number of his necessities, from firearms, saddle, and boots, to canned goods and reading material. The railroad, a major link with civilization, prompted the great trail drives that gave employment to thousands of ranch hands. In contrast, home-made and handmade items accompanied the llanero and gaucho. Likewise, the Mexican vaquero often made his own saddle and tack. The gaucho plaited quirts and lariats. Isolated from distant centers of manufacturing, the llanero also had to improvise and make his own gear. The railroad, which provided employment for cowboys, in contrast hastened the decline of the gaucho by supplanting long livestock drives to Buenos Aires markets with cattle cars and by facilitating the spread of agriculture across the pampas.[23]

The three groups of horsemen also faced different political climates and economic prospects. With thrift, hard work, and a bit of luck, a cowboy could gather a small herd of his own and perhaps find a piece of grazing land not already occupied by one of the large outfits. But a politically powerful elite in Argentina maintained tight control of land and thus prevented the gaucho or small farmer from joining the ranks of the propertied.[24]

The gaucho and llanero also faced political and military disruptions largely unknown in the American West. Although an Indian attack or gang of rustlers could force a cowboy into trading the lasso for the six-shooter, he did not face chronic civil wars and the consequent threat of military conscription. On the llanos and the pampas, military commanders could sweep into a ranch, draft the hands, and hold them in service indefinitely. Such uprooting and violence made the ranch hand's existence a most precarious one.[25]

Overall, we see clear resemblances among the great horsemen of North and South America. Virtues and vices of these three groups transcend national borders and time. But major differences also mark their historical evolution, and such elements still call out for study. What remains evident is the continuing importance and impact of cowboy culture in all nations where the cowboy, llanero, and gaucho rode. These figures, colorful and intriguing in historical perspective, continue to be a significant source of ideas and inspiration for many people today. The more we know about them as historical figures, the more we will know about ourselves as peoples of the Americas.

Chapter 6

Frontier Institutions

Western Saloons and Argentine Pulperías

Rural society lacks the extensive network of institutions that characterizes urban life. Thus the institutions that do exist in rural society play vital, varied roles. This chapter compares the social and economic functions of the saloon in the western United States with its counterpart, the pulpería, *on the pampas of Argentina. Similar male-dominated "saloon cultures" developed in both countries.*

Only a limited number of social institutions functioned in sparsely populated nineteenth-century cattle frontier regions of the Americas. The ranch, as a central socioeconomic complex, took on added importance. Ranch owners often took upon themselves political and legal powers exercised by civic officials in more settled areas. In the cattle regions of the American West and the pampas of Argentina, taverns were important local institutions. A comparison of social activities in the western saloon and the Argentine *pulpería*—combination country store and tavern—reveals strong similarities. As frontier institutions, they served analogous multiple functions, and their cowboy and gaucho patrons behaved according to the norms of similar "saloon cultures."[1]

Beyond their intrinsic importance as frontier institutions, the saloon and the pulpería helped to shape many of the

Gaucho knife fight. Photograph by F. Rimathe, circa 1885. (Archivo General de la Nación, Buenos Aires, Argentina)

Gauchos sipping *mate* and playing cards, circa 1910. (Author's collection)

Gauchos often engaged in singing duels at the pulpería. Caricature by Florencio Molina Campos. (Author's collection)

Card game at a pulpería. Caricature by Florencio Molina Campos. (Author's collection)

negative stereotypes of the cowboy and the gaucho—the itinerant cattle hunter and ranch hand of the pampas. It was in the saloons of western cow towns that eastern journalists formed their judgment of cowboys as wild and drunken. A writer in the *Cheyenne Daily Leader* described cowboys in 1882: "Morally, as a class, they are foulmouthed, blasphemous, drunken, lecherous, utterly corrupt." The newspaper found their behavior in town particularly reprehensible because there "liquor has the ascendancy over them." Relatively comfortable taverns, rich with gossip and news, held considerably more attraction for eastern writers than did the hot dusty plains, so it is not surprising that writers spent more time in the saloon than in the saddle.[2]

Similarly, European travelers on the pampa saw gauchos lounging, drinking, gambling, and fighting at pulperías. Outsiders formed equally unflattering estimates of the gaucho character. One mid-nineteenth-century visitor opined that "gambling is the moving spirit of existence and enjoyment in the real gaucho. Indeed the veritable camp gaucho is a sort of loafer, hanging about pulperías, looking out for gaucho-flats to fleece of whatever they have about them, drinking caña and gin, now and then ripping up somebody with his knife after a dispute of the most insignificant nature."[3]

By viewing cowboys and gauchos at rest and play, rather than at work in the saddle, many observers recorded biased conclusions about their character and way of life. For most cowhands of Argentina and the United States, idling and drinking at public houses represented only a small, if more highly visible, portion of their lives. Like other elements of cowboy life, the time spent "hellin' 'round town" became exaggerated and romanticized.

Origins and Functions

Many aspects of tavern life in Argentina and the North American West were similar, including the origins of the institutions. Western saloons grew from urban roots in colonial America, where taverns and hotels provided both lodging and liquor. Such institutions served as important political and social meeting places during the colonial period. For instance, in 1788 the Hillsborough Convention voted that the capital of North Carolina had to be built within ten miles of a tavern located on Isaac Hunter's plantation. As a result, Raleigh, in Wake County, was laid out as the state's capital in 1792.[4]

The etymology of the word *saloon* includes the sense of an abode (German *saal*), a large room (French *salon*), or hall (Dutch *zaal*). The term, meant to conjure up images of a lavish French salon, came into general use in the United States during the 1840s. As the settlers moved westward, state laws were changed in the 1830s and 1840s to permit the sale of alcohol without lodging facilities. Richard Erdoes identifies New Orleans, St. Louis, Chicago, and San Francisco as especially important in shaping the nature of the western saloon. At the cutting edge of the moving frontier, the saloon carried urban values and practices westward. It also served as a principal theater where western and eastern ideas and practices met, melded, and clashed.[5]

Argentine pulperías also first operated in towns, where they sold liquor and incidentals. On the pampa, where vast distances separated settlements, they served as way stations. Although the western saloon often shed the historic lodging function of the tavern, the rural pulpería added the services of posthouse for travelers. In his fine novel of gaucho life,

Don Segundo Sombra, Ricardo Güiraldes describes a typical country tavern of the pampa: "It was a single building, rectangular-shaped; the taproom was an open room on the right with benches where we sat side by side like swallows on a wire. The storekeeper handed out the drinks through a heavy iron grating that caged him in with tiers of brightly labeled bottles, flasks, and jugs of every kind. Skin sacks of *mate* leaf, demijohns of liquor, different-shaped barrels, saddles, blankets, horse pads, lassos, covered the floor."[6]

Accommodations at these posthouses remained rudimentary through the nineteenth century. Guests could partake of a spartan meal and sleep on the floor amid hordes of ravenous insects and bold rats. Although similar to the businesses operating in Buenos Aires and other towns, rural pulperías—those frequented by gauchos—took on a different character. Gauchos, avoiding contact with civic and military officials whenever possible, preferred the remoteness of the rural public house. Families of the landed elite often owned the pulperías and operated them through managers as adjuncts to their ranching and mercantile interests. Although a few bottles of cheap French wine occasionally graced the shelves of these crude country stores, pulperías held few other accoutrements of urban or European civilization.[7]

In some ways, the pulpería resembled the road ranch (or "ranche") of the Great Plains. These way stations offered humble shelter to plains transients benighted between towns. A Cincinnati banker, James F. Meline, described a Nebraska road ranch in 1866 as "not a dwelling, nor a farmhouse, nor a store, nor a tavern, but all of these and more." These rude structures often carried colorful, suggestive names, such as "Dirty Woman's" and "Fort Wicked" in Colorado. (An important historical footnote to the road ranches is that they showed that cattle could forage for enough dried prairie grass to survive Great Plains winters.) But unlike the pulpería, which supported local area gauchos and transients, the road ranch catered almost entirely to passing migrants.[8]

Despite some differences, however, western saloons and Argentine pulperías both fulfilled a variety of functions. The public house in American history has operated as courtroom, church, political arena, barber shop, trading post, post office, and library, in addition to its usual services. Since cash flowed into taverns on the specie-short frontier, many saloon keepers took advantage of the lack of banks by making loans. One Denver tavern owner, "Uncle Dick" Wootney, charged up to 20 percent interest per day. Saloons also provided a logical and convenient site for illicit activities, including prostitution, gambling, and fencing stolen goods.[9]

Pulperías, while not quite as varied in their functions as the whiskey mills of the American West, also provided a diverse set of services. The proprietors, or *pulperos*, sold liquor, basic necessities, and the gaucho's favorite *vicios* (his vices of *mate* tea and tobacco). Pulperías functioned as hiring halls: A rancher in need of hands for a roundup could count on finding unemployed and willing peons at the local pulpería. The seasonal nature of ranch work left gauchos without wage income for months at a time, so the pulpero often extended credit. Travel restrictions and internal passport requirements imposed on gauchos helped to secure the pulpero's outlay. Some ranches issued tokens for payment of wages that circulated locally as currency at stores on the specie-short pampa. Thus the pulpería added banking functions to its other activities. Although the sale of liquor and incidentals brought in some income, the real profits of a pulpería came through its function as a trading post. Pulperos paid for hides and ostrich feathers, usually asking few questions about origin, brands, or ownership. Pulperías became important collection points for licit and illicit livestock produce—cattle and horsehides, tallow, and bones—that eventually reached merchant houses in Buenos Aires for shipment to European markets. Salted beef went to feed slaves in Brazil and Cuba.[10]

It would seem that gauchos had somewhat better access to illicit gains than did North American cowboys. Rural pulperías, spread far across the pampa, operated beyond the pale of adequate policing. In addition, mobile stores (*pulperías volantes*), run by itinerant merchants, exchanged liquor and goods for hides and feathers—far from the watchful eye of the justice of the peace. The landed elite lobbied strenuously for repression of the traveling merchants. They charged that the itinerant traders encouraged drunkenness, disorder, and theft. Pulperías volantes also offered unwelcome competition for the *estanciero*'s own country store. Buenos Aires Province banned the traveling traders in 1831; bans followed in Corrientes in 1833 and Santa Fe in 1836. None of the bans was successful, however, and the maligned, itinerant *mercachifles* continued their profitable, illicit activities.[11]

Because of the substantial market for illicit livestock produce, Argentine gauchos could earn a marginal living by cooperating with corrupt pulperos and ranchers in the contraband capitalism of the pampa. Additionally, European fashion fads had created a demand for ostrich feathers, which were gathered by bands of gaucho hunters. Thus, gauchos had access to sources of income (albeit meager) that cowboys lacked. Unemployed cowboys on the drift might well butcher someone else's beef (calling it a "slow elk" or a "big antelope") for a meal. And a mavericker could build a herd from the calves of other people's animals. Rustling and poaching occurred in the American West, but they were not on the same scale nor considered as acceptable as similar activities on the pampas.[12]

Thomas Noel identified a number of illegal business activities in the saloons of Denver. Fencing stolen goods provided additional income to some tavern keepers. At Denver's more unscrupulous saloons, drunk customers were sometimes rolled for whatever remaining cash they possessed. Such activities did not decrease a saloon's attractiveness, however. As another observer has noted: "It is a curious historical fact that vile gambling joints peopled by knaves, sharpers, ropers, and steerers have only served to heighten the excitement and increase their patronage."[13]

Drinking, Machismo, and Violence

Despite the multifunctional nature of barrooms, most patrons frequented them to drink and to gamble. Behavior in taverns in both the American West and Argentina seems to bear out partially David G. Mandelbaum's cross-cultural observations about drinking. He found that drinking (*a*) tends to be a male activity, (*b*) is normally a social rather than a solitary pursuit, (*c*) occurs usually among peer groups and age cohorts, and (*d*) cements social solidarity and amity. Only on the last point did saloon and pulpería behavior differ markedly. Although amity could be the outcome of drinking, aggression and conflict were much more likely, particularly in the pulpería.[14]

As sites of predominantly male activity, taverns provided a logical showcase for exhibitions of manliness or machismo. Lionel Tiger's notion of "male bonding" is faulty historically and biologically, but clearly "treating" or "buying drinks for the house" represented a means of temporarily uniting a group of drinking men. It was a gross breach of barroom etiquette to refuse a proffered drink, although in the United States one could sometimes get away with substituting coffee for liquor. Toasting, or calls of "bottoms up," provided another communal activity that brought drinkers together in a brief shared moment. Recent research on alcoholism has shown a correlation between participation in masculine activities and problem drinking in the United States. The cultural links between "manliness" and the consumption of alcohol appear to be pervasive and enduring.[15]

The rosy glow induced by friendly social drinking, however, often turned to the vivid red of violent anger. Saloons earned their widespread reputations as sites of fighting and death. The temporary bonds of communal drinking often gave way to contests of dominance, competition, and conflict. Rousing, furniture-smashing saloon fistfights ("dog fights") were largely creations of the Western movies; real cowboys disdained fisticuffs. (As one old-timer remarked, "If the Lord had intended me to fight like a dog, He'd a-give me longer teeth and claws.") But a cowboy did not hesitate to fight with a knife and a "manstopper" (gun). Some cattle-country saloons became infamous. Violence at the original "Bucket of Blood" saloon, owned by Shorty Young in Havre, Montana, led cowboys to apply the term to any tough whiskey mill. Elliott West found similarly high levels of homicide in the saloons of Rocky Mountain mining towns.[16]

Argentine pulperías became justifiably famous for bloody knife fights. Gauchos skillfully wielded long, deadly swordlike knives (*facones*) well after firearms reached Argentina. One rancher of the pampas suggested in 1856 (with some exaggeration) that 99 percent of homicides, injuries, and disorders occurred at pulperías. Police and justice of the peace records are full of cases in which knife duels ended in the wounding or death of one combatant and the precipitous flight of the other to more remote areas of the frontier. Despite the fact that the traditional goal of gaucho knife duels was simply to mark an opponent's face, drunken fights often went far beyond the rituals of dueling.[17]

William B. Taylor noted the same combination of machismo, drink, and violence in taverns and *pulquerías* of colonial Mexico. Arguments and contests of dominance often spawned fights. During the late colonial period in Mexico City, patrons battled one another in lower-class bars. Forty-five percent of all arrests in the city in 1798 were alcohol-related. In the Mexican countryside or the capital, refusal of a drink could be taken as a serious affront to manly honor and could precipitate a fight. William and Claudia Madsen found the same potent forces of machismo, verbal duels, drinking, and aggression among mestizos in contemporary Mexico.[18]

Alcohol-related violence at one barroom helped seal the doom of the western saloon. In the Texas town of Richmond (just southwest of Houston) stood the nondescript Brahma Bull and Red Hot Bar. In 1889 drunken patrons violently beat a man named David Nation. The victim and his wife, Carry Nation, moved to Kansas thereafter. Her bar-smashing crusade in that state pushed ahead the ultimately successful drive for national Prohibition of alcohol. In 1920 the Eighteenth Amendment to the U.S. Constitution went into effect, thereby killing the already ailing western saloon as an institution.[19]

Barroom violence did not stem from mere physiological changes induced by alcohol. Although alcohol impairs sensorimotor capabilities, it does not necessarily act as a disinhibiting agent, nor does it necessarily suspend moral judgment. Rather, social conventions influence drunken comportment, just as they do the behavior of sober persons. Mandelbaum points out that cultural expectations regulate emotional as well as physiological reactions to liquor. A link clearly exists between increased aggression and the consumption of alcohol. But even that relationship is not a matter of strict physiology. Men who drink distilled spirits show higher levels of aggression than those who consume beer. But so do men given a placebo who think that they are consuming a distilled beverage.[20]

Violence and lack of accountability for one's actions are part of a different set of "time-out" norms. In the case of the saloon culture, the "time-out" norms represent the values and behaviors of an exaggerated machismo. For example, the killing of a gaucho in a drunken duel was considered to be a *desgracia*—an unfortunate accident. In the eyes of his peers, the killer deserved sympathy, not blame. In a sense, alcohol was used as a convenient excuse to escape the restrictive conventions of society and embrace other norms of the saloon culture. These norms, different from those of "proper society" outside the tavern, shaped the actions of drinking men. Assertive and domineering machismo, verbal and physical aggression, and gambling with abandon were part of the saloon culture of both the northern and southern frontiers. Despite somewhat different cultural heritages, frontier barrooms of North and South America show marked similarities as theaters of excessive machismo.[21]

Anglo-American cowboys carried the cultural baggage of a Protestant work ethic that revered and rewarded hard work and distrusted idleness. Nevertheless, Americans drank pro-digiously during the colonial period. Rum and homemade whiskey were especially popular for slacking thirst in the eighteenth century. Drinking probably increased in the nineteenth century, and alcohol became one of the many targets of religiously motivated social reformers. Like sailors home from the sea, cowboys engaged in spree drinking when the rare opportunity presented itself. The end of a long trail drive or of a roundup and branding season provided two such opportunities. But drinking bouts were separated by long dry periods. Liquor was often unavailable outside of towns, and some ranchers insisted on sobriety on the ranch. "Teddy Blue" Abbott relates the story of a rancher who offered his foreman one hundred head of cattle to stay sober for a year. American social critics identified vagrancy, idleness, and tavern-going as vices associated with the "unworthy" poor. Although spree drinking was pardoned, if not entirely condoned, no working cowboy could afford (in monetary or social terms) to idle away his days at the saloons.[22]

The abstemious Spanish Roman Catholic heritage also condemned excessive drinking. The epithet of "drunkard" was an extreme insult. But ritualized drunkenness in connection with festivals was permissible. According to one foreign observer, "feast days are strictly kept by the gauchos in their own peculiar way," which meant accompanied by much drinking. But the great number of Catholic feast days provided many more opportunities for acceptable drunkenness than the sparse Protestant religious calendar and the seasonal work schedule on the ranch. During his long dictatorship as governor of Buenos Aires Province, Juan Manuel de Rosas issued decrees to eliminate some of the many holidays that provided excuses for drinking and idleness.[23]

One minor difference between cowboys and gauchos was in the types of beverages consumed. Gauchos drank fermented *caña* or gin at the pulpería. Caña, the favorite, was distilled from sugar cane juice. The juice of palm trees could also be processed into an alcoholic drink. Pulperos also sold other beverages. One late nineteenth-century visitor to the pampa recalled a pulpería where "vermuth, absinthe, squarefaced gin, Carlon, and *vino seco* stand in a row, with a barrel of Brazilian caña, on the top of which the *pulpero* ostentatiously parades his pistol and his knife."[24]

Cowboys at western saloons favored whiskey—bourbon, rye, or corn—which they generically termed "bitters." Texas cowboys referred to whiskey as "Kansas sheep-dip" in honor of the cow towns where they quaffed drinks at the end of a trail drive. Near Utah, cowboys called very strong whiskey a "Brigham Young cocktail," because "one sip and you're a confirmed polygamist." Other colloquial names for liquor included tornado juice, coffin varnish, mountain dew, red eye, red ink, snake poison, and tanglefoot. Beer enjoyed great popularity toward the end of the nineteenth century as breweries moved into the West[25]

Prices charged for beverages at saloons segregated western bars by social class. Denver saloons charged from five to twenty-five cents for a mug of beer. Cowboys gathered at the cheap saloons, while cattlemen, buyers, and other business-men gathered at fancier bars in hotels. The physical layout of saloons could also separate customers by class. In addition, racial segregation excluded Chinese, discriminated against Hispanics, and isolated blacks in separate establishments. In short, the same class and racial divisions that cut through frontier society also obtained in the western whiskey mills[26]

The Gambling Spirit

Honoré de Balzac wrote that "the gambling passion lurks at the bottom of every heart." Ubiquitous throughout history, gambling was epidemic among cowboys and gauchos. Like heavy drinking, aversion to footwork, and machismo, it represented another element of cowboy culture. Tavern keepers were more than happy to host games of chance. Card

games played in cattle frontiers traced their origins to Europe.
Spain, perhaps the card-playing capital of medieval Europe,
numbered many fanatical players. Soldiers, sailors, and even
clerics played cards enthusiastically. Canasta, a variant of
rummy, had many adherents. That popular game, and many
others, traveled from Spain to Spanish America with the
conquistadors.[27]

In Spanish America, regional favorites appeared. In Mexico,
both men and women of all classes patronized *salas* or
gambling halls. Women often worked as dealers. Spanish
monte, played like short faro, reigned as the most popular
card game of Mexico. In Argentina, William MacCann noted
that at the pulperías, the gauchos' "chief amusement is card
playing, and they are confirmed gamblers." On the pampa,
however, the most popular card game was *truco*. Played with
a forty-card deck, it included a good bit of clever signaling,
witty table talk, and verbal sparring. In some cases, players
also sang verses back and forth as part of the game.[28]

The dandified Mississippi riverboat gambler is the most
colorful representative of western gaming, but every saloon
included a number of busy card tables. One Denver pioneer
wrote in an 1859 letter that "there is more drinking and
gambling here in one day than in Kansas City in six—in fact
about one-half of the population do nothing else but drink
whiskey and play cards." But by 1872 Kansas City, the
"Cowboy Capital," offered a range of lavish establishments,
including the Alhambra, Lady Gay, Alamo, and Lone Star.
Gamblers enjoyed the hospitality of the Gold Room in
Cheyenne and the Bull's Head in Abilene.[29]

Cowboys favored the simplicity and clarity of poker,
especially draw and stud. The games of faro and monte also
held favor with many gamblers. Cowboys distrusted compli-
cated gambling machinery or fancy card games, just as they

distrusted other artifacts of eastern culture. Many cowboys lost their hard-earned wages to more skillful gamblers at saloon tables. As one Montana cowboy recalled, "When I would get into a town I wanted to have a good time. I usually took a few drinks, and sometimes got into a game of poker, and generally left town 'broke.'" Cheating in many guises was commonplace. A "card mechanic" might "jump the cut" and deal himself an especially good hand. "Buying chips" came to mean jumping into a fight—evidence of the close relationship between gambling and fighting. Many ranchers prohibited gambling at the home place, so sprees in town came as a welcome relief. Cowboys also enjoyed poker games around a roundup campfire, if the roundup boss permitted it.[30]

For the gaucho card playing was only a small part of his gambling activity. As Thomas Hutchinson commented, gambling was the "life, soul, and very existence" of gauchos. In addition to cards, gauchos enjoyed playing *taba*. In this ancestor of modern dice games, players threw the knuckle or anklebone (the *tali* or *astragali*) of cattle or horses. The outcome of the throw—heads or tails—determined the winner. As elsewhere in Latin America, cockfights drew large, boisterous crowds. In addition, gauchos participated in and bet on a number of contests on horseback. By sponsoring a horse race, ostrich hunt, or similar event, a pulpero could draw patrons from great distances on the pampas.[31]

Prostitution

Drinking and gambling occupied most patrons, but taverns also offered other activities to attract customers and to generate additional profits. Prostitution provided a natural adjunct to liquor sales. Richard Erdoes notes that "Westerners divided women into two categories—good ones and bad ones." A Virginia City newspaper reporter, Alfred Doten, wrote a revealing journal entry in 1870 about a benefit ball held to aid Benito Juárez and the Mexico liberals: "The women were principally whores, altho there were some decent women among them." The sexual imbalance toward males in frontier regions dictated that most men, especially poor, working cowboys, socialized only with "bad ones."

An Argentine commentator, Ezequiel Martínez Estrada, pointed out a similar circumstance on the pampa. Of women on the plains, "there were only two extremes, immured chastity and prostitution." The demands of ranch work, as well as powerful negative pressures from the landed elite, condemned most gauchos to enforced bachelorhood, or, at best, to serial concubinage. Some ranchers discouraged or even prohibited women from living on the ranch because they aroused jealous conflict between the men. Gauchos lived mobile lives to meet the requirements of ranch work and to escape military conscription. Barred effectively from land ownership, gauchos had few opportunities to set up a stable home life. Prostitutes were often their only opportunity for female companionship.[32]

The "fallen angels," "soiled doves," or "calico queens" of the West graced most cow towns, despite city ordinances and the determined efforts of civic and religious reformers. Abilene, the notable exception, made a largely successful effort to exclude prostitutes in 1870. The term *red light district* supposedly originated in one of the foremost cow towns, Dodge City. As the *Rocky Mountain News* lamented in 1889, saloons "were the most fruitful source for breeding and feeding prostitution." Though some sanitized memoirs of life in the Old West discreetly omit this element of cowboy life, others are more forthright. "Teddy Blue" Abbott devotes an entire chapter of his memoirs to the cowboy's relationship with prostitutes. Some, such as Cattle Annie, with her heart of gold, became legends. Besides prostitutes, saloons employed "hurdy-gurdy" girls who danced with patrons and brought them drinks—for a price.[33]

If the local population near a pulpería did not suffice to support resident prostitutes, an itinerant madam and her charges probably serviced the area. The arrival of such an entourage in a high-wheeled oxcart signaled the beginning of an impromptu fiesta that quickly drew gauchos from far and wide. Setting up small tents for the clients and women, the madam sold candles of varying lengths that measured the time allotted to each patron. Because of the lack of employment opportunities for women in the countryside, many moved to towns and worked as prostitutes. Most towns passed ordinances that regulated the business and required periodic health inspections. With a nod to social propriety, some municipalities prohibited solicitation on the street.[34]

Demise of the Saloon and Pulpería

As frontier institutions, the pulpería and the saloon were as vulnerable to the encroachments of "civilization" as other elements of frontier life. Along with the ranch, the tavern served essential social and economic functions in the absence of more specialized institutions. But as frontier regions became more settled, taverns, like their cowboy patrons, went into decline. The twin forces of regulation and specialization doomed the frontier saloon and pulpería by the early twentieth century. Modernizing elites in Argentina legislated away much of the gaucho's life, including favored equestrian games, ostrich hunts, and cockfights. Other laws restricted the gaucho's movements or forced him into obligatory military service. With the taming of the gaucho population, the pulpería became a relic of the past. A few have been preserved as museum sites by traditionalist groups, but, as with other elements of gaucho life, the form, not the substance, remains.[35]

Similar forces altered and eclipsed the western saloon. In the United States, municipal reform and temperance movements set about to uplift society. The Women's Christian Temperance Union movement, founded in 1874, made the prohibition of liquor its avowed goal the following year. Led by the vigorous Frances E. Willard, the WCTU targeted local saloons and taverns for attack. Funded by churches and led by clergy, the Anti-Saloon League joined the WCTU in its fight in 1895. These groups and other reform movements coalesced in the Progressive Era and gradually succeeded in altering American politics and in banning prostitution, gambling, and finally, with the coming of Prohibition, alcohol. The Eighteenth Amendment sounded the death knell for 177,790 saloons throughout the land in January 1920. Carry Nation gained revenge on the barroom brawlers of Richmond, Texas, who had beaten her husband three decades before. One old Arizona gambler complained bitterly in 1908 of the new "milksop frontier": "The buttermilk boys have driven us into the ditch."[36]

In addition to the effects of Progressive reform and other social change, the growth of cities spawned new specialized services and institutions that supplanted the multifunctional saloon. As "civilization" overtook the frontier, saloons of the West and pulperías of the pampa lost both their clientele and their monopoly on services. While they lasted, they had similar functions and similar saloon cultures. But in the twentieth century, both institutions became museum relics, symbols of a lost frontier of the past, frequented by soda-sipping tourists, not hard-drinking cowboys or gauchos.[37]

Part Two

Techniques
and Methods

Chapter 7

Turner's Influence
in Canada and Latin America

In 1893 Frederick Jackson Turner "created" a new field of historical inquiry with his frontier thesis. A legion of scholars has analyzed the impact of the frontier thesis on historiography in the United States. This chapter, however, compares the diffusion, influence, and criticism of Turner's thesis on twentieth-century Canadian, Latin American, and Spanish Borderlands historiographical debate. I conclude that, despite shortcomings in Turner's formulation, the concept of the frontier remains a viable, important analytical tool. Further, I suggest that the examination of historical theory in different cultural contexts can add new critical insights to the theory.

During the past century, scholars have relished, then revised, and finally reviled Frederick Jackson Turner's frontier thesis. I seek neither to praise Turner nor to bury him. Instead I show the wide-ranging impact of Turnerian thought on historians throughout the Western Hemisphere. Thinkers in many nations of the Americas tested Turner's thesis. Most historians have ignored the fact that Turner intended to explain characteristics peculiar to the development of the United States. Unlike Walter Prescott Webb's later formulation, Turner never aspired to explain global history. Nevertheless scholars from the Canadian prairies to the pampas of Argentina developed Turnerian views of the frontier in many different countries.

The concept of the frontier thus generated important historiographical debate across the Americas.[1]

Canada

Canadian historians developed three broad interpretations of the nation's past that relate in some way to the Turner thesis. Two of these perspectives are strongly Turnerian. Canadian scholar J. M. H. Careless calls the first view the "the Environmentalist School, or North Americans All." Like Turner, some Canadians wished to demonstrate Canada's distinctiveness from its European ancestry. For them a focus on the "native North American environment" seemed appropriate.[2]

The second view, a modified frontier thesis, accepted the importance of both frontier and extrafrontier forces. Writers, often exhibiting a degree of nationalism, conceived Canada's past as distinct from both the United States and Europe. The third view, metropolitanism, posited Canada's eastern, urban centers as wielding greater influence in the nation's history than did its frontiers.

Applying Turner's thesis to Canada is not such a far-fetched notion. As Gilman Ostrander has pointed out, "Turner may be said to have been a Canadianist before he was an Americanist." Turner's doctoral thesis at Johns Hopkins emphasized the importance of riverine access in shaping Canada's history. Turner argued that Canada faced no formidable Appalachian barrier that held back inland expansion.[3]

Walter Sage set forth a direct application of Turner in 1928. He erased the boundary between the United States and Canada and presented North American expansion as a single great movement. Marcus Lee Hansen and John Bartlett Brebner presented a similar interpretation. The title of their text emphasized their theme: *The Mingling of the Canadian and American Peoples.*[4]

Chilean rodeo. (Prints and Photographs Division, Library of Congress)

Canadian cowhands relaxing, Bar U Ranch, Alberta. (Glenbow Archives, Calgary, Alberta, NA-285-4)

In 1935 Frank Hawkins Underhill published a study that placed Canada's east-west political conflict within a Turnerian framework. In similar fashion Edmund Henry Oliver in *Winning the Frontier* (1930) traced frontier influences on religion in Canada.[5]

A. L. Burt illustrated strong, pervasive frontier influences in New France, an area often cited by Canadian scholars as defying Turner's thesis. Burt pointed to many factors distinguishing New from Old France. New France exhibited a weak feudal system, settler defiance of church and state power, and a degree of local political participation. As Burt explained, "In contrast to that of the Old World, which developed out of a mass struggle to gain freedom which existing conditions of life denied, the democracy of this continent has existed because the individual would not surrender the freedom which the very conditions of life conferred upon him. It was the freedom of the frontier."[6]

Arthur Lower framed a modified version of the frontier thesis. He acknowledged that a certain class leveling, which he termed *social* democracy, might emerge from any frontier environment, regardless of the ethnicity of the actors. *Political* democracy, however, arose only in societies with a prior democratic tradition. Unlike Sage, Lower found significant differences between Canadian and American democracy. He attributed the stronger democratic impulse in the United States to Canada's briefer frontier experience, its stronger European ties, and its parliamentary form of government.[7]

In his 1946 textbook *Colony to Nation*, Lower described the "spirit of the New World" in strongly Turnerian language:

> While the New World has not had the power to make different things the same, it has had great power to modify, to change old institutions and give them new form and spirit.

In all pioneer agricultural society, where nature was strong and man was weak, social equality was the rule, a sturdy sense of personal values prevailed, an empiric rather than a traditional measurement of men's value. North American democracy was forest-born.[8]

George Stanley turned his focus from Old France to the Canadian West. He found major differences between western Canada and the American West. He argued that the Turner thesis did not fit Canada's development. Canadian settlement never pushed beyond the reach of government organization and law. Western Canada did not suffer frontier lawlessness and violent conflicts. Far from completely rejecting Turner, however, Stanley developed a middle ground. He concluded that while the environment had conditioned economic affairs, European tradition had shaped politics: "The history of Western Canada cannot be explained in terms of either of these factors alone."[9]

Although the frontier thesis clearly influenced Canadian historiography, few scholars accepted it uncritically. Most historians pointed to Canada's closer European ties and to the stronger influence of outside events. Canada had a relatively short frontier experience. French Canada exhibits a cultural background distinct from the Anglo-Saxon. Even though many Canadian historians stressed "environment" as a major factor in Canadian history, the frontier represented only a single element of that environment. Unlike Turner, Canadians did not neglect the importance of transmitted tradition and acquired ideas.

In the late 1940s, Morris Zaslow took stock. He concluded that "despite all the criticisms and modifications, something of the frontier hypothesis seems to have entered into the work of recent Canadian historiography and seems destined to leave its mark upon the writing of the future."[10]

During the 1940s, scholars increasingly questioned the earlier Turnerian and neo-Turnerian interpretations. Metropolitanism, the third view of the Canadian past, stood the frontier thesis on its head. In *The Rise of Toronto, 1850–1890* Donald Campbell Master emphasized Toronto's growing domination over its hinterland. Toronto-Montreal competition, according to Master, reshaped the nation's economic and political face.

Donald Grant Creighton focused on the attempts of the St. Lawrence metropolitan area to extend its economic control. He denied the applicability of the frontier theory as a general explanation of Canada's past. Despite his Laurentian emphasis, he did accept the importance of the frontier during certain historical periods.

Canadian historian J. M. S. Careless explicitly laid out the metropolitan view in 1954. He stressed the importance of eastern, urban factors over the forces of Canada's western and northern frontiers in shaping the nation's development. Metropolitan centers came to dominate the hinterland by supplying capital, transportation, and markets. "The frontier's culture, too," wrote Careless, "originally stems from a metropolitan community; at root, learning and ideas radiate from there."[11]

Turning from eastern to western Canada, we find that Turnerian thought received other challenges. In 1976 David Breen pointed out that Canada's western agrarian frontier opened and closed very quickly—within the space of two decades. A twentieth-century phenomenon, the settlement process had little of the personal and social isolation that Turner imputed to the U.S. frontier.[12] Breen also considered the cattle frontier that preceded western farming. Again, he found little evidence to support Turner. The frontier did not alter preexisting class stratification and strong British cultural values.[13]

As in the United States, recent decades of Canadian historiography have turned distinctly anti-Turnerian. In 1977 Robin W. Winks concluded that "the total meaning of the frontier experience for Canada was quite different from that of the United States." He found no support for Turner's thesis in any of Canada's frontiers.[14] Turner's ideas, however, strongly shaped historiographical debate in Canada, as they did in the United States, for more than half a century.

Latin America

The diffusion of Turnerian thought into Latin America paralleled its spread through Canada. Many Latin American thinkers tested the frontier hypothesis for their region. While revealing some similarities, their works generally concluded that Turner's version of the frontier did not operate in Latin America.

Interestingly, some Latin Americans anticipated Turner's thinking. In 1888 the Brazilian-born French writer Emilio Daireaux described the powerful effect of plains frontiers. He argued that plains frontiers around the world "imprint" their inhabitants with common characteristics, including a "passion for independence."[15]

João Capistrano de Abreu (1853–1927) focused on the dry inland plains of Brazil's northeast, the *sertão*, just as Turner focused on the frontier. This rugged "backlands," lying between the narrow coastal plain and the Amazon basin, became central to his explanation of Brazilian history. Capistrano viewed the sertão as a place of racial and social democracy. His nationalism and "New Worldism" resonate well with Turner's vision.[16]

In 1923 Victor Andrés Belaúnde examined "The Frontier in Hispanic America."[17] He found that Spanish and British colonial settlement patterns contrasted sharply. The Spanish quickly built cities across their vast continental empire. The English, in contrast, colonized only the narrow Atlantic coastal strip. Not until the late eighteenth century did Americans push westward across the Alleghenies.

Belaúnde also contrasted the history of the Mississippi River valley with the Amazon basin. The Mississippi basin yielded fertile soils for farming and easy riverine access. The Amazonian tropical rain forest provided no such bounty of arable land. Access to much of the region proved difficult because of the Andes Mountains and the nature of the rain forest itself.

Belaúnde concluded that only the Río de la Plata and southern Brazil offered regions appropriate for comparison with the U.S. The flat topography and water access made them readily accessible to European immigration. The temperate climate, coastal farmland, navigable rivers, and lack of high mountain barriers paralleled conditions in the United States.

Despite the geographical similarities, however, Belaúnde identified significantly different frontier effects. Spanish policy purposefully created large estates. In contrast, individuals and settler families established a tradition of smaller land parcels in the United States. "Individualism and equality of opportunities, the two great derivations of the frontier principle," did not arise in the Río de la Plata as they did in the U.S. Belaúnde presciently linked land tenure and politics: "large estates continue to be the great obstacle in the way of democracy."

Silvio Zavala, familiar with Belaúnde's essay, shifted his focus to Mexico's vast northern frontier. He asked whether the northern frontier "may be considered a source of the Mexico national type." He concluded that the "North can be considered only a source of social peculiarities," not of Mexican national identity. He found no Turnerian parallels for Mexico.[18]

In contrast, in a 1940 essay Arthur Scott Aiton found a significant basis for comparing frontiers in Latin America and the United States. Aiton recognized the preexistence in Latin America of highly developed, sedentary civilizations. He also noted that, unlike Anglo-Americans, the Spanish absorbed indigenous populations into a new mestizo society as much as possible. Despite such differences, he reached a Turnerian conclusion: "Frontier conditions in Latin America, as elsewhere, developed individualism, self-reliance, democracy, initiative, and willingness to experiment despite closer controls."[19]

Scholars, including Caio Prado, Jr., Gilberto Freyre, and J. F. Normano, have analyzed Brazil's frontier heritage. Freyre, for example, wrote in Turnerian language that "the 'moving frontier' in Brazil has meant the creation of new ways of life and new combinations of culture."[20]

Turner, of course, explained the influence of the frontier on American national character. In 1981 Argentine historian Hebe Clementi examined "National Identity and the Frontier." Unlike most recent scholars, she supported Turner's linkage of the frontier and national identity.[21]

Clementi compared the role of the frontier in the formation of national identity in the United States, Brazil, and Argentina. She focused on the Brazilian slave hunter and explorer (the bandeirante), the Argentine gaucho, and the pioneer of the American West. These frontier figures became national archetypes in their respective nations. Clementi concluded that each "helps to define his nation's character through his participation in the appropriation of empty land, and through his contact with the frontier."[22]

In contrast to Clementi, Brazilian Clodomir Vianna Moog argued that the pioneer of the American West and the bandeirante were antithetical figures. Moog attributed the

great differences not to frontier impact but to different
Portuguese and English approaches to frontier resources. The
English brought "an initially spiritual, practical, and con-
structive spirit in the development of North America." The
Portuguese approached Brazil with "a predatory, extractive
and almost only secondarily religious spirit." Moog attributed
much of the greater material progress of the United States to
these differing approaches toward New World frontiers and
resources. The national archetypes described by both
Clementi and Moog are unduly stereotypical and reduc-
tionist. They do point up, however, the force of frontier
mythology in several nations of the Americas.[23]

Spanish Borderlands

In contrast to Canadian and South American scholars, most
historians of the Spanish Borderlands ignored Turner. This
indifference came despite the exhortation of Herbert Eugene
Bolton, dean and founder of Borderlands studies, to use a
Turnerian lens. "For him," wrote Bolton in 1917, "who inter-
prets, with Turner's insight, the methods and the significance
of the Spanish-American frontier, there awaits a recognition
not less marked or less deserved." Bolton did not practice
what he preached. In *The Spanish Borderlands*, which
appeared four years later, he emphasized the persistence of
Hispanic culture on the frontier.[24]

Only in Alta California did Bolton see a marked alteration
of Spanish imports by the frontier environment. The region's
mild climate, fertile soil, ample Indian labor, and great
distance from markets, said Bolton, combined to produce
atypically "idle" Hispanic frontiersmen. Idle they may have
been, but, Bolton suggested, the *californios* were superior to
other Mexicans. Their isolation gave them a "greater degree of

independence, social at least if not political." Bolton thought that he detected a "mellower spirit" in California.[25]

Neither did Bolton's legion of students apply the Turner thesis. Some Borderlands works, however, shared Turnerian assumptions. In *Los Paisanos*, a 1979 examination of northern New Spain, Oakah L. Jones, Jr., used a Turnerian perspective without mentioning Turner. He concluded that conditions on New Spain's far northern frontier changed Spanish society dramatically. Hispanic frontiersmen over time "became more self-reliant, more individualistic, less class conscious, and more conservative in their political outlook than the people of central New Spain."[26]

After reviewing Turner's impact on Borderlands scholars, David Weber concluded that the Turner thesis "seems even less likely to gain their interest in the future. The thesis has been modified to the point that historians have difficulty either embracing it as an explanatory device or using it as a foil."[27]

Placing Frontiers in Context

Turner's frontier hypothesis failed as "metatheory" throughout the Western Hemisphere. Even if the hypothesis is wanting as a general explanatory device, however, the frontier concept itself offers intriguing and continuing possibilities for analyzing differential development in the Americas.

Revisionist historians notwithstanding, the frontier as an analytical construct remains important in framing the history of the Western Hemisphere. I believe it is counterproductive to bury the concept of frontier simply because Turner's formulation has proved incorrect (see chapter 10).

Several generations of writers rightly criticized Turner's depiction of the frontier as "the meeting point between savagery and civilization." The stark either/or formulation of the frontier thesis and the metropolitan school distorts the importance of interactions across frontiers. These constructs also ignore variations among different types of frontiers (see chapter 1).

Latin American thinkers both anticipated and echoed Turner's pithy concept of the frontier. Interestingly, South American philosophers and novelists, more than historians, highlighted the importance of frontier interactions. The relationship of city and country, or as Domingo F. Sarmiento formulated it, "Civilization and Barbarism," is an old, but useful theme. In 1902, Euclides da Cunha penned *Rebellion in the Backlands*, another classic study of conflict between people of the backlands and the forces of urban modernization.[28] Rómulo Gallegos made the battle between civilization and barbarism the central motif of his powerful 1929 novel, *Doña Bárbara*. The hero, Santos Luzardo, from the city, confronts the powerful witch of the Venezuelan llanos, Doña Bárbara. Civilization triumphs over barbarism, but Gallegos also reveals the close ties and crosscurrents between the two.

Silvio Duncan Baretta and John Markoff moved the motif from the realm of fiction to sociology. They creatively explored the complex interactions between urban "civilization" and cattle frontier "barbarism" in their oft-cited 1978 article. They demonstrated that civilization was "not only the 'mother of barbarism'; it was also its child."[29]

Walter Prescott Webb expanded the concept of frontiers to encompass the entire Western Hemisphere: *The Great Frontier* juxtaposed New World frontiers with European metropolises. I consider his vision a forerunner of world-systems analysis.[30]

Thomas D. Hall and others are giving world-systems analysis some fine tuning. Hall gives new life and significance to frontier analysis by developing a more nuanced look at the periphery. Frontier areas range from weakly incorporated ("contact periphery") to moderately incorporated ("region of refuge"). Hall's analysis accommodates important frontier variations as well as intrafrontier processes and conflicts.[31]

Hall revitalizes the frontier concept by placing it within a world-systems framework. "A frontier," he writes, "is where, in social and geographical space, incorporation occurs." By identifying levels of interaction and incorporation, Hall engenders the frontier with an analytical richness lacking in Turner's simple dualism. "Frontiers are integral parts of world-systems, even though they are—by definition—on the fringe."[32]

Recent presidents of the Western History Association (WHA) have agreed that the frontier concept should be refined, not buried. In his 1987 presidential address, Martin Ridge reminded historians that "the history of frontier theory is too valuable to abandon."[33]

In his 1992 WHA presidential address, Richard Maxwell Brown recast and reinvigorated the frontier concept. He placed Indian-white frontier conflict within the context of incorporation, a view consonant with Hall's work. "From 1850 to 1920, the conservative, consolidating authority of modern capitalistic forces infused the dynamics of the Western Civil War of Incorporation."[34]

Brown drew from recent research on frontier social marginals, including cowboys and bandits, to pose a broad question: "Did a nineteenth-century Western Hemispheric Civil War of Incorporation extend all the way north from the cattle spreads of Chile and Argentina to the prairies of western Canada? The intriguing evidence in Richard W. Slatta's recent comparative study of cowboys of South and North America suggests an affirmative answer."[35]

The study of frontiers has been enriched by framing them within the process of incorporation. As Baretta and Markoff have shown, strong forces operated across the porous cultural membranes typical of frontiers. We need to identify and analyze these forces, some indigenous, some European in origin. Frontier social changes and interactions need more probing. Even if we acquiesce to burying Turner, we should demur from burying the concept of the frontier with him.

Chapter 8

Gaúcho and Gaucho

Comparative Socioeconomic Change
in Rio Grande do Sul and
Buenos Aires Province, 1869–1920

*Frontier regions present special demographic challenges. Because of
their distance from centers of political power and record keeping, cattle
frontiers do not generate very complete demographic records.
Nevertheless we can use census records and economic data to examine
socioeconomic changes for nineteenth-century cattle frontiers.*

*This chapter compares nineteenth-century socioeconomic change in
two important South American cattle-raising regions: Buenos Aires
Province, Argentina, and Rio Grande do Sul, Brazil. By about 1900 the
demographic profiles of the two regions had begun to diverge
substantially. I remain convinced that comparative demographic study
is an important area of frontier research. I am now less sanguine,
however, about how well the theory of the demographic transition
explains the nature and direction of the changes described below.*

Complex socioeconomic changes dramatically altered the
composition and functioning of ranch society in Rio Grande
do Sul and Buenos Aires Province during the late nineteenth
and early twentieth centuries. I compare some of the major
socioeconomic and demographic changes that reshaped
those regions and test the validity of the theory of the
demographic transition for both. Protests by the Brazilian
nationalist Moysés Vellinho to the contrary notwithstanding,
the pampean cattle regions of southern Brazil and Argentina
displayed remarkably similar cultural characteristics and

Gaucho and dogs, Buenos Aires Province, Argentina, 1890. (Archivo General de la Nación, Buenos Aires, Argentina)

Gauchos roasting meat and drinking *mate*, 1927. (Archivo General de la Nación, Buenos Aires, Argentina)

Gauchos enjoyed a variety of equestrian games, including *la sortija*, the ring race. Caricature by Florencio Molina Campos. (Author's collection)

patterns of development. Differences arose in timing and degree, but both areas "modernized" according to the same general pattern and both populations experienced the changes associated with the beginning of the demographic transition to lowered mortality and fertility. Their most significant difference lay in the realm of national politics. Rio Grande had a relatively weak voice in national policy making compared to the political hegemony of pampean cattle ranchers in Argentina.[1]

Dense clouds of myth and symbol, exciting and occasionally half-true but at variance with social realities, obscure the histories of both Rio Grande and Buenos Aires Province. Demographic data, principally from published censuses, offer a useful scalpel to slice through the veil of romanticism and reveal how both societies changed from the late 1800s to the early twentieth century.

Gaúcho and *gaucho*—even defining the terms is as difficult as determining the social realities encompassed by them. The word *gaucho* has been in use since the last quarter of the eighteenth century in the Río de la Plata and most frequently referred to vagabond horsemen who chased, killed, and skinned wild livestock and traded the hides illicitly. The term implied marginality and criminality, but by the nineteenth century it broadened to include virtually all rural horsemen who owned no land. The etymology and usage of the Brazilian term *gaúcho* parallels that of gaucho and also suffers from a number of conflicting interpretations.[2] I will use both terms in a nonpejorative sense throughout this chapter to indicate the rural ranch workers of Rio Grande do Sul and Buenos Aires Province.

Hoary myths of frontier individualism, independence, and egalitarianism clothe both Brazilian and Argentine horsemen. Mythical knights of the pampa pervade literature in both areas. *Riograndense* writers praise the gaúcho as "virile, unafraid, rustic, strong, and chivalrous," and romanticize him as a eugenic paradigm—"a splendid animal of combat" who was at the same time jovial and noisily happy. This mythical, equestrian superman supposedly possessed a democratic spirit evidenced in the equal sharing of ranch work and in the "equality and familiarity between patrons and servants" that precluded the formation of rural social classes.[3]

Myth and romance also dominate the image of the Argentine gaucho. Twentieth-century nationalists rehabilitated the once maligned horseman and cast him as the idealized paragon of Argentine national virtues. The lord of the pampa putatively exhibited generosity, valor, binding friendship, honesty, independence, and a tremendous latent energy and dynamism. "Free air and fat meat," the ringing cry of the gaucho, supposedly bespoke the elegant simplicity of his straightforward, uncomplicated values and desires.[4]

Such romantic depictions contain kernels of truth but reduce the gaúcho and gaucho to static, unidimensional caricatures. By analyzing demographic and socioeconomic changes as revealed in successive censuses, we may eschew the traditionalist fascination with the heroic, epic, and mythic and turn instead toward a more empirical examination of ranch society. Demographic variables indicate the rate, direction, and intensity of change. In general, the demographic similarities of Rio Grande and Buenos Aires underscore their cultural commonalities and point to differences in degree rather than type of social change.[5]

Of the three major regions within Rio Grande—the serra, littoral, and campanha—the latter most clearly manifests the state's cattle culture. Since the eighteenth century, the rolling hills of the campanha, luxuriant with grasses and *umbu* trees, have nourished livestock, prized first for their hides, later for jerked beef, and finally for high-quality chilled and processed meat. The *municipios*, or counties, of the campanha include Alegrete, Bagé, Dom Pedrito, Livramento, Quarahy, Rosario, and Uruguayana. Of all Brazilian counties in 1920, those in the campanha ranked first in number of horses (Alegrete), first in sheep (Uruguayana), and first, second, and third in cattle (Alegrete, Uruguyana, and Livramento).[6]

Argentina's cattle culture, spread over twenty-one million hectares of some of the world's richest, deepest topsoil, presented a more extensive but nevertheless distinctive region. Buenos Aires Province, because of its political hegemony and the ready access of its port to overseas markets, dominated livestock production throughout the nineteenth century. The province presents a useful unit to compare to the campanha, but because of the disparity in size, selected *partidos*, or counties, will be analyzed more closely. These southern counties—Arenales, Ayacucho, Azul, General Alvear, Lobería, Olavarría, Tandil, and Tapalqúe—contained large ranches and vast herds of livestock like the campanha and lay a sufficient distance from the national capital to dilute its powerful, urban influence.[7]

Turbulent civil wars disrupted the campanha and Buenos Aires Province in the mid-nineteenth century as uncompromising factions battled for economic and political control. In the riograndense civil wars of 1833 to 1845, the cattle-ranching elite struggled unsuccessfully for the regional autonomy necessary to modernize the area's economy and to compete favorably with Uruguay and Argentina. In 1852 a coalition of Argentine modernizers, who sought to attract European immigrants, capital, and markets, banded together with the Federalist caudillo from Entre Ríos, General Justo José de Urquiza, to oust Juan Manuel de Rosas. Thereafter the processes of modernization began to transform both regions.

New technologies, including wire fencing, windmills, hybrid livestock breeding, railroads, and refrigeration, altered the traditional concentration upon hides and jerked beef. Both areas experienced the compelling forces of technological change as well as an infusion of foreign influences. The impact came earlier and with greater force to Buenos Aires Province, but both regions changed profoundly[8]

Both Brazilian and Argentine ranchers eagerly pursued new markets and technological improvements to increase profits and consolidate their economic and political power. Argentine ranchers successfully operated as a dynamic, flexible, directing elite whose political might ensured favorable tax, land, immigration, and labor policies. Provincial and national governments played a positive, supportive role for the landed elite by promoting immigration, railroad building, land control, territorial expansion, and other policies consonant with rancher interests[9]

Riograndense ranchers harbored similar ambitions and sensed their deteriorating competitive position vis-à-vis neighboring Uruguay and Argentina. But coffee *fazendeiros* in Río de Janeiro and São Paulo ably wielded political clout to maintain taxes and duties that discriminated against cattle interests in the south. The revolution of 1893–1895 in Rio Grande may have signaled the ranchers' violent reaction to the long-term political marginality that hindered the economic growth of the region[10] More than any other single factor, the political hegemony of ranchers in Buenos Aires Province versus the marginality of campanha landowners in national affairs accounts for the relatively slower and less extensive modernization of Rio Grande.

Argentine estancieros, confidently controlling the national and provincial political machinery throughout the nineteenth century, responded creatively to changing world market

TABLE 1   Selected Argentine Exports (× 1000 Tons), 1876–1914

| Year | Beef | | | Wool | Wheat |
	Dried	Live	Chilled		
1876	30	110	–	89	0.02
1878	34	86	–	88	3
1880	26	55	–	98	1
1882	27	54	–	111	2
1884	19	78	–	114	108
1886	37	128	0.5	132	38
1888	26	95	0.04	132	179
1890	43	150	0.7	118	328
1892	45	125	0.3	155	470
1894	43	220	0.3	162	1,608
1896	46	383	3	188	532
1898	22	359	6	221	645
1900	16	151	25	101	1,930
1902	22	118	70	198	645
1904	12	129	98	169	2,305
1906	5	71	154	149	2,248
1908	7	61	175	176	3,636
1910	9	90	245	151	1,884
1912	9	261	318	165	2,629
1914	2	116	328	117	981

demands. Exports shifted from the traditional emphasis on hides and jerked meat to chilled beef production. Table 1 illustrates this shift from 1876 to 1914. The traditional meat export, jerked beef, peaked in 1896 and dropped rapidly thereafter because of Uruguayan and Brazilian protectionism and because chilled beef shipped to Europe yielded a higher return. Sheep, prized for both mutton and fine wool, continued as an export mainstay. Live cattle shipments overseas had a precarious existence because of the constant threat and ultimate reality of quarantines enacted by the United States and Great Britain to halt the spread of hoof-and-mouth disease.[11]

The most dramatic success story on the Argentine pampa came in cereals production. In addition to an impressive export tonnage (see table 1), the relative proportion of total Argentine exports contributed by cereals shows a marked trend toward rural diversification. For the period from 1880 to 1884, livestock accounted for 89 percent of total Argentine exports and agriculture only 7 percent. Twenty years later the contribution of agriculture had risen to 47 percent of the total, and by 1920–1924 agriculture provided 59 percent of total exports and livestock 37 percent. The rural economy of Buenos Aires Province prospered and modernized as ranchers skillfully utilized foreign capital, markets, tenant farmers, and agricultural laborers but still maintained control of the land.[12]

Campanha ranchers, unable to manipulate Brazilian policies in their favor, could not provide the same inviting milieu to foreigners. Economic growth and diversification lagged behind Argentina. Jerked beef production (*charque*) remained the mainstay of the campanha economy well into the twentieth century. Rio Grande still maintained thirty-one *charqueadas* producing jerked beef in 1920. Eleven functioned in the campanha. As Argentina vacated the charque market in favor of chilled beef, Rio Grande expanded, a trend shown clearly in table 2. Six charqueadas were established in Bagé alone between 1897 and 1914. Although the first chilled beef processing plant opened in Rio Grande in 1903, only a decade after similar developments in Argentina, not until mid–World War I did Armour and Swift commence truly large-scale operations in Livramento and Rio Grande (city), respectively. These modern plants pointed the future direction

TABLE 2   Number of Animals Processed at Saladeros
and Charqueadas, 1890–1907 (Animals Processed × 1000)

Year	Buenos Aires Province	Rio Grande do Sul
1890	371	380
1891	438	455
1892	443	485
1893	381	450
1894	352	380
1895	328	280
1896	210	215
1897	250	320
1898	106	340
1899	101	270
1900	92	232
1901	141	210
1902	181	375
1903	8	360
1904	?	412
1905	?	305
1906	?	375
1907	?	458

Source: Argentine Republic, Censo agropecuário nacional: La ganadería y la agricultura en 1908, 3 vols. (Buenos Aires, 1909), 3: 370–71.

of the livestock industry because together they could process more cattle than all the charqueadas in the state. Meatpackers further altered traditional livestock management by lending technical assistance to breeders to improve the quality of the animals and to render them more suitable for chilled beef production.[13]

Extensive cereal production came to the campanha later than to the Argentine pampa, but in both regions the inexorable advance of wheat brought dislocation and marginalization to the ranch labor force. The technologically unemployed gaúcho exchanged his horse for a tractor, watched livestock trails widened to accommodate trucks, and heard the clank of machinery shatter the pastoral peace of the campanha grasslands. Long denied access to land ownership, the gaúcho, like his Argentine counterpart, suffered the loss of his means of livelihood—tending cattle and sheep.[14]

Large landholdings remained a constant on both the rio-grandense and Argentina pampa despite the welter of rapid, complex changes. Some Argentine estancias had been established with land grants as large as 65,000 hectares or more. During the 1820s Santiago Tobal received nearly 46,000 hectares in Tandil, Bartolo Pereyra 54,000 hectares in Lobería, and Juan M. Silva nearly 65,000 in Azul. In 1914, 93 percent of rural landholdings in the southern Argentine counties listed earlier contained only 53 percent of the land, while a mere 7 percent of the holdings held nearly half the land. Absentee ownership accompanied land monopoly as hired managers administered more than 58 percent of all ranches and farms.[15]

The concentration of landownership in Rio Grande showed an even greater imbalance. In 1920, 93 percent of all native landholders controlled only 30 percent of the land, while the largest 7 percent controlled the other 70 percent of land. The top 3 percent of all landholdings accounted for 50 percent of the land. The rate of absentee ownership ran far below that of Buenos Aires Province. Salaried managers ran only 6 percent of the land.[16] Riograndense ranchers personally managed their estates more often than their Argentine counterparts. The proximity of the Argentine national capital and the early development of an extensive rail network radiating out from Buenos Aires permitted estancieros to enjoy both the income and prestige of land owning and the amenities of cosmopolitan urban life in the port city.

The major demographic processes—migration, fertility, and mortality—reinforce the similarities evident in land tenure and cultural traits of the two regions. Immigration, however, played a greater role in Buenos Aires Province and can be assessed the most significant social difference between the two regions, and after the differential in political power within the nation, the second most important factor overall. After the fall of Rosas at Caceros in early 1852, liberal immigration policies together with the attractiveness of New World economic opportunity brought a flood tide of Europeans to the Argentine pampa. The percentage of foreigners in Buenos Aires Province climbed from 20 in 1869 to 31 in 1895 and reached 34 by 1914.[17] This trend also appeared in Rio Grande until 1900 but then reversed itself. The percentage of foreign and naturalized persons rose from 9 in 1872 to 12 in 1900 but then fell back to 7 percent in 1920. European immigrants to Rio Grande most often settled in the littoral in agricultural colonies such as São Leopoldo. These prosperous farming settlements of German and Italian immigrants aided in the growth and diversification of the state's economy, however, relatively few immigrants ventured into the campanha ranching region.[18]

The foreign-born populations of the two ranching areas exhibited the skewed age and sex distributions characteristic of European immigration to the Americas at the time. Adult males constituted a disproportionally large share of the population. The resulting surplus of labor depressed wages and reduced the bargaining power of rural workers. Argentine price inflation further reduced the bargaining power of rural workers and outstripped real wages. Rural employers increased profit margins at the expense of workers. A similar but less acute circumstance obtained among native workers in Rio Grande. According to Wolfgang Hoffmann-Harnisch, a

German traveler, the gaúcho cared nothing about money but rather concerned himself only with living a free, unfettered life.[19] This viewpoint only partially represents the true gaúcho mentality, but it hints at a broader economic fact. Lack of effective bargaining power, not simply lack of pecuniary interest, shaped the workers' seeming indifference to money matters. Ranchers could dictate conditions and wages, and laborers could accept them or seek employment elsewhere.

A social manifestation of the age-sex imbalance among the immigrants was enforced bachelorhood for many rural males because of the relative shortage of young adult women. In 1914 men in Buenos Aires Province aged twenty to thirty-nine outnumbered women of the same age by a ratio of three to two. Among foreigners the ratio stood at seven to three. The sex ratio for Rio Grande do Sul ran about even for the total population between the ages of twenty-one and thirty-nine, but foreign men outnumbered foreign women three to two.[20]

Other demographic changes in addition to immigration affected and were affected by the many processes of modernization. The theory of the demographic transition—first formulated by Warren Thompson in 1929, and refined by Donald Cowgill and others—summarizes the major relationships between demographic change and other aspects of modernization. Because of improved health, better medical care, developing contraceptive technology, and changing values, mortality and fertility decline during modernization. Mortality decline precedes fertility decline thereby prompting a rise in the rate of natural population increase during the early stages of the transition. A society also becomes on the average "older," more evenly balanced between men and women, and more urban. This change from high mortality and high fertility toward lower rates of both creates major social changes for a modernizing society.[21]

The pattern of demographic change in Buenos Aires Province appears consonant with this theory. The population became older on the average: The percentage of children under age ten in the total population of Buenos Aires Province fell from 33 to 28 between 1869 and 1914. The percentage of older adults above the age of sixty rose from 2.2 to 4.3 for the same period. Rio Grande seemingly represents an anomalous case because the percentage of children apparently rose from 15 to 31, while that of older adults dropped from 14 to 4 from 1872 to 1920. In a 1943 evaluation of past censuses the eminent Brazilian demographer Giorgio Mortara concluded that enumerators in 1872 undercounted children under age six and overstated the ages of the elderly. The age-sex structure for Rio Grande in 1872 should probably conform closely to that of the southern Buenos Aires counties in 1869, but further demographic study is necessary.[22]

As the populations became older or more mature on the average, the proportion of women also increased. The trend is clearest for Rio Grande where the masculinity ratio (number of males per 1,000 total population) dropped from 521 in 1872 to 508 in 1900 and fell to 506 in 1920. Although immigration disrupted the even balance of the sexes, especially in Buenos Aires Province, the native populations there and in the campanha tended to equalize. The masculinity ratio for native Argentines in the province stood at 509 in 1914—close to the 506 registered for Rio Grande in 1920.[23] By the second decade of the twentieth century, both regions had commenced the journey toward more mature, sexually balanced societies characteristic of modern nations.

Change in fertility—a demographic measure of central importance—can be gauged by a fertility ratio: that is, the number of children aged zero to five per 100 women aged fifteen to forty-nine. For the free population of Rio Grande the rate stood at a very low twenty-two for the under-enumerated census of 1872. The figures for Buenos Aires ran higher—eighty-nine for the province and 102 for the counties in 1869. This discrepancy must be at least partially attributable once again to errors in the Brazilian census of 1872. Later the fertility ratios of the two areas converged with the Argentine ratio at sixty-nine in 1914. Simply stated, native women on the Argentine pampa appear to have been considerably more fertile than those of Rio Grande do Sul.[24]

This fertility differential cannot be explained simply in terms of Brazilian underenumeration of children. Higher infant mortality figured into the lower Brazilian fertility rate. Infant mortality in Rio Grande exceeded 104 deaths per 1,000 births until 1914 (peaking at 139 in 1909) and did not drop below eighty-five until 1922. The crude birth rate (number of live births per 1,000 total population) in Rio Grande lagged far behind that of Buenos Aires Province until World War I. The Argentine rate fluctuated within a narrow range between thirty-four and thirty-nine. The crude birth rate for Rio Grande dipped during the first five years of the twentieth century then climbed rapidly from a low of twenty-three to thirty-six in 1915—a figure nearly equal to the Argentine rate. Long-term fertility decline in Rio Grande commenced about 1918 when the rate began to fall from its high point of thirty-six. Argentina also made an initial transition to lower fertility during World War I.[25] Other factors, notably age of marriage, require investigation for a better understanding of Rio Grande's generally lower fertility during the period.

Mortality trends, like fertility rates, appear consistent with the theory of the demographic transition. During the first two decades of the twentieth century, the crude death rate (number of deaths per 1,000 total population) declined in Buenos Aires Province, while it rose in Rio Grande until it coincided with the Argentine rate from 1912 to 1915. Long-term decline in Rio Grande's mortality figures began after 1918 when it peaked at sixteen deaths per 1,000 population. The Argentine rate, except for a brief rise from 1903 to 1907, showed a similar decline after the turn of the century. Once again the demographic changes appear to begin earlier on the Argentine pampa than in the campanha. The rates of natural increase (births minus deaths) climbed in both areas, although the Argentine figures showed signs of leveling off just prior to World War I. The "fit" of the data is perfect in neither region, but the theory of the demographic transition seems to hold explanatory potential.[26]

Urbanization forms an integral part of the transition process. Both the campanha region and Buenos Aires Province urbanized, albeit less extensively than other parts of Brazil and Argentina. In the campanha the administrative seat of the municipio usually represented the only urbanized area in the county. The city of Uruguayana, described in unflattering terms by a traveler in the 1880s as "a large cemetery," likely resembled other towns of the campanha. It boasted the best theater on the border, the "Carlos Gomes," but unplastered buildings and poor street lighting marred the town's appearance. Inconstant mail and telegraph service and inadequate rail connections, chronic problems in the entire region, also plagued Uruguayana. Similarly, a traveler on the southern Argentine pampa in 1875 described Olavarría as "a sad desert." On a return visit four years later he found a town of 1,000 people with simple buildings of sun-dried brick and no planted gardens despite the rich soil of the pampas.[27]

From these humble origins, some towns grew to modest size. In the campanha, Bagé grew to a population of 12,500 and Uruguayana to 12,000 by 1900, but a rural ambience remained. When juxtaposed with the burgeoning centers of the littoral, the dispersed campanha towns appeared backward and relatively static in population well into the twentieth century. At the turn of the century, the region continued to be 66 percent rural, with Rosario still 94 percent rural.

Urbanization in Argentina followed the same general pattern as county seats grew into the only significant towns of each partido. Lobería, 100 percent rural in 1869, remained 75 percent rural in 1914 as did Olavarría. Of the counties of the southern pampa, only Azul, with 39 percent of its population residing in the countryside, could be classified more urban than rural in 1914. Larger towns such as Azul grew to 20,000 and Tandil to 16,000 in 1914, but most county seats ranged from 2,400 to 8,000 inhabitants. The entire province of Buenos Aires moved from 82 percent rural in 1869 to 65 percent rural in 1895 to 46 percent in 1914, but most pampean towns survived by serving the rural economy and generated few self-sustaining features.[28]

Serial discussion of these factors obscures their interrelationships. For example, the concentration of landownership blocked an important avenue to economic well-being and forced many people to migrate to cities, which stimulated urbanization. Furthermore, the social dimensions of demographic change are far more significant than the figures themselves. Lowered mortality influences cultural mores such as mourning practices, religious beliefs, and fertility. Large numbers of children, prized during high mortality eras as a form of old-age social security and as a necessity to the survival of the lineage, appear less necessary as more people live to an older age. Thus declines in mortality and fertility closely interact. As the age composition of a society shifts toward maturity, the average age and hence flexibility of the labor force increases and consumption patterns alter because "younger" societies must devote relatively more income to services for dependent children.[29]

These putative advantages of a more mature society, however, were largely attenuated in the two regions by the continued domination of large landowners. The rural masses reaped few of the advantages of "modernization." Class mortality differentials—what has been termed the "social inequality of death"—meant that the wealthier segment of the rural population benefited more. Improvements in medical knowledge, health care, and technology were not distributed equally over the entire population. Comparative class differentials in rural mortality, fertility, and social measures require further examination.[30]

The skewed sex composition of the campanha and the Argentine pampa, with a disproportionate percentage of adult males, probably increased fertility by encouraging women to marry at an earlier age. Massive immigration, the factor responsible for sexual imbalance, disrupted rural society, sometimes to the point of violent nativism. One such outbreak occurred in 1872 in Tandil on the southern Argentine pampa when a xenophobic horde of gauchos massacred about seventeen foreigners. Immigration also intensified competition for jobs and land, further constricted economic opportunity, and necessitated migration to larger cities, usually along the coast.[31]

Given the general conformity of Rio Grande do Sul and Buenos Aires Province to the demographic transition theory, other changes associated with the theory perhaps apply. According to the theory, individualism should gain and familialism decline as core social values. The division of labor should become more complex as economic and social structures become more specialized and differentiated. Faced with longer life expectancies, people should marry at a later age thereby automatically reducing total fertility. Geographical mobility, rural to urban migration in particular, should increase as men and women seek better employment and more promising marital prospects in larger cities.[32]

These theoretical conjectures go beyond the bounds of empirical research at it now stands. But the socioeconomic and demographic data presented above indicate that the ranching societies of Brazil and Argentina presented a more complex and variegated fabric than the simplistic mythology of the areas would indicate. The colorful, romantic stereotypes of the gaúcho and gaucho popularized in myriad fictional works did not actually ride the southern pampas. On the other hand, the composition of the rural workforce who lived on the pampas changed, and the relative concentration of these workers in various sectors of the economy was altered. Migratory gauchos, termed a "dying or extinct class" by a Briton in 1911, were transformed into sedentary ranch hands with altered equipment and reduced numbers. The rural division of labor from peon up to manager and land-owner became more complex and specialized as modernization and mechanization altered the nature of ranch work.[33] Women, the forgotten half of rural society, also played significant economic roles. They often operated country stores and taverns, served as midwives and teachers, husked corn and reaped wheat on farms, and sheared sheep on ranches.[34]

Ranching areas of Rio Grande do Sul and Buenos Aires Province exhibited many socioeconomic and demographic similarities that appear to conform to the broad outlines of the theory of the demographic transition. As one scholar has noted, "the press of hard times and the opportunities of happier periods are reflected in historical demography like images in a camera obscura."[35] Census and other statistical data, however imprecise and incomplete, add further pieces to the mosaic of history for the two regions. Theories, such as the demographic transition, provide useful working hypotheses that turn the image of ranching society away from the realm of myth and toward that of historical study and empirical understanding. The true gaúchos and gauchos of the South American pampas will then emerge.

Chapter 9

Social History
in the Saddle

Trailing Cowboys
of the Americas

In this chapter I highlight some of the source problems that confront the social historian researching rural frontier history in the Americas. Sparsely populated frontier regions, lacking the public and private institutions of urban areas, do not offer the sort of documentation that historians traditionally rely on. I describe the means of meeting and overcoming these source problems, and I conclude by summarizing recent findings and revisions about frontier history in North and South America. Most of the examples come from the history of the cowboy and cattle frontiers.

The cowboy is a vivid, internationally recognized symbol. People around the globe associate the cowboy with the United States, but skilled and daring horsemen also played important roles in the history and culture of many other nations. Gauchos rode the pampas of Argentina and Uruguay. Llaneros herded cattle and fought battles on the tropical llanos of Colombia and Venezuela. Vaqueros and charros created parallel equestrian traditions in Mexico. These various cowboy types provide research and source challenges for the social historian seeking to represent their lives faithfully.[1]

First I want to emphasize that we are not dealing only with dead people and a long-disappeared culture. Pundits have been declaring the cowboy dead or disappeared for more than a century. Howard T. Lee, writing in the Denver *Friday Evening Times* (July 14, 1905), declared that "the cowboy of today is a lackey. . . . He is no longer the King of the range. His duties are mainly branding, keeping fences in repair, and doctoring the disabled. He is Samson after a haircut."

Assumptions of the cowboy's death remain widespread today. Texan Buster McLaury, a working cowboy, recently put it this way: "There's a lot of people in the world that don't know there are still real cowboys who are out there livin' and workin' on a ranch, makin' their livin' taking care of cattle. They don't have any idea. They think their beef comes from a grocery store."[2]

The cowboy is not dead, and cowboys have been riding the ranges of North and South America far longer than many people realize. Because of their importance in battling the Moors during the reconquest of Spain, horsemen—like the legendary "El Cid"—gained very high status. This religious warfare, lasting from the eighth century until the Spanish Catholic victory in 1492, made the cavalryman a national hero. Spanish kings had themselves depicted on horseback. The equestrian pose emphasized power, heroism, and high status.[3]

On his second voyage in 1493–1494, Christopher Columbus brought horses and cattle to the New World. Horses played an important military role in the conquest of Mexico and other parts of Latin America. The horse initially shocked Native Americans. They quickly adopted the "big dog," however, thereby expanding their military power and economic options. Equestrian life quickly became important both to many native tribes and to the European newcomers.[4] But how do we trail these New World horsemen?

Cowboys in Cloudcroft. (Rio Grande Historical Collections, New Mexico State University Library, Las Cruces)

Traditional cowboy songs, such as those performed by Texas singer Red Steagall, offer insight into old-time cowboy culture. (© 1993 Warner Bros. Records)

Cowboy poets like Waddie Mitchell preserve important oral traditions of the West. (© 1992 Warner Bros. Records)

Autobiographies and memoirs, like Andy Adams's *The Log of a Cowboy* (1903), provide telling details of cowboy life. (Author's collection)

Montana poet Wally McRae (*left*) and Canadian singer Ian Tyson help keep traditional cowboy culture alive. (1991 photograph by the author)

Material culture, including this western stock saddle with long *tapaderas*, shows the strong Hispanic influence on American cowboy life. (Photograph by the author)

The Problem of Sources

Unlike elites, commoners do not leave long, wide, convenient paper trails. For researching a nonelite social group like cowboys we have a limited store of primary sources. Usually illiterate, Latin American ranch hands did not leave diaries, letters home, or memoirs. Fortunately, many cowboys on the ranges of western Canada and the United States were literate and left firsthand accounts of their lives. Cowboy writings vary widely in reliability, but they offer unique insights. As with other types of evidence, the historian verifies them by checking against other sources.[5]

Ranching frontiers tend to be located some distance from urban centers of power and record keeping. Historical documents pile up in towns where public offices and businesses congregate. Likewise, newspapers of the past and present devote disproportionate space and attention to city matters.

When government officials did take an interest in the countryside, cowboys generally met them with distrust and reserve. Latin American governments often conscripted cowboys into the army, since the ranch hand's equestrian skills made him an excellent cavalryman. Thus cowhands would run from officials, sometimes even fleeing to live among Indians. Local officials in Argentina's Buenos Aires Province complained during the 1820s that gauchos fled en masse to escape being drafted to fight Brazil. As a result, ranchers and farmers faced severe labor shortages.[6]

A dispersed, migratory, rural labor force, cowboys generated none of the documents commonly used in labor history. It is difficult to track cowboy careers, movements, or even the proportion of time they worked each year. Cowboys did not form mutual aid societies, nor did they successfully form unions, so we have no lists of dues-paying members, minutes from meetings, nor other documents from labor organizations.[7]

As lower-class rural workers, cowboys accumulated few worldly goods. They seldom left the plethora of historical documents associated with death. We find no wills, inventories, bank accounts, safety deposit boxes, probate records, or catalogs of library books. The old cowboy song "When the Work's All Done This Fall" aptly conveys a cowboy's last will and testament:[8]

> Fred, you take my saddle, George, you take my bed,
> Phil, you take my pistol after I am dead.

Writing in 1918 Englishman Charles Darbyshire accurately described a typical gaucho funeral. "The gaucho, as a rule, cannot read or write. When he dies—after possibly 30 or more years service—he leaves no effects, no savings bank account; the owner of the estancia puts together a rude coffin, and a bullock-cart takes the corpse to the nearest cemetery."[9]

Historians have long made excellent use of church documents that track major life-cycle events, notably birth, marriage, and death. Unfortunately, cowboys rarely had the inclination or opportunity to grace the inside of a church. Working on the remote reaches of the frontier, cowboys lived outside the realm of most civil and religious institutions. Not understanding this problem, I spent days poring over nineteenth-century church records in Argentina. I found merchants, lawyers, ranchers (who often lived in town), and others, but no poor, working cowhands.

Given the lack of sources generated by cowboys themselves, we must turn to writings left by outsiders. Unfortunately, ethnocentrism, ignorance, and overt hostility toward cowboys color most of these outside observations. Many outsiders dismissed the cowboy as an uncouth barbarian. Edmond Temple, a British mining engineer who visited the pampas in 1823, termed gauchos "little better than a species of carnivorous baboon."[10]

Other observers succumbed to the romanticism dominant during much of the nineteenth century. They presented the cowboy as a noble savage or as the latter-day incarnation of a bold, heroic, medieval knight. In other cases, writers imposed their own Victorian morality on the cowboy. Some carefully suppressed coarser elements of old-time cowboy life. Folklorist John A. Lomax, for example, cleaned up the often bawdy lyrics of cowboy songs before publishing them. Cowboy R. S. Scott noted that "In the singing about camp, a cowboy would often cut loose with a song too vile to repeat; great cheers and hurrays would usually follow and there would be calls for more."[11]

Other writers carefully failed to mention the cowboy's association with the "soiled doves of the plains," the prostitutes who often provided the only female companion-ship available to poor working men. Thanks to the frank recollections of hands such as "Teddy Blue" Abbott, we have a more realistic understanding of the cowboy's relationship with prostitutes.[12] In short, many outsiders tended to demean or glorify the cowhand, making it difficult to locate the genuine article.

Solutions to the Lack of Traditional Sources

To resolve the source problems of rural social history, one adopts a two-pronged strategy. First, seek out additional sources beyond the range of traditional printed documents and manuscripts. Second, make novel use of traditional sources.

Despite the dangers of ethnocentrism and bias noted earlier, the writings of outsiders, including foreigners, can provide excellent contemporary descriptions of ranch life. By reading a large number of travelers' books and memoirs, we can filter out the untrustworthy and corroborate better observations with other sources.[13]

Scientists could be acute observers of ranch life. German naturalist Alexander von Humboldt traveled the tropical plains of the llanos in 1799. He also left a valuable ethnographic record for early nineteenth-century New Spain (Mexico). Humboldt ably described many facets of llanos life:

> The cattle, oxen, horses, and mules, are not penned, but wander freely over an extent of several square leagues. There is nowhere any enclosure; men naked to the waist, and armed with a lance, ride over the savannahs, to inspect the animals, bring back those that wander too far from the pastures of the farm, and mark with a hot iron all that do not already bear the mark of the proprietor. These Mulattoes, who are known by the name of *Peones Llaneros*, are partly freed men and partly slaves. There does not exist a race more constantly exposed to the devouring heat of the tropical Sun. Their food is meat dried in the air, and a little salted; and of this even their horses sometimes eat. Always in the saddle, they fancy they cannot make the slightest excursion on foot.[14]

Charles Darwin traveled the pampas of Uruguay and Argentina. In late October 1832, Darwin revealed to his sister Caroline his joy of gaucho life. "I never enjoyed anything so much as Ostrich hunting with the wild Soldiers, who are more than half Indians.—They catch them, by throwing two balls, which are attached to the ends of a thong, so as to entangle their legs: it was a fine animated chace.—They found the same day 64 of their eggs."[15]

We can use one source to help evaluate another. Writing to Caroline in early November 1832, Darwin noted "I intend to have some good gallops over the Pampas.—I suppose you all well know [Sir Francis Bond] Head's book [*Rough Notes Taken during Some Rapid Journeys across the Pampas and among the Andes*, 1826]—for *accuracy* & animation it is beyond praise."[16]

Darwin, of course, could not observe everything firsthand. He also relied on informants. Writing to J. S. Henson from East Falkland Island in March 1834, he noted that he had heard about another yet unsighted species of ostrich. "All the Gauchos & Indians state it is the case: & I place the greatest faith in their observations."[17]

Darwin also ably described a rancher's house near Maldonado, Uruguay, in 1832:

> After witnessing the rude wealth displayed in the number of cattle, men, and horses, Don Juan's miserable house was quite curious. The floor consisted of hardened mud, and the windows were without glass; the furniture of the sitting-room boasted only of a few of the roughest chairs and stools, with a couple of tables. The supper, although several strangers were present, consisted of two huge piles, one of roast beef, the other of boiled, with some pieces of pumpkin: besides this latter there was no other vegetable, and not even a morsel of bread. For drinking, a large earthenware jug served the whole party.[18]

Nineteenth-century paintings and photographs show the evolution of equipment, clothing, and other dynamics of cowboy life. Paintings of the gaucho illustrate the increasing foreign influence on clothing. By the mid-1800s imported British textiles replaced the gaucho's hand-woven Indian poncho. Machine-woven *bombachas*, bloused trousers, replaced the traditional *chiripá*, a baggy, diaper-like cloth. By late in the century machine-made European boots supplanted the traditional *botas de potro*, crafted from the hind leg skin of a colt.[19]

As with written accounts, the historian who relies on images needs to be aware of biases introduced by social class, culture, and artistic license.

Painters and photographers have found the cowboy an irresistible subject. Romanticism lent a rose-colored tinge to many nineteenth-century paintings and photographs. Some photographers, however, such as Erwin E. Smith, left a valuable corpus of documentary works. Born in 1886 in Honey Grove, Texas, Smith captured the end of open-range life in his remarkable black-and-white photographs. W. S. Perryman's *Indian Territory* reprints photographs of American Indians in Oklahoma.[20]

The wealth of photographs increases during the twentieth century. We benefit from works by Michael Rutherford, Dudley Witney, Barbara Van Cleve, and many other talented photographers. Many western archives preserve important photographic records of ranch life.[21]

Newspapers certainly do not provide an error-free window on the past, but the press can be useful in many ways. Partisanship and the quest for advertising revenue have long colored the editorial pages. But something as easily over-looked as a newspaper's classified ads provide insights into rural social life. Help-wanted ads in nineteenth-century newspapers reveal the relative demand for various types of workers. Wet nurses, especially European immigrants, could earn a handsome wage in Argentina. Ads reveal a strong market for slaves in Argentina through the 1840s. Despite the rhetoric of freedom that accompanied Argentine indepen-dence, slavery continued through a variety of subterfuges until 1853. Thanks to the mysterious disappearance of police records in 1831, many Afro-Argentines remained enslaved long after they should have been freed. Newspaper classifieds document this long persistence of slavery.[22]

More skilled reporters recorded telling details of cowboy life. A writer for the *Gunnison Review* (Colorado, August 14, 1880) described "Saturday Night in a Kansas Cattle Town":

> Everywhere the cowboys made themselves manifest, clad now in the soiled and dingy jeans of the trail, then in a suit of many buttoned corduroy, and again in the affluence of broadcloth, silk hat, gloves, cane and sometimes a clerical white necktie. And everywhere, also, starred and shone the Lone Star of Texas—for the cowboy, wherever he may wander, and however he may change, never spends his money or lends his presence to a concern that does not in some way recognize the emblem of his native State; so you will see in towns like New Sharon a general pandering to this sentiment, lone stars abound of all sizes and hues, from the big disfiguring white one painted on the hotel front down to the little pink one stitched in silk on the cowboy's shilling handkerchief.

Cowboys escaped many but not all forms of government record keeping. They often found their way into police, judicial, and military records. Cowboys seemed to have a penchant for blowing off steam in ways that city folks found objectionable. We can examine arrest and trial records, wanted posters, internal passports, work papers, military records, and conscription lists.

Police records tell us something about the cowboy's tastes in recreation. For Latin America, such public documents also give us important demographic information about ranch hands. Military and judicial documents often included a detailed physical description (*filiación*). Internal passports identified the color of the bearer's skin, eyes, and hair. The document also described the nose, mouth, face, stature, eyebrows, forehead, and beard, if any. These demographic sources reveal that the overwhelming majority of cowboys in Latin America were men of color. This evidence runs sharply counter to the mythology of Uruguay and Argentina that depicts the gaucho hero as a white Spaniard. Places of birth and residence are often given, revealing something about internal migration patterns for ranch hands.[23]

Governments often took more interest in getting an accurate count of animals than of people. Latin American ranchers paid taxes based on the size of their herds so officials periodically conducted animal censuses. We can use a cattle census to estimate the number of cowboys on the range. From ranch records we can approximate the number of full-time and seasonal hands required to handle a given number of animals. Projecting that ratio to the entire cattle population for a region yields a reasonable estimate of the cowboy population. At any given time, of course, a portion of hands would be between jobs.

Unlike cowboys, who left relatively few firsthand records, many ranchers kept detailed accounts of their operations. Ranch account books and letter books show cowboy wages, the work calendar, purchases, and cattle prices. These records underpin much of our understanding of the economic and social character of ranch life. For example, a shopping list for Alberta's Cochrane Ranch (February 21, 1885) reveals a staple diet similar to that of the American cowboy. William F. Cochrane ordered 200 pounds of green coffee, twenty sacks of flour, 500 pounds of bacon, twenty pounds of green tea, 100 pounds of rice, canned corn and tomatoes, and a miscellany of spices.[24]

Account books and written orders to ranch managers reflect the worker stratification on most ranches. During busy roundup seasons, ranchers added temporary hands paid by the day. A much smaller permanent group of year-round hands handled routine chores. On many ranches some men labored on foot while others did mounted work. Experience and type of work determined a laborer's wages. Letters also reveal the special concerns and problems of ranchers, such as rustling. A letter dated September 21, 1892, from the files of Alberta rancher A. E. Cross, summarized the "rules for stock inspector." The list of rules concluded with broad instructions to "Look thoroughly after any suspicious characters owning or branding stock. Investigate anything that looks not right."[25]

Even though they seldom labored as wage cowhands, women left important sources for the history of the ranching frontier. As Patricia Nelson Limerick correctly observed, "exclude women from Western history, and unreality sets in. Restore them, and the Western drama gains a fully human cast of characters—males and females whose urges, needs, failings, and conflicts we can recognize and even share." Limerick added, however, that "'the pioneer woman' is a generic concept imposed on a diverse reality" that included white, black, Hispanic, Chinese, and Indian women.[26]

Men outnumbered women by a wide margin in cattle frontiers, but ranch wives, widows, daughters, and, by the twentieth-century, a few working cowgirls, populated the frontier. Many ranch women left diaries and letters, providing valuable female perspectives on a predominately male world. In *Tenderfoot Bride* (1920) Clarice E. Richards recounted Colorado ranch life. Mary Kidder Rak provided an often humorous look at Arizona ranch life in *A Cowman's Wife* (1934). In 1941 Agnes Morley Cleaveland published her memoirs of New Mexico ranch life. J. Frank Dobie called Cleaveland's *No Life for a Lady*, the "best book on range life from a woman's point of view ever published."[27]

Laura V. Hamner offered a glimpse of ranch life in the Texas Panhandle in *Short Grass and Longhorns* (1943). Monica Hopkins provided a glimpse at the Alberta range in *Letters from a Lady Rancher* (1981). More recently Alice Mariott gathered interviews with ranch women in *Hell on Horses and Women* (1993). Elizabeth Maret examined *Women of the Range: Women's Roles in the Texas Beef Cattle Industry* (1993).

As noted, cowboys seldom showed up in church documents. One type of ranch worker, however, did make it into church records—Indian neophytes who tended cattle on Spanish missions. As early as the mid-sixteenth century the Roman Catholic Church in New Spain received royal grants of land and cattle. By the early 1600s Indians herded cattle on Jesuit estancias in Sinaloa and Sonora. During the last two decades of the seventeenth century Father Eusebio Kino established five mission ranches in northern Sonora and what is today southern Arizona. In California Franciscans built five missions between 1769 and 1773 where Indians tended cattle.[28]

If cattle frontiers are somewhat light on paper sources, they make up for it with leather. Material culture—saddles, tack, boots, hats, clothing, weapons, equipment—often survives long after the owners are deceased and paper has disintegrated. Fortunately, every country has museums and private collections where items of material culture—"the totality of physical objects made by a people for the satisfaction of their needs"—have been preserved. The Ranching Heritage Center in Lubbock, Texas, includes authentic buildings, a corral, windmills, and other elements of ranching architecture. Similar centers throughout the West preserve other objects from the past.[29]

Cowboy material culture and ranch terminology reveal the profound debt that American ranch culture owes to Mexico. Tack includes a *bozal*, usually rendered bosal, the nose band of a hackamore. The latter term, a headstall, is from the Spanish term *jáquima*. Chaps, the cowboy's distinctive leather leggings, pronounced "shaps," is from the Spanish *chaparreras*.

The ever-present lariat comes from *la reata*; McCarty (a fine horsehair rope) from *mecate*. "Theodore" (a small-diameter rope used on a horse as a chin-strap or throat latch) is a corruption of *fiador*.[30]

Architecture, the built environment, likewise confirms the importance of the Spanish heritage in Texas and elsewhere in the Southwest. Lubbock has many fine examples of Spanish revival-style buildings, mostly constructed during the 1920s. The Baker Building on Thirteenth Street and much of the Texas Tech University campus well represent Spanish revival architecture. Missions, ranch houses, fences, and other structures throughout Texas stand as striking evidence of the state's Spanish and Mexican past.[31]

Oral tradition transmits many important cultural values and helps fill in the blanks left by the lack of conventional documents. Argentine politician and writer José Hernández penned *Martín Fierro*. This two-part epic poem about the gaucho appeared in 1872 and 1879. The long work (305 pages in translation) reveals myriad, important, accurate details of daily life on the pampa:

> There was porridge of corn in steaming pots,
> And free-baked bread galore,
> And broth and stew, and a barbeque,
> And caña or wine as it suited you,
> No wonder I sigh for the days gone by,
> the times that shall come no more.[32]

The poem also aptly summarized government persecution of the gaucho:

> And give yourself up for lost, my boys,
> If the Mayor nooses you;
> They'll drag you off with a hail of blows,
> Though why neither God nor the Mayor knows,

> And they finish you quick if you stand and draw,
> As the gaucho used to do.[33]

Incidentally, "draw" refers to a knife, not a revolver. Vaqueros and gauchos considered firearms unmanly and delayed using them long after they had become available.[34]

Since the mid-1980s cowboy and increasingly cowgirl poetry has made a spirited comeback. Many poems are honest, straightforward chronicles of cowboy and ranch life. As with music, we find cowboy humor, values, interests, and concerns. Spurred by the popularity of the Cowboy Poetry Gathering in Elko, Nevada, similar gatherings have multiplied throughout the West. Montana poet Wally McRae voices the environmental concerns of many westerners faced with rapid mining and commercial development. Baxter Black's comic genius communicates the humorous side of cowboy life. From the ranch house to the bunk house, from the rodeo arena to the movie theater, poets share their feelings about life, death, work, and play.[35]

Composers, professional and amateur, set many cowboy poems to music. The lyrics of songs offer another valuable and very enjoyable window on cowboy culture. Fortunately, western singers have kept the old songs alive over the decades. Although born in New Jersey, Don Edwards became an adopted Texan at age seventeen. Since 1961 he has been singing cowboy tunes. Dallas-born Michael Martin Murphey and Gainesville-born Red Steagall have been major forces since the mid-1980s in reviving traditional cowboy music. All three singers currently record on the Warner Western label, created after the great success of Murphey's 1990 album *Cowboy Songs*.[36]

Steagall, talented singer and poet, recently began a radio program called "Cowboy Corner." "Everybody, regardless of where they live or their walk of life, is fascinated with the cowboy image," says Steagall, "because the cowboy exhibits independence, individualism, and freedom. Those are the things that everybody wants to feel like they have in this world." Of course these singers join a long line of musical Texas talents from Bob Wills, Ernest Tubb, Gene Autry, Jimmy Dean, Buddy Holly, Roy Orbison, and Lefty Frizzell to Mac Davis, Larry Gatlin, George Jones, Tanya Tucker, Freddy Fender, Johnny Rodriguez, Willie Nelson, Waylon Jennings, and George Strait.[37]

Cowboys are still alive and working, but no one lives forever. I recall this historical truism to remind us that we must take care to record, on audio- or videotape, the memories, stories, and wisdom of the older generation—before it is too late. Writer Jane Pattie, for example, spent twenty years interviewing talented western spur makers. By the time she published *Cowboy Spurs and Their Makers* in 1991, all the artisans she interviewed had died. Legendary JA Ranch cowboy Tom Blasingame died in 1991. In the realm of popular cowboy culture, in the fall of 1994 we lost actor Noah Beery, Jr.[38]

Oral history, like other methodologies, has its limits. As with all historical inquiry, it requires the careful evaluation of evidence and the use of multiple sources. In *The Last Cowboys* (1993), Connie Brooks used oral history interviews in an attempt to challenge many prevailing views of cowboys. Unfortunately, her limited sample of only thirty-two cowboys who settled in Lea County, New Mexico, is inadequate to support her sweeping, revisionist interpretations. In addition, she interviewed mostly family members of deceased cowboys, not the actual subjects themselves.[39]

Popular fiction generally offers much more entertainment than history. For the historian, the value of popular cowboy writers, like Louis L'Amour, Zane Grey, Max Brand, and countless others, lies in their manipulation and alteration of the cowboy's heroic image. Some novels do contain excellent descriptions and evocations of real cowboy life. During the late nineteenth century Javier de Viana produced naturalistic novels of Uruguayan gaucho life.[40] Argentine writer Ricardo Güiraldes captured the essence of gaucho values in his 1926 novel *Don Segundo Sombra*. In 1927 Venezuelan Rómulo Gallegos published his haunting portrait, *Doña Bárbara*, which brilliantly evokes the powerful dangers and deep superstitions of llanos life.

Myth and Historical Reality

Social history research often undercuts widely believed elements of popular culture and mythology. Myth underpins much of what many people assume they know about history. Nations and peoples need myths to bind them together. Myth offers a "useful" collective past. It provides a sense of security from the uncertainties of the present and future. White Southerners, for example, long ago crafted a mythological view of their antebellum past. Benevolent, paternalistic white planters and docile, loyal, but uncivilized black slaves populated this mythical Old South of "moonlight and magnolias."[41]

The mythical Old South was a happy, ordered world—an organic society where rich and poor, powerful and powerless, knew their respective places and lived in general peace and harmony. The Civil War, according to this view, resulted not from a desire to maintain slavery but from the agitations of northern radicals—abolitionists and Republicans—who sought to undo the protections of the Constitution. Like civil rights workers of the 1950s and 1960s, abolitionists and

Republicans sought to remake the South in the image of the North, in the process destroying the cherished southern way of life. Thomas Nelson Page (*The Old South*, 1892) propounded this view. Even the brilliant "scientific" historian Ulrich B. Phillips succumbed to much of the seductive mythology in his award-winning *Life and Labor in the Old South* (1929).[42]

Like the South, the West has its own powerful mythology based on popular culture, political machinations, and wishful thinking. Rugged individualists built the mythical West largely unassisted. William Perry Pendley's *War on the West: Government Tyranny on America's Great Frontier* (1995) is the latest example of this right-wing myth making. As historian Michael P. Malone correctly notes, the West's "exceptional reliance upon the federal government" is one the region's major identifying characteristics.[43]

The federal government funded expeditions by Meriwether Lewis and George Clark, Stephen Long, John Charles Frémont, and others. Public monies paid for maps, charts, reports, paintings, and photographs documenting the West. As Ron Tyler, director of the Texas State Historical Association, has noted, "between 1843 and 1863, the federal government alone published almost thirty different illustrated survey reports relating to the trans-Mississippi West containing a total of approximately 24.5 million prints."[44]

The U.S. Cavalry controlled the Indians and provided markets for beef and mounts. Army engineers also built an extensive network of federal wagon roads, especially in Texas, Utah, and New Mexico. Railroads, with the exception of the Great Northern, received huge land subsidies—to the tune of 200 million acres of land. The Butterfield Overland Mail received a million dollar annual federal subsidy. Federal lands have provided cheap, abundant grazing, mineral exploitation, and timber. Dams and federal irrigation projects have watered the arid West.[45]

The story was similar in the Canadian West. The Canadian government spurred the growth of Alberta ranching with beef purchases for soldiers at military posts, Indians, and railroad workers. Security, in the form of the federal Mounted Police, meant that ranchers could concentrate their energies on cattle, not on marauding Indians and rustlers. In the early 1880s Senator Matthew Henry Cochrane lobbied successfully for government leasing and tariff policies favorable to his ranching fortunes.[46]

A More Inclusive West

Thanks to ongoing research we have a more accurate, inclusive view of the nature of frontier societies. The mythical West was a world of dominating white Anglo-Saxon males. But social history research has restored the significance of the Spanish heritage in cowboy life throughout the Americas. Oregon and Nevada cowboys still call themselves "buckaroos" (from the Spanish term *vaquero*). Saddles, bridles and other tack, the organization and conduct of daily labors, roundups, roping techniques, names for the colors of horses, and ranch lingo all reflect a strong Spanish heritage.

Ethnically diverse, cowboys came from native, black, and white backgrounds. Nonwhite cowboys predominated in Latin America. Gauchos, llaneros, and vaqueros reflected a mixture of Indian, African, and to a lesser extent white ancestry. In the United States, Native American cowboys are common in many areas, notably Oklahoma, South Dakota, and New Mexico.[47]

More probing research is revealing the presence and roles of African Americans in the West. Bill Pickett, famed as the inventor of bulldogging, broke horses and worked as a featured performer in the Miller Brothers 101 Show. He died following a horse accident on the Miller Ranch in 1932. Ex-slave John Ware migrated to Alberta, Canada. He cowboyed and succeeded in building his own ranch. A number of geographical place names commemorate his career. Another ex-slave, George McJunkin, cowboyed in the Folsom, New Mexico, area. In 1908 he made a major archeological discovery—10,000-year-old bones from a huge, extinct bison.[48]

Other historians have revealed a Jewish presence in the West generally not visible in traditional studies or popular culture. Meyers Cohen, a Prussian Jew, figured among early homesteading ranchers in Bannock County, Idaho. These hardy pioneers began settling in Marsh Valley in the 1860s. In 1887 Henry Altman and Dan McIlvain bought the famed Swan Land and Cattle Company after Texas fever and a hard winter wiped out most of the cattle. Over the next three decades they built a prize herd of Herefords. Some western merchants, like David Levy (Prescott, Arizona) and William Koshland (Signal, Arizona) accepted cattle for payment of debts. In this fashion they got into the cattle business as well as mercantile trade. And, of course, many a cowboy worked in denim jeans created by Levi Strauss.[49]

Frontier Differences and Similarities

Cowboys in different countries exhibited important similarities. We must not, however, overlook significant regional variations. Gauchos of the great flat pampas used a very flat multilayered saddle (*recado*). Their counterparts in the dry, brushy, thorny northern province of Salta added *armas*—flaring, stiff leather protectors to the sides of their saddles. Vaqueros of Baja California used similar leather protection to shield themselves against desert vegetation. Cowboys inventively adapted their clothing, equipment, and work techniques to a wide range of natural conditions. On the llanos of Colombia and Venezuela, where monsoon rains fell six months a year, cowboys survived by being excellent boatmen and swimmers.[50]

Another important point of divergence between cowboy life in North and South America is the time span involved. Wildcattle hunting and open-range ranching was already well established in much of Latin America by the mid-sixteenth century. Gauchos, llaneros, and vaqueros rode the range for two to three centuries before the appearance of Anglo cowboys in the American West. The American cowboy enjoyed a brief heyday that lasted barely a generation.[51]

Donald E. Worster quotes Montana rancher Granville Stuart to show how quickly things changed on the northern ranges: "In 1880 no one had heard tell of a cowboy in 'this niche of the woods' and Charlie Russell [the famous cowboy artist of Montana] had made no pictures of them; but in the fall of 1883, there were 600,000 head of cattle on the range. The cowboy . . . had become an institution." Just five years later bitter winter weather, overstocking, and overgrazing brought open-range ranching into quick decline.[52]

Similar forces brought an end to open-range ranching throughout the Americas. The introduction of refrigeration created a chilled beef boom. The hardy, lean Longhorn gave way to Herefords and other breeds that provided more and better fresh beef. Ranchers from Alberta to Argentina adjusted to the changing world market demands, with some variation in timing.[53]

Along with new cattle breeds came barbed-wire fencing to promote selective breeding. Cowboys everywhere responded with instant dislike to fencing. Alberta cowmen voiced a widely held opinion concerning the advent of fencing: "Oh, I wouldn't say sheep were so bad. I'd say barb wire is what ruined this country. At first we could keep it out pretty well, and use the posts for firewood, but it got so, after a while, they were putting up the d——— stuff faster than a guy could cut it down."[54]

As I noted at the beginning of this chapter, part of popular mythology is that cowboys and cowboying are dead. But we still find ranch hands tending cattle and horses throughout North and South America. True, some methods have changed. A propane tank might now heat branding irons. Cattle receive innoculations unknown a few decades ago. But cowboy life and cowboy culture is still very much alive. Large and growing attendance at the National Cowboy Symposium and Celebration, in Lubbock; the Cowboy Poetry Gathering, in Elko, Nevada; Cowboy Songs and Range Ballads, in Cody, Wyoming; and hundreds of other annual events attest to the vibrancy of cowboy culture today.

Historical research remains diverse and dynamic. English historian John Tosh well summarized the varieties of historical research as now practiced: "It concerns both events and structures, both the individual and the mass, both mentalities and material forces. Historians themselves need to combine narrative with analytical skills, and to display both empathy and detachment. Their discipline is both re-creation and explanation, both art and science."[55]

Serious historical study, however, does not mandate scorning or abandoning our joy of B Western movies, Louis L'Amour western fantasies, rodeo, or cowboy poetry. On the contrary, one of the many fascinating realms of exploration is the intersection between cowboy social history, popular culture, and mythology. Fiction, film, painting, and mythology can sometimes capture some element of historical "truth," but they are not history. "Cowboy myth and history both have a place, but we must try to distinguish between them."[56]

Doing social history in the saddle, like cowboying itself, requires a great deal of adaptation, ingenuity, and occasional recourse to a strip of rawhide or a length of bailing wire. The effort is worth it. In recapturing the real cowboy past we enhance our understanding of and appreciation for today's vibrant cowboy culture throughout the Americas.

Chapter 10

Dangers of Frontier Overrevisionism

Cautionary Notes from Alberta to Abilene to Argentina

Historical revisionism has added important new dimensions and nuances to our understanding of frontier societies. In some cases, however, researchers have plunged into "overrevisionism." This chapter critiques recent frontier historiography that goes beyond the bounds of sound historical method and good use of sources. I summarize recent scholarship on frontiers throughout the Americas, including Canada. Although I am sympathetic with the general historiographical trend toward a more inclusive and socially complex vision of frontier societies, I warn against the overzealous rejection of all prior research in the search for a new, improved history that uncritically embraces untested theory.

Once again, the West has become a battlefield. This time around, however, it's *writers* of the purple sage flinging ink, not lead. Revisionist historians and a new breed of western novelists and poets are challenging old "truisms" of western mythology.[1]

The traditional western narrative was "John Wayne" history. Hardy, brave white men singlehandedly brought civilization to the western deserts. Too frail for such rigors, white women appeared only after men had secured the frontier. In this "White Man's West," Native Americans and Hispanics appeared only in caricature.

During the 1980s, Patricia Nelson Limerick (*The Legacy of Conquest*) and other historians challenged the old narrative. These revisionists began exploring the lives and actions of the invisible westerners—women, working-class people, African Americans, Hispanics, Chinese, and others. Historian Frederick Jackson Turner and his disciples had depicted a West of triumphant progress. It seems, however, that violent conquest and exploitation rather than civilization and progress more often typified the flow of western history. With *"It's Your Misfortune and None of My Own"* (1991) Richard White synthesized *A New History of the American West*.

Long before the current crop of historians, however, Dee Brown was pioneering western history revisionism. A Native American, Brown wrote some of the first widely read histories of western women (*The Gentle Tamers*, 1958) and Native Americans (*Bury My Heart at Wounded Knee*, 1970).

In general, I find the trend toward western history revisionism a healthy one. I would caution, however, against the excesses of "overrevisionism" that pose the danger of trivializing, distorting, or losing sight of larger events, processes, and issues.

Without question, traditional historiography, with its myopic focus on elite white males, slighted the roles of women and ethnic minorities. But we should not overcompensate by interjecting social groups where they did not actually exist. For example, I found no nineteenth-century ranch record in any country listing women as ranch hands. It would be ahistorical to interject "cowgirls" (defined as the female equivalent of cowboys) into a study of ranch hands. Women certainly lived and worked on ranches—as daughters, wives, and widows—but not as salaried cowhands. Things did change a bit in the twentieth century. For example, Georgie Sicking, of Fallon, Nevada, worked much of her adult life as a cowhand.[2]

Luna ranch hands. (Rio Grande Historical Collections, New Mexico State University Library)

Canadian cowboys. (Glenbow Archives, Calgary, Alberta, NA-2927-1)

Bronco busting, 1904. (Prints and Photographs Division, Library of Congress)

Women, like this Wyoming ranch woman, lived and worked in cattle regions, but seldom as salaried cowhands. (Prints and Photographs Division, Library of Congress)

British versus Hispanic Roots of Ranching

Terry G. Jordan provided an example of overrevisionism with *Trails to Texas* and other writings during the 1980s. Reacting to what he viewed as overemphasis on the Hispanic influences of western cattle ranching, Jordan traced putative influences from the Old South westward into the Texas Gulf coast. Ignoring a wealth of linguistic and material culture, Jordan built a very feeble case that convinced few readers.

In a more thoroughly researched book, *North American Cattle-Ranching Frontiers* (1993), Jordan corrected some of his earlier mistaken notions. For example, in 1988 he asserted that "the word *cowboy* possibly originated as a term for a slave herder, just as *buckaroo* and *corral* perhaps entered the American ranching vocabulary by way of Gullah *buckra* and Angolan-Portuguese *kraal* (*crawl*)." In 1993 he acknowledged the Spanish origin of the term *corral*. He also rather indirectly admitted riding up another wrong trail: "Earlier attempts to link it [the word *buckaroo*] to the African West Indian and Carolina-derived slave-cowpen culture," he owned up, "were misguided."[3]

Jordan's errors remind us of the continued usefulness of Ockham's razor: "What can be accounted for by fewer assumptions is explained in vain by more." The case for direct linguistic diffusion from Mexican Spanish to Texas is much stronger and clearer than the route he posited in the 1980s, which would have taken words from Africa (perhaps with a stop in the Caribbean), westward through the Old South.[4]

An important part of Jordan's argument in *Trails to Texas* rested on his assertion that black slaves, who had tended cattle in the Carolinas, carried their skills and work habits westward to Texas. In *North American Cattle-Ranching*

Frontiers Jordan again recants an earlier supposition of his. He clearly comments on the lack of evidence for significant African influence on the western range-cattle industry: "Claims that 'Africans shaped [the] American cattle industry' and that the Texas cowboy 'is indebted to the Negro for his culture' are exaggerated."[5]

Jordan has also argued that Texas has been overemphasized as a source of western cattle raising. This is something of a specious argument, because in making it, Jordan dilutes a major point—the pervasiveness of Hispanic influence in the West. As his own analysis shows, Hispanic influence reached the American West from many paths: by way of Texas northward but also from California, Arizona, New Mexico, Louisiana, and Florida. Hispanic influence even crossed the Pacific Ocean in the 1830s when vaqueros from Spanish California taught Hawaii's cowboy, the *paniolo*, how to handle cattle.[6]

Deconstruction on the Range

"The West as America: Reinterpreting Images of the Frontier," an exhibit held at the Smithsonian's National Museum of American Art in 1991, represented another example of over-revisionism. The captions and text panels ignored or violated the historical integrity of artworks. Some viewers empathized with the revised vision of the past, but many viewers left pointed criticisms: "Your comments are attempts to put twentieth-century sensibilities and beliefs on people of the nineteenth century. W. S. R. Springfield, VA." In *Prints of the West* (1994), Ron Tyler offers a much more historically based analysis of nineteenth-century images.[7]

Blake Allmendinger's deconstruction of the cowboy (*The Cowboy: Representations of Labor in an American Work Culture*,

1992) provided another example of overrevisionism. First formulated by Jacques Derrida, deconstructionism surfaced in the 1970s in reaction to structuralism. Vincent Leitch provides an intelligible description of what often appears to be unintelligible theory:

> For the deconstructionist, language is everything. The world itself is "text." Language directs humanity and creates human reality. (A reality that cannot be named or described is illusory, at best.) Yet, upon close examination, words seem to have no connection with reality or with concepts or ideas.
>
> Related to textuality, the notion of intertext refers to the broader cultural background, the context that saturates the text with innumerable and nonverbal conventions, concepts, figurations, and codes. Given the silent and hidden links of a text to its cultural and social intertext, the text's content and meaning are, essentially, indeterminate. Texts, therefore, are unreadable, and the practice of interpretation may be defined as misreading.[8]

Paul de Man became the leading American apostle of deconstructionism. Revelations of his feet of clay helped turn many thinking people against such theories. He wrote anti-Semitic tracts for a Belgian collaborationist publication during World War II. These actions and other character flaws seemed to offer "evidence that deconstruction is inherently ahistorical and ultimately immoral."[9]

In their more honest moments, most mortals will admit to not understanding the new literary theories. Ben Yagoda notes correctly that "part of theory's sexiness was its daunting difficulty." One had to wade through and pretend to understand a bewildering plague of terms and constructs. Of course, possessing what is perceived to be difficult, esoteric knowledge is part of what the academy is all about, so "the intellectual groupies swooned."[10]

Allmendinger's book consists of four largely unconnected chapters with no apparent unifying logic. The chapter titles warn the reader that the author is looking at things in a very different way:

"1. Skin Grammar: Cattle Branding and Symbolic Wounds." "If brand owners also own, silence, or dispossess cowboys, then cowboys subvert the brand owners' notions of ownership by using brands not to indicate their economic submission, but to suggest their religious elevation in heaven" (p. 29). I've heard branding described in many ways but never as a religious experience.

"2. Frontier Gender: Livestock Castration and Square Dancing." "During this hundred-year history, men and women represented but at the same time confused gender, alternately revealing, concealing, and metaphorically castrating themselves and each other while role-playing, acting out functions conferred on them by heterosexuality, homosexuality, cross-dressing, and castration" (p. 81).

"3. Dual/Dueling Identities: Rustlers and Cowboy Detectives." Jacques Derrida would be proud of this play on words, a common conceit among postmodernists.

"4. Where Seldom is Heard a Discouraging Word: Orphanhood and Orality at Home on the Range." Alliteration is likewise a favorite deconstructionist pastime. I fear that many a cowboy poet will be quite discouraged to learn from Allmendinger what their deconstructed words "really" mean.[11]

Brand me a reactionary (only symbolically, please), but I have many objections to the self-indulgent babble and loose, sloppy nomenclature that typifies deconstructionism. Real people, real historical actions, time, causality, and the critical analysis of evidence get lost in a maze of codes, texts, intertexts, and language. As labor historian David Zonderman put it, Allmendinger's "presentation of the literary and cultural material makes great leaps of faith, works through obscure metaphors rather than logic, and creates a chronology which is often free roaming at best."[12]

Text becomes anything any individual reader wants it to be. This is the antithesis of the historian's work, which hinges on uncovering, validating, and analyzing sources within their own historical context. Zonderman well summarizes the historian's objection: "Looking for cultural representations is crucial for understanding a society and its working people; but if we are not told much about the social structures and daily practices these people are trying to represent, then the analysis has little value to historians studying working-class lives and thought." In short, as Vincent Leitch rightly notes, "deconstruction has been regularly attacked as childish philosophical skepticism and linguistic nihilism."[13]

Postmodernist posturings notwithstanding, the critical use of sources remains at the heart of the historian's job. Some revisionists have utterly rejected official government documentation, viewing official documents as mere expressions of cultural and policy hegemony. Such scholars often uncritically embrace "popular" sources as authentic voices of the people. The analysis of bandits, quintessential frontier figures, offers yet another example of the dangers of overrevisionism.[14]

Popular sources, folklore, and firsthand reports by "just plain folks," can be fraught with difficulties (see chapter 9). Erick Langer's observation for Bolivian historiography applies well to any society. Peasant stories, notes Langer, "exhibit a selective memory that emphasizes only certain traits among bandits. No tale deals with robbing other peasants."[15]

For the United States the history and mythology of "Billy the Kid" offers an instructive example. The tangled mass of myth, fiction, and historical fragments surrounding William Bonney well illustrates the potential dangers in using "popular" sources. As part of a New Mexico Writers' Project in the 1930s, government-paid interviewers questioned residents who claimed firsthand knowledge of Billy the Kid. Some respondents avowed personal knowledge of episodes in the Kid's life created by fiction writers. Faulty memory and vivid imagination shaped many of the recollections. Many of the respondents probably came to believe the fictions they had created and embellished over the decades. Jeff Dykes summed it up this way: "I thought I had heard about all the tall tales, figments of the imagination, faulty recollections, and down-right lies about him [Billy]. Not so! Examples from these interviews . . . clearly indicate that legends do not die—they just grow."[16]

Bury the Frontier?

I also question the strain of overrevision that relegates the concept of the frontier to historiographical oblivion. Richard White has written that "the New Western historians differ from the old Western historians in their preference for inter-preting the West as a region rather than as a frontier." In 1987 Patricia Nelson Limerick wrote that "frontier, then, is an unsubtle concept in a subtle world."[17] I disagree. True, Turner's formulation of the impact of the frontier has been found wanting, but recent work by a number of scholars points to the continued vitality of the frontier concept. The West can be studied to good effect as both frontier and region (see chapter 7).

Since writing off the frontier, Limerick appears to have changed her mind about the viability of what she had often termed "the f-word." Writing in 1994, Limerick reviewed "The Adventures of the Frontier in the Twentieth Century." Although remaining critical of Turnerian thought, Limerick had become impressed with the pervasiveness and power of the frontier concept. Obviously one could not simply wish away this ubiquitous idea.

> As a mental artifact, the frontier has demonstrated an astonishing stickiness and persistence. It is virtually the flypaper of our mental world; it attaches itself to everything— healthful diets, space shuttles, civil rights campaigns, heart transplants, industrial product development, musical innovations. . . . Whether or not it suits my preference, the concept works as a cultural glue—a mental and emotional fastener that, in some very curious and unexpected ways, works to hold us together.[18]

Argentina's Divisive Frontier

Divisions and polemics have long colored Argentina's historiography. Following Domingo F. Sarmiento's lead, the traditional "liberal" view depicts Argentina's past as a battle between "civilization and barbarism." According to this view, Europeanized leaders in Buenos Aires finally prevailed over backward, federalist caudillos. Juan Manuel de Rosas, Facundo Quiroga, and their "barbarous" gaucho hordes fell in defeat. In the twentieth century Ricardo Levene and others continued the nation's liberal historical tradition.[19]

Beginning in the 1930s, partisans of Rosas attacked the liberal orthodoxy. The so-called revisionists presented the dictator in a positive light as a prototypical nationalist and populist. Many revisionists marshaled their evidence to lend support to a very conservative, authoritarian political order. Beginning in the 1950s, comparisons between Rosas and Juan Perón added another layer to the nation's historical polemic.[20]

Political scientist Fred Murphy recently has added another twist to this longstanding polemic. According to Murphy,

Rosas's fall and the subsequent ascendancy of central over provincial governments "can be thought of as a revolution." He poses the question: "Why did this mid-nineteenth century Argentine revolution usher in a central state with a parliamentary regime?"[21]

Perhaps because I have taught a course on Latin American revolutions for more than a decade, I question Murphy's appropriation of the term. Cuba in 1959: that's a revolution. Nicaragua in 1979: that's a revolution. I see no widespread social or political restructuring in the 1850s in Argentina. Like the polemics of Rosistas and liberals, Murphy's injection of a fictive "revolution" obscures major continuities of the country's nineteenth century history. For example, after the fall of Rosas, many Rosista justices of the peace retained their positions of power in rural society.[22]

Research by María Sáenz Quesada, Mark Szuchman, John Lynch, and David Rock highlights the continuation of elite political power, the expansion of latifundia, and tight social control of the rural and urban masses. They find no sharp break, much less a revolution, occurring with the fall of Rosas.[23]

Pollyanna Pampa

Two strains of attempted revisionism converge on the questions of the rural social order and land tenure. Jonathan Brown (*Socioeconomic History of Argentina*, 1979) argued that inexorable market forces operated positively and in accord with Adam Smith's economic rules. Labor shortages on the pampas brought rural workers higher wages, personal autonomy, and other putative advantages. Brown paints a "Pollyanna Pampa" with gauchos and landowners, large and small, all sharing in the benefits of an expanding export economy.[24]

The livestock economy did indeed expand under Rosas. Lyman Johnson, with his trademark empirical thoroughness, deals a fatal blow to Brown's interpretation of that expansion. Using estate inventories from probate records, Johnson clearly demonstrates that under Rosas income inequality increased dramatically in rural Buenos Aires Province. This is precisely the period when Brown hypothesizes generalized socioeconomic progress in rural society. Instead, the rich got richer; much richer.[25]

Increased seasonal demands for rural labor did give gauchos some economic leverage. However Brown erred in assuming that gauchos readily translated potential economic clout into improved social conditions. On the contrary, ranchers needed gauchos as peons. The government needed gauchos for military service. A barrage of repressive mechanisms successfully limited the gaucho's economic options, geographic mobility, and even his dress and recreation. Records from justices of the peace, police, and military archives reveal a crear pattern of successful rural social control. Government officials constructed an elaborate labyrinth of legal constraints. Vagrancy laws, required work papers, and internal passports were already in place in the mid-eighteenth century. Ricardo Rodríguez Molas and Gastón Gori thoroughly documented governmental legal and extralegal coercion for the eighteenth century; I've done so for the nineteenth.[26]

Brown seems to have recognized the error of his earlier interpretations. In a 1994 essay he paints a less rosy, more accurate picture: "The frontier did not create a social democracy in which all residents enjoyed equal chances to get ahead. Economic boom went hand in hand with effective repression that curtailed the economic opportunities of mestizos, mulattoes, and blacks." This new view brings Brown in line with Rodríguez Molas, Gori, and other historians of the pampas. Brown now recognizes that "postrevolutionary society did not shake its colonial mentalities; social discrimination once again influenced how Argentines shared the products of economic development."[27]

Land Tenure and Rural Power

In 1981 John Lynch demonstrated that sixty estancieros held 76 percent of the settled lands in Buenos Aires Province in 1830. Brown argued that rural land concentration decreased thereafter. Brown presented three maps that show progressively smaller estancias but he omitted a crucial piece of evidence—the family names shown on the original maps.[28] These names reveal interlocking networks of prominent extended families.

Maps for the *partidos* (counties) of Balcarce and Tandil in 1863 show that certain family names recur on many "different" estancias. We find repetitive patterns of names, such as Peña and Sosa. Members of the Pereyra Iraola family have estancias in both counties. The names Santamarina and Anchorena dot the Tandil countryside. Property may have appeared to be subdivided, but marital and family ties kept elite wealth and power intact.[29]

Again, Brown's more recent work (1994) admits to the highly unequal distribution of resources in rural society, including land: "Sons of estancieros and immigrant Europeans usually benefited from the spread of landownership; native-born peons did not." Mark Szuchman notes the persistence of land concentration in the 1820s: "New lands were given to men who were already among the most prominent estancieros; therefore, the addition of available land was not successfully converted into an opportunity to expand the number of landowners."[30]

A parallel phenomenon occurred in neighboring Uruguay. Spanish colonial policy promoted land concentration and the marginalization of the gaucho. Rich, landed families—Viana, de la Quadra, and others—came to dominate the countryside, and, after independence, the country. Justices of the peace, obedient to landed interests, wielded civil and military authority on behalf of the elite. Ranchers organized the Uruguayan Rural Association to promote their interests at the national level.[31]

Carlos Mayo has demonstrated that large estancias did not completely dominate the countryside of eighteenth-century Buenos Aires Province. He also noted that the area's livestock business was an economic backwater compared with the much larger number of hides exported from the Banda Oriental (Uruguay). John Chasteen provides similar evidence for nineteenth-century Rio Grande do Sul.[32]

The existence of small ranches, however, does not negate the reality of large rancher power and influence. Put another way, just because small ranches existed in south Texas doesn't mean that Richard King was not powerful. Without question, the rancher elite emerges as politically and economically powerful in nineteenth-century Argentina. Historians still need to trace the roots of that power. Eduardo Azcuy Ameghino's thesis is certainly worth testing: "Latifundist appropriation of rural space effectively determined during the colonial period the general features that characterized the economy and society of the Buenos Aires countryside before and after independence."[33]

Power to the People

Another strain of revisionism that I term "power to the people," seeks to remove the rural lower classes from a position of passive victimization and to portray them as active historical agents. A commendable goal, but over-revisionism rides again. Using data from a single ranch, the Estancia de las Vacas, Ricardo Salvatore and Jonathan Brown examine the seasonality of ranch work and other elements of estancia administration. They conclude that "the power of the gaucho on the prairies of the Banda Oriental was great enough to defy the economic impositions of those prophets of capitalism, the hacendados."[34]

Fortunately Jorge Gelman also minutely examined the same records. He systematically undermines the Salvatore/Brown arguments and reveals a complex web of agricultural and ranch labor patterns in the Banda Oriental. Gelman also acknowledges the exceptionality of the Estancia de la Vacas. Elsewhere on the pampas, "the presence of a more scattered rural population, with few agricultural activities and with more opportunities for illegal activities, made itself felt significantly." In short, this one estancia is a poor basis for generalizing about rural life on the pampas.[35]

Establishing human agency for the rural masses is no problem. The historical records of gaucho murders, knife duels, military desertion, and banditry clearly establish their agency. After poring over hundreds of cases involving gaucho violence and resistance, I would hardly depict them as passive victims.[36]

Brown's more recent work still insists that, despite the welter of repressive legislation directed against them, gauchos enjoyed some freedom of opportunity and movement. Brown's fundamental problem is that he halts his research during the 1850s. If he had continued to examine the impact of the Buenos Aires Rural Code of 1865 and of the successful repression of the gaucho in the 1870s and 1880s, he would not paint such a rosy picture of rural society. José

Hernandez's epic poem of the 1870s, *Martín Fierro*, offers excellent insights into the decline of the gaucho. Brown's conclusion to his 1995 essay is most revealing: "Native-born persons of color—be they mestizos, blacks, or mulattoes—found opportunities galore, but at the bottom of the rural social ladder."[37] Not much had really changed since colonial times.

No one debates whether gauchos resisted victimization—they did so repeatedly and in many ways. Unfortunately for them, they lost. Officials working on behalf of the landed elites fought and ultimately won a century-long war of oppression against the gaucho. No empowerment or agency theory can change the reality of their subjugation. Brown himself described the reality of rural social relations: "The biggest estancieros in a particular sector of the countryside, especially in the sparsely settled frontier areas, effectively dominated the entire area through their monopolies of *pulperías* and the means of transportation, carriages, and carts."[38]

Historians of Argentina, as elsewhere, have overstressed the exceptionalism of the nation's past. Exceptionalists should consult studies of rural societies beyond a single country. Miguel Izard on Venezuela, David McCreery on Guatemala, José P. Barrán and Benjamín Nahum on Uruguay, and Michael J. Gonzalez on Peru reveal rural social conflict and coercion comparable to the Argentine case. The general conclusion is clear: the nineteenth-century rural masses did not live a Pollyanna existence.[39]

Canada's Ranching West

Canada's cattle ranching frontier has also undergone historiographical transformation. Traditional studies presented ranch life in Alberta as a simple, straightforward northern extension of the American West. In important studies published in the 1970s and early 1980s David H. Breen challenged this erasure of the border. He pointed up many elements of eastern Victorian culture that moved intact from eastern to western Canada.[40]

Other scholars have in turn challenged Breen's emphasis on the eastern Victorian roots of the Canadian cattle frontier. Simon Evans provides evidence of substantial influence moving from the American ranching complex northward into southeastern Alberta and southern Saskatchewan. Warren M. Elofson has shown that Canadian ranchers valued cowboy and ranching expertise imported from the United States. As elsewhere, diverse influences and environments shaped the Alberta ranching frontier.[41]

A hemispheric perspective is appropriate for studying livestock frontiers. Many of these regions went through similar changes in technology and world markets. Tom Hall's revision of world-systems theory and his use of the concept of incorporation offer a workable, comparative framework for such a vast hemispheric undertaking.[42]

Despite the dangers of overrevisionism, the general historiographical trend leaves us with a clearer, more accurate picture of frontiers throughout the Americas. The history of the cowboy and of the West in general needs continued work. As Brian Dippie reminds us, "Easterners prefix everything western with the all-purpose pejorative 'cowboy'—cowboy music, cowboy stories, cowboy art, cowboy history—the easier to ignore." The awarding of MacArthur Fellowships to Patricia Limerick and Richard White in 1995 drives home the error of eastern snobbery. As recent historiography clearly shows, students of western and frontier history have absolutely no reason to hang their heads.[43]

Notes

Preface

1. Herbert Eugene Bolton, "The Epic of Greater America," *American Historical Review* 38, 3 (April 1933): 448–74; Walter Prescott Webb, *The Great Frontier* (Austin: University of Texas Press, 1951); Owen Lattimore, *Studies in Frontier History: Collected Papers, 1928–1958* (London: Oxford University Press, 1958); Walker D. Wyman and Clifton B. Kroeber, eds., *The Frontier in Perspective* (Madison: University of Wisconsin Press, 1957).

2. William G. Robbins, "Laying Siege to Western History: The Emergence of New Paradigms," and Walter Nugent, "Frontiers and Empires in the Late Nineteenth Century," in Patricia Nelson Limerick, Clyde A. Milner II, and Charles E. Rankin, eds., *Trails: Toward a New Western History* (Lawrence: University Press of Kansas, 1991).

3. Philip D. Curtain, "Depth, Span, and Relevance," *American Historical Review* 89, 1 (February 1984): 1–9; Walter Nugent, "Frontiers and Empires in the Late Nineteenth Century," *Western Historical Quarterly* 20, 4 (November 1989): 393–408; Richard Maxwell Brown, "Western Violence: Structure, Values, Myth," *Western Historical Quarterly* 24, 1 (February 1993): 5–20. For further discussions of comparative history, see Richard W. Slatta, *Cowboys of the Americas* (New Haven: Yale University Press, 1990), 1–2, 6–8; Lewis Hanke, ed., *Do the Americas Have a Common History? A*

Critique of the Bolton Theory (New York: Knopf, 1964); Marvin W. Mikesell, "Comparative Studies in Frontier History," in Richard Hofstadter and Seymour Lipset, eds., *Turner and the Sociology of the Frontier* (New York: Basic Books, 1968), 152–71; Peter Kolchin, "Comparing American History," in Stanley I. Kutler and Stanley N. Katz, eds., *The Promise of American History: Progress and Prospects* (Baltimore: Johns Hopkins University Press, 1982), 64–81; Magnus Morner et al., "Comparative Approaches to Latin American History," *Latin American Research Review* 17, 3 (1982): 55–90; Donald P. Warwick and Samuel Osherson, eds., *Comparative Research Methods* (Englewood Cliffs: Prentice-Hall, 1973), esp. 3–88; George M. Fredrickson, "Comparative History," ' in Michael Kammen, ed., *The Past Before Us: Contemporary Historical Writing in the United States* (Ithaca: Cornell University Press, 1980).

1. Historical Frontier Imagery in Canada, the United States, and Latin America

Much of this chapter appeared as my essay "Historical Frontier Imagery in the Americas" in Lawrence A. Herzog, ed., *Changing Boundaries of the Americas* (La Jolla: University of California, San Diego, Center for U.S.-Mexican Studies, 1992), 25–46. The section on the Great Plains is based on my book *Cowboys of the Americas* (New Haven: Yale University Press, 1990), 59–61, 66–67.

1. On the frontier in the United States, see Herbert Eugene Bolton, "The Epic of Greater America," *American Historical Review* 38, 3 (April 1933): 448–74; Ray Allen Billington, *America's Frontier Heritage* (New York: Holt, Rinehart and Winston, 1966); Billington, *The Frontier Thesis: Valid Interpretation of American History?* (Huntington, N.Y.: Robert E. Krieger, 1966); Billington, "The American Frontier" in Paul Bohannan and Fred Plog, eds., *Beyond the Frontier: Social Process and Cultural Change* (Garden City, N.Y.: Natural History Press, 1976); Billington, *Land of Savagery; Land of Promise: The European Image of the American Frontier in the Nineteenth Century* (New York: Norton, 1981); Walter Prescott Webb, *The Great Frontier* (Austin: University of Texas Press, 1951); Webb,

"The Western World Frontier," in Walker D. Wyman and Clifton B. Kroeber, eds., *The Frontier in Perspective* (Madison: University of Wisconsin Press, 1957); Jack D. Forbes, "Frontiers in American History," *Journal of the West* 1, 1 (July 1962): 63–73; Frederic L. Paxon, "A Generation of the Frontier Hypothesis: 1893–1932," *Pacific Historical Review* 2, 1 (March 1933): 34–51; Wilbur R. Jacobs, *On Turner's Trail: 100 Years of Writing Western History* (Lawrence: University Press of Kansas, 1994). Criticism of the Turner hypothesis has been gathered into a single convenient volume, Richard Hofstadter and Seymour Martin Lipset, eds., *Turner and the Sociology of the Frontier* (New York: Basic Books, 1968). See also chapter 7.

2. On Latin American frontiers, see Victor Andrés Belaúnde, "The Frontier in Hispanic America," *Rice Institute Pamphlet* 10, 4 (October 1923): 202–13; Herbert Eugene Bolton, "The Epic of Greater America," *American Historical Review* 38, 3 (April 1933): 448–74; Silvio Zavala, "The Frontiers of Hispanic America" in Wyman and Kroeber, *The Frontier in Perspective*; Isaiah Bowman, *The Pioneer Fringe* (New York: American Geographical Society, 1931); Richard J. Morrisey, "The Shaping of Two Frontiers," *Americas* 3, 1 (January 1951): 3–6, 41–42; Martin T. Katzman, "The Brazilian Frontier in Comparative Perspective," *Comparative Studies in Society and History* 17, 3 (July 1975): 266–85; Mary Lombardi, "The Frontier in Brazilian History: An Historiographical Essay," *Pacific Historical Review* 44, 4 (November 1975): 437–57; Hebe Clementi, "National Identity and the Frontier," *American Studies International* 19, 3–4 (1981): 36–44; Silvio Duncan Baretta and John Markoff, "Civilization and Barbarism: Cattle Frontiers in Latin America," *Studies in Comparative Society and History* 20 (October 1978): 587–620; Alistair Hennessy, *The Frontier in Latin American History* (Albuquerque: University of New Mexico Press, 1978).

3. On defining the frontier, see Owen Lattimore, "The Frontier in History," in *Studies in Frontier History: Collected Papers, 1928–58* (London: Oxford University Press, 1958); Fulmer Mood, "Notes on the History of the Word Frontier," *Agricultural History* 22, 2 (April 1948): 78, 80–81; Lucien Febvre, "Frontière: The Word and the Concept," in Peter Burke, ed., *A New Kind of History from the Writings*

of Lucien Febvre, trans. K. Folca (London: Routledge and Kegan Paul, 1973), 208–09; Katzman, "Brazilian Frontier," 275–81.

4. Donald D. Brand, "The Early History of the Range Cattle Industry in Northern Mexico," *Agricultural History* 35, 3 (July 1961): 133.

5. George M. McBride, *The Land Systems of Mexico* (1923; repr., New York: Octagon, 1971), 38, 154; Terry G. Jordan, *North American Cattle-Ranching Frontiers: Origins, Diffusion, and Differentiation* (Albuquerque: University of New Mexico Press, 1993), 126–32.

6. William Eugene Hollon, *The Great American Desert Then and Now* (New York: Oxford University Press, 1966), 5.

7. Jordan, *North American Cattle-Ranching Frontiers,* 221–27.

8. Richard White, *"It's Your Misfortune and None of My Own": A New History of the American West* (Norman: University of Oklahoma Press, 1991), 183–86.

9. L. P. Guichon, "A Brief Summary of the History of the Cattle Industry in British Columbia," *Canadian Cattlemen* 1, 3 (December 1938): 111, 138.

10. John Macoun, *Manitoba and the Great Northwest* (Guelph, Ont.: World Publishing, 1882), 255.

11. Sheilagh S. Jameson, "The Era of the Big Ranches: The Romantic Period of Southern Alberta's History," MS, Glenbow Archives, Calgary, D 636.081 J31, May 1968, 3; reprinted as "Era of the Big Ranches," *Alberta Historical Review* 18, 1 (summer 1970): 1–9.

12. Mary Ella Inderwick, "Letter to Alice, May 13, 1884, from North Fork Ranch, Alberta," Glenbow Archives, Calgary, M 559; reprinted in "A Lady and Her Ranch," *Alberta Historical Review* 15, 4 (autumn 1967): 1–9.

13. Walter Prescott Webb, "The American West, Perpetual Mirage," *Harper's Magazine,* May 1957, 26, 29; Hollon, *Great American Desert,* 5; Susan Rhoades Neel, "A Place of Extremes: Nature, History, and the American West," *Western Historical Quarterly* 24, 4 (winter 1994): 489–506.

14. R. Douglas Francis, "From Wasteland to Utopia: Changing Images of the Canadian West in the Nineteenth Century," *Great*

Plains Quarterly 7, 3 (summer 1987): 179–81. See also R. Douglas Francis, "Changing Images of the West," *Journal of Canadian Studies* 17 (fall 1982): 5–19. On conflicting plains imagery in the United States and Canada, see "The Desert and the Garden," pt. 5 of Brian W. Blouet and Merlin P. Lawson, eds., *Images of the Plains: The Role of Human Nature in Settlement* (Lincoln: University of Nebraska Press, 1975), 125–88.

15. Macoun, *Manitoba*, 252.

16. Francis, "Wasteland to Utopia," 187–89; Paul F. Sharp, "The American Farmer and the 'Last Best West,'" *Agricultural History* 21, 2 (April 1947): 65–75.

17. Sharp, "American Farmer," 65–75. For more on the Canadian frontier, see Michael S. Cross, ed., *The Turner Thesis and the Canadas: The Debate on the Impact of the Canadian Environment* (Toronto: Copp Clark, 1970).

18. Wallace Stegner, *Wolf Willow: A History, a Story, and a Memory of the Last Plains Frontier* (Toronto: Macmillan, 1962), 96.

19. Juan Iturbe, "Nuestros llanos: Apuntes fisiográficas, biológicas y agro-pecuarias," pamphlet (Caracas: La Nación, 1942), 5, 33; John V. Lombardi, *People and Places in Colonial Venezuela* (Bloomington: University of Indiana Press, 1976), 22. Frederick Gerstacker compares the llanos, pampas, and Great Plains, in *Viaje por Venezuela en el año 1868*, trans. Ana María Gathmann (Caracas: Universidad Central de Venezuela, 1968), 67.

20. Pablo Vila, *Geografía de Venezuela*, 2d facsimile ed. (Caracas: Ministerio de Educación, 1969), 236–39. See also Jane M. Rausch, *A Tropical Plains Frontier: The Llanos of Colombia, 1531–1831* (Albuquerque: University of New Mexico Press, 1984), and Jane M. Rausch, *The Llanos Frontier in Colombian History, 1830–1930* (Albuquerque: University of New Mexico Press, 1993).

21. Karl Sachs, *De los llanos: Descripción de un viaje de ciencias naturales a Venezuela*, trans. José Ezquierdo (Caracas and Madrid: Edime, 1955), 94, 236. On llanos floods and epidemics, see Manuel Landaeta Rosales, *Gran recopilación geográfica, estadística e histórica de Venezuela*, 2 vols. (Caracas: Banco Central de Venezuela, 1963), 2: 230–31; Iturbe, "Nuestros llanos," 25–27.

22. No works comparable to Rausch's *Tropical Plains Frontier* and *The Llanos Frontier in Colombian History* exist for Venezuela. On llanos historiography, see Richard W. Slatta and Arturo Alvarez D'Armas, "El llanero y el hato venezolano: Aportes bibliográficas," *South Eastern Latin Americanist* 29, 2–3 (September 1985): 33–41.

23. Manuel Tejera, *Venezuela pintoresca e ilustrada* (Paris: Librería Española, 1875), 247.

24. Agustín Codazzi, *Resumen de la geografía de Venezuela* (Caracas: Ministerio de Educación Nacional, 1940), 90; Luis J. Alfonso, *Breve analisis del pasado de Venezuela* (Caracas: Imprenta Nacional, 1872), iii.

25. Rómulo Gallegos, *Doña Bárbara*, trans. Robert Malloy (New York: Peter Smith, 1931).

26. Quoted in Adolfo Rodríguez, "Los mitos del llano y el llanero en la obra de Rómulo Gallegos," pamphlet (San Fernando, Venezuela: Cronista del Estado, 1979), 5; Laureano Vallenilla Lanz, *Disgregación e integración* (Caracas: Universal, 1930), 66.

27. Rómulo Gallegos, *Cantaclaro* (Caracas: Ministerio de Educación Nacional, 1945), 246; Rómulo Gallegos, "Necesidad de valores culturales," in *Una posición de la vida* (Mexico: Humanismo, 1954), 84–85; Marco Aurelio Vila, *Las sequías en Venezuela* (Caracas: Fondo Editorial Común, 1975), 95–129.

28. Robert P. Matthews, Jr., "Rural Violence and Social Unrest in Venezuela, 1840–1858: Origins of the Federalist War" (Ph.D. diss., New York University, 1974); Miguel Izard, *El miedo de la revolución: La lucha por la libertad en Venezuela, 1777–1830* (Madrid: Tecnos, 1979); Manuel A. Machado, Jr., *The Northern Mexican Cattle Industry, 1910–1975: Ideology, Conflict, and Change* (College Station: Texas A&M University Press, 1981), 7–28.

29. See Rausch, *Tropical Plains Frontier*.

30. Carl E. Solberg, "A Discriminatory Frontier Land Policy: Chile, 1870–1914," *The Americas* 26, 2 (October 1969): 115; Brian Loveman, *Chile: The Legacy of Hispanic Capitalism* (New York: Oxford University Press, 1979), 48, 61, 73–74.

31. Loveman, *Chile*, 142–43.

32. Arnold Bauer, "Chilean Rural Labor in the Nineteenth Century," *American Historical Review* 76, 4 (October 1971): 1070.

33. Loveman, *Chile*, 123-24.

34. On perceptions of Southern Cone Indians, see Kristine L. Jones, "Nineteenth-Century British Travel Accounts of Argentina," *Ethnohistory* 33, 2 (1986): 195-211.

35. Solberg, "Discriminatory Frontier Land Policy," 125-27; Charles C. Griffin, "Francisco Encina and Revisionism in Chilean History," *Hispanic American Historical Review* 37, 1 (February 1957): 1-28.

36. Carl E. Solberg, *Immigration and Nationalism: Argentina and Chile, 1890-1914* (Austin: University of Texas Press, 1970), 139-46. See also Hugo F. Castillo, "Agrarian Structures in a Region of Recent Colonization: La Frontera, Chile, 1850-1920," (Ph.D. diss., University of North Carolina at Chapel Hill, 1983).

37. Richard W. Slatta, *Gauchos and the Vanishing Frontier* (Lincoln: University of Nebraska Press, 1983), 18-19.

38. Ezequiel Martínez Estrada, *X-Ray of the Pampa*, trans. Alain Swietlicki (Austin: University of Texas Press, 1971), 6-7.

39. See chapter 2.

40. Slatta, *Gauchos*, 15-24.

41. Domingo F. Sarmiento, *Life in the Argentine Republic in the Days of the Tyrants; or, Civilization and Barbarism*, trans. Mrs. Horace [Mary] Mann (1845; repr., New York: Hafner, 1971).

42. Ricardo Rodríguez Molas, *Historia social del gaucho* (Buenos Aires: Marú, 1968), 136; Daniel Granada, *Reseña histórico-descriptiva de antiguas y modernas supersticiones del Río de la Plata* (Montevideo: Barreiro y Ramos, 1896); Slatta, *Gauchos*, 11-13.

43. Quoted in José Antonio Wilde, *Buenos Aires desde setenta años atras (1810-1880)* (Buenos Aires: EUDEBA, 1966), 78.

44. Henry Marie Brackenridge, *Voyage to South America*, 2 vols. (Baltimore: Cushing and Jewett, 1819), 1: 222; Slatta, *Gauchos*, 21-25.

45. On Argentine agriculture, see James R. Scobie, *Revolution on the Pampas: A Social History of Wheat* (Austin: University of Texas

Press, 1964); Slatta, *Gauchos*, 150–60; David Rock, *Argentina, 1516–1987: From Spanish Colonization to Alfonsín*, 2d ed. (Berkeley: University of California Press, 1987), 135–40.

46. On repressive laws, see Buenos Aires Province, *Registro oficial* (Buenos Aires, 1822), 69, 170, 277; Benito Díaz, *Juzgados de paz de la campaña de la Provincia de Buenos Aires, 1821–1854* (La Plata: Universidad Nacional de La Plata, 1959), 105–06, 202–03; Slatta, *Gauchos*, 106–25, 141–60.

47. Estrada, *X-Ray of the Pampa*, 205. On barriers to gaucho family life, see Slatta, *Gauchos*, 58–60.

48. On the Indian frontier, see chapter 3 as well as Roberto H. Marfany, *El indio en la colonización de Buenos Aires* (Buenos Aires: Comisión Nacional de Cultura, 1940); Juan Carlos Walther, *La conquista del desierto*, 2d ed. (Buenos Aires: Círculo Militar, 1964); Richard W. Slatta, "Civilization Battles Barbarism: Argentine Frontier Strategies, 1516–1880," *Inter-American Review of Bibliography* 39, 2 (1989): 177–94. On rural banditry, see Richard W. Slatta, ed., *Bandidos: The Varieties of Latin American Banditry* (Westport, Conn.: Greenwood Press, 1987).

49. See also chapter 6. Buenos Aires Province, Comisión de Hacendados del Estado de Buenos Aires, *Antecedentes y fundamentos del proyecto de código rural* (Buenos Aires, 1864); letter from Mauricio Díaz, Bahia Blanca, 6 March 1850, juez de paz de Azul 9-4-4; reports of juez de crimen 1872, 38-4-313; Archivo Histórico de la Provincia de Buenos Aires "Ricardo Levene" (La Plata, Argentina); police reports of March, June, July 1852, Policía 1852, Archivo Histórico Municipal de Tandil (Tandil, Argentina).

50. Slatta, *Gauchos*, 12–13, 118–19; John C. Chasteen, "Violence for Show: Knife Dueling on a Nineteenth-Century Cattle Frontier," in Lyman L. Johnson, ed., *The Problem of Order in Changing Societies: Essays on Crime and Policing in Argentina and Uruguay, 1750–1940* (Albuquerque: University of New Mexico Press, 1990), 47–64.

51. Scobie, *Revolution on the Pampas*, 53–54, 58–60, 162.

52. Solberg, *Immigration and Nationalism*, 24; Rock, *Argentina*, 179.

53. See also chapter 8. Michael G. Mulhall, *Rio Grande do Sul and its German Colonies* (London: Longmans, Green, 1873), 24. On the

colonial history of Rio Grande do Sul, see Oliveira Viana, *O campeador riograndense*, vol. 2 of *Populações meridionais do Brasil* (Rio de Janeiro: Paz e Terra, 1972).

54. Alfredo Castellanos, *La cisplatina, la independencia y la república caudillesca, 1820–1838*, vol. 3 of *Historia uruguaya*, 2d ed. (Montevideo: Banda Oriental, 1975), 7, 30–33, 59–64, 82.

55. Catherine LeGrand, *Frontier Expansion and Peasant Protest in Colombia, 1850–1936* (Albuquerque: University of New Mexico Press, 1986), 8–9. On southern Brazil, see Sergio da Costa Franco, "A campanha," and Paulo Xavier, "A estancia," in *Rio Grande do Sul: Terra e povo* (Pôrto Alegre, Brazil: Editora Globo, 1963). For contemporary descriptions of Brazil, see May Frances, *Beyond the Argentine, or, Letters from Brazil* (London: H. W. Allen, 1890); Charles G. Hamilton, "English-Speaking Travelers in Brazil, 1851–1887," *Hispanic American Historical Review* 40, 4 (November 1960): 533–47.

56. Lombardi, "Frontier in Brazilian History," 448, 456.

57. See John C. Chasteen, *Heroes on Horseback: A Life and Times of the Last Gaucho Caudillos* (Albuquerque: University of New Mexico Press, 1995); Moises Vellinho, *Brazil South: Its Conquest and Settlement* (New York: Knopf, 1968).

58. Caio Prado, Jr., *The Colonial Background of Modern Brazil*, trans. Suzette Macedo (Berkeley: University of California Press, 1971), 197, 213–41.

59. Lombardi, "Frontier in Brazilian History," 441–42, 447–48; Febvre, "Frontière," 209–11.

60. See also chapter 7. Lombardi, "Frontier in Brazilian History," 453–54. For both contemporary and modern views of the slave hunters, see Richard M. Morse, ed., *The Bandeirantes: The Historical Role of the Brazilian Pathfinders* (New York: Knopf, 1965).

61. Euclides da Cunha, *Rebellion in the Backlands (Os Sertões)*, trans. Samuel Putnam (1902; repr., Chicago: University of Chicago Press, 1944), 54; E. Bradford Burns, "The Destruction of a Folk Past: Euclides da Cunha and Cataclysmic Cultural Clash," *Review of Latin American Studies* 3, 1 (1990): 17–36.

62. See also chapter 7. Clementi, "National Identity," 40–41; Lombardi, "Frontier in Brazilian History," 444, 449–51.

63. Morrisey, "Shaping of Two Frontiers," 3–6, 41–42.

64. Hofstadter and Lipset, *Turner and the Sociology of the Frontier,* 15–42, 120–51, 172–200.

65. Zavala, "Frontiers of Hispanic America," 45, 56.

66. Scobie, *Revolution on the Pampas,* 45–46; Slatta, *Cowboys of the Americas,* 180–82.

67. Webb, *Great Frontier,* 8–28; David M. Potter, *People of Plenty: Economic Abundance and the American Character* (Chicago: University of Chicago Press, 1973), 124, 155–65.

68. Slatta, *Cowboys of the Americas,* 9–12.

69. For an excellent model of seeing both sides of the frontier, see Thomas D. Hall, *Social Change in the Southwest, 1350–1880* (Lawrence: University Press of Kansas, 1989).

70. John Hemming, *Red Gold: The Conquest of the Brazilian Indians* (Cambridge: Harvard University Press, 1978); Hemming, *Amazonian Frontier: The Defeat of the Brazilian Indians* (Cambridge: Harvard University Press, 1987); Julio Aníbal Portas, *Malón contra malón: La solución final del problema del indio de la Argentina* (Buenos Aires: La Flor, 1967); Kristine L. Jones, "Conflict and Adaptation in the Argentine Pampas, 1750–1880" (Ph.D. diss., University of Chicago, 1984); Ricardo Ferrando Keun, *Y así nació la frontera: Conquista, guerra, ocupación, pacificación, 1550–1900* (Santiago: Editorial Antártica, 1986). Scholarship on the Indian frontier in South America lags behind that in the United States and Canada. See, for example, Ray Harvey Pearce, *The Savages of America: A Study of the Indian and the Ideal of Civilization* (Baltimore: Johns Hopkins University Press, 1965); Richard Drinnon, *Facing West: The Metaphysics of Indian-Hating and Empire-Building* (Minneapolis: University of Minnesota Press, 1980); Brian M. Fagan, *Clash of Cultures* (New York: W. H. Freeman, 1984); Olive Patricia Dickason, *The Myth of the Savage and the Beginnings of French Colonialism in the Americas* (Edmonton: University of Alberta Press, 1984).

71. Forbes, "Frontiers in American History," 63–73; Jack D. Forbes, "Frontiers in American History and the Role of the Frontier Historian," *Ethnohistory* 15, 2 (spring 1968): 203–35; David J. Weber,

"Turner, the Boltonians, and the Borderlands," *American Historical Review* 91, 1 (February 1986): 81; Baretta and Markoff, "Civilization and Barbarism," 593–95.

72. Weber, "Turner, the Boltonians, and the Borderlands," 70, 73; John Francis Bannon, *The Spanish Borderlands Frontier, 1513–1821* (New York: Holt, Rinehart, and Winston, 1970), 5; Herbert Eugene Bolton, *The Spanish Borderlands: A Chronicle of Old Florida and the Southwest* (New Haven: Yale University Press, 1921), 233–34.

73. Marvin W. Mikesell, "Comparative Studies in Frontier History," *Annals of the Association of American Geographers* 50, 1 (March 1960): 62–74; Slatta, *Gauchos*, 7–8, 78–80, 87; Félix Coluccio, *Diccionario folklórico argentino*, 2 vols. (Buenos Aires: Luis Lasserre, 1964); José Antonio de Armas Chitty, *Vocabulario del hato* (Caracas: Universidad Central de Venezuela, 1966).

74. William Norton, "The Cultural Landscape of the Historical Frontier," *Journal of Cultural Geography* 3, 2 (September 1983): 119; Dietrich Gerhard, "The Frontier in Comparative Perspective," *Comparative Studies in Society and History* 1 (March 1959): 205–29; Donald Denoon, *Settler Capitalism: The Dynamics of Dependent Development in the Southern Hemisphere* (New York: Oxford University Press, 1983); John Fogarty, "Staples, Super-Staples, and the Limits of Staple Theory: The Experience of Argentina, Australia, and Canada Compared," in D. C. M. Platt and Guido di Tella, eds., *Argentina, Australia, and Canada: Studies in Comparative Development, 1870–1965* (London: Macmillan, 1985), 1–18.

2. Indian Equestrian Economies: A Hemispheric Perspective

I presented an earlier version of this chapter at the Western History Association meeting in Albuquerque, October 21, 1994.

1. Defining regions, such as the "Greater Southwest" or the "Borderlands" remains problematic. For a probing discussion of such difficulties, see James W. Byrkit, "Land, Sky, and People: The Southwest Defined," *Journal of the Southwest* 34 (autumn 1992): 257–387. On ethnographic source and research problems, see Thomas E. Sheridan, "How to Tell the Story of a 'People Without

History': Narrative versus Ethnohistorical Approaches to the Study of the Yaqui Indians through Time," *Journal of the Southwest* 30 (summer 1988): 168–89. For this comparative overview, I must disregard band and tribe diversity. The Apache, for example, include six groups: the Western Apache, Chiricahua, Mescalero, Jicarilla, Lipan, and Kiowa Apache. Similar difficulties arise in defining the pampas, as this great plain extends through portions of Argentina and virtually all of Uruguay. In keeping with usual historiographical practice, I will also refer to the southern frontier as the Río de la Plata.

2. Alvar W. Carlson, "Environmental Overview," in Ellwyn R. Stoddard, Richard L. Nostrand, and Jonathan P. West, eds., *Borderlands Sourcebook: A Guide to the Literature on Northern Mexico and the American Southwest* (Norman: University of Oklahoma Press, 1983), 75–78; Conrad Joseph Bahre, *A Legacy of Change: Historic Human Impact on Vegetation in the Arizona Borderlands* (Tucson: University of Arizona Press, 1991), 29.

3. Elizabeth A. H. John, *Storms Brewed in Other Men's Worlds: The Confrontation of Indians, Spanish, and French in the Southwest, 1540–1795* (College Station: Texas A&M University Press, 1975), 12; Carlson, "Environmental Overview," 75–78; Marc Simmons, *Coronado's Land: Essays on Daily Life in Colonial New Mexico* (Albuquerque: University of New Mexico Press, 1991), 68–70; David J. Weber, *The Spanish Frontier in North America* (New Haven: Yale University Press, 1991), 310–11; Thomas E. Sheridan, "The Limits of Power: The Political Ecology of the Spanish Empire in the Greater Southwest," *Antiquity* 66 (March 1992): 155; Robert J. Hard and William L. Merrill, "Mobile Agriculturists and the Emergence of Sedentism: Perspectives from Northern Mexico," *American Anthropologist* 94 (1992): 601–20. On contemporary problems of aridity, see Patricia Paylore and Richard A. Haney, eds., *Desertification: Process, Problems, Perspectives* (Tucson: University of Arizona Office of Arid Lands Studies, 1976).

4. Ted J. Warner, ed., *The Domínguez-Escalante Journal: Their Expedition through Colorado, Utah, Arizona, and New Mexico in 1776*, trans. Fray Angelico Chavez (Provo, Utah: Brigham Young University Press, 1976), 15.

5. David Rock, *Argentina 1516–1987: From Spanish Colonization to Alfonsín*, rev. ed. (Berkeley: University of California Press, 1987), 3–5; Richard W. Slatta, *Gauchos and the Vanishing Frontier* (Lincoln: University of Nebraska Press, 1983), 17–19, 23–25; Liberio Justo (Quebracho), *Pampas y lanzas* (Buenos Aires: Editorial Palestra, 1962), 12–14.

6. Kristine L. Jones, "Indian-Creole Negotiations in the Southern Frontier," in Mark D. Szuchman and Jonathan C. Brown, eds., *Revolution and Restoration: The Rearrangement of Power in Argentina, 1776–1860* (Lincoln: University of Nebraska Press, 1994), 105–6.

7. Alfred J. Tapson, "Indian Warfare on the Pampas during the Colonial Period," *Hispanic American Historical Review* 42 (February 1962): 2–3; Lorenzo R. Parodi, *La agricultura aborigen argentina* (Buenos Aires: EUDEBA, 1966), 16.

8. Robert B. Cunninghame Graham, *The Conquest of the River Plate* (Garden City, N.Y.: Doubleday, 1924), 196; Antonio Serrano, *Los aborígenes argentinos: síntesis etnográfica* (Buenos Aires: Editorial Nova, 1947), 188, 204; John M. Cooper, "The Araucanians," in Julian H. Steward, ed., *Handbook of South American Indians. Vol 2. The Andes* (New York: Cooper Square Publishers, 1963), 756; Tapson, "Indian Warfare," 6. On ethnographic sources, see Meinrado Hux, *El indio en la llanura del Plata: guía bibliográfica* (La Plata: Archivo Histórico "Ricardo Levene," 1984).

9. Tapson, "Indian Warfare," 5; James Lockhart and Stuart B. Schwartz, *Latin America: A History of Colonial Spanish America and Brazil* (Cambridge: Cambridge University Press, 1983), 56.

10. Tapson, "Indian Warfare," 2–4; Serrano, *Los aborígenes argentinos*, 182–89; Ricardo Rodríguez Molas, *Historia social del gaucho* (Buenos Aires: Marú, 1968), 23–24; Roberto H. Marfany, *El indio en la colonización de Buenos Aires* (Buenos Aires: Comisión Nacional de Cultura, 1940), 62–63.

11. J. Ignatius Molina, *The Geographical, Natural, and Civil History of Chili*, vol. 2, trans. 1808 (1787; repr. New York: AMS Press, 1973), 64; Salvador Canals Frau, "Expansion of the Araucanians in Argentina," in Steward, *Handbook of South American Indians*,

761–66; Robert C. Padden, "Cultural Change and Military Resistance in Araucanian Chile, 1550–1730," in Patricia J. Lyon, ed., *Native South Americans: Ethnology of the Least Known Continent* (Boston: Little, Brown, 1974), 327–42.

12. Padden, "Cultural Change," 333–35.

13. Tapson, "Indian Warfare," 5–6; Graham, *Conquest*, 275; Marfany, *El indio*, 67–68; Serrano, *Los aborígenes argentinos*, 182–89; Rodríguez Molas, *Historia social del gaucho*, 23–24.

14. Lizárraga and Cattaneo, reprinted in José Luis Busaniche, ed., *Estampas del pasado: Lecturas de historia argentina* (Buenos Aires: Solar-Hachette, 1971), 65, 120–21.

15. Graham, *Conquest*, 267. Graham cites Pierre François de Charlevoix's *Histoire du Paraguay* (Paris, 1756), 158.

16. Thomas Falkner, *A Description of Patagonia and the Adjoining Parts of South America* (1774; repr., New York: AMS Press, 1976), 39.

17. Translated and quoted by Graham, *Conquest*, 291.

18. Graham, *Conquest*, 294.

19. See Peter J. Iverson, *The Navajo Nation* (Westport, Conn.: Greenwood Press, 1981); Peter J. Iverson, "The Emerging Navajo Nation" in Alfonso Ortiz, ed., *Handbook of North American Indians. Vol. 10. Southwest* (Washington, D.C.: Smithsonian Institution, 1983), 636–40; Peter J. Iverson, *The Navajos: A Critical Bibliography* (Bloomington: Indiana University Press, 1976); Peter J. Iverson, "Native Americans" in Stoddard, *Borderlands Sourcebook*, 285–89; D. C. Cole, *The Chiricahua Apache, 1846–1876: From War to Reservation* (Albuquerque: University of New Mexico Press, 1988), 46–50; Stephen Trimble, *The People: Indians of the American Southwest* (Santa Fe: School of American Research Press, 1993). For contemporary perspectives, see José Cortés, *Views from the Apache Frontier: Report on the Northern Provinces of New Spain*, trans. John Wheat (Norman: University of Oklahoma Press, 1989).

20. D. W. Meinig, *Southwest: Three Peoples in Geographical Change, 1600–1970* (New York: Oxford, 1971), 14–15; Jack D. Forbes, *Apache, Navajo, and Spaniard* (Norman: University of Oklahoma Press, 1960), 29–30, 34–35, 73–74, 109; LaVerne Harrell Clark, *They Sang for Horses: The Impact of the Horse on Navajo and Apache Folklore*

(Tucson: University of Arizona Press, 1966), 8–9. Literature on the northward diffusion of horses includes Jack Douglas Forbes, "The Appearance of the Mounted Indian in Northern Mexico and the Southwest to 1680," *Southwestern Journal of Anthropology* 15 (1959): 189–212; Francis Haines, "The Northward Spread of Horses among the Plains Indians," *American Anthropologist* n.s., 40 (1938): 429–37; Francis Haines, "Where Did the Plains Indians Get their Horses?" *American Anthropologist* n.s., 40 (1938): 112–17; Donald E. Worcester, "The Spread of Spanish Horses in the Southwest," *New Mexico Historical Review* 19 (1944): 225–32, and 20 (1945): 1–13.

21. Edward H. Spicer, *Cycles of Conquest: The Impact of Spain, Mexico, and the United States on the Indians of the Southwest, 1533–1960* (Tucson: University of Arizona Press, 1962), 546–47; LaVerne Harrell Clark, "Early Horse Trappings of the Navajo and Apache Indians," *Arizona and the West* 5 (1963): 235–36. María Soledad Arbelaez attempts to measure the real impact of raids in "The Sonoran Missions and Indian Raids in the Eighteenth Century," *Journal of the Southwest* 33 (autumn 1991): 366–86.

22. Kristine L. Jones, "Comparative Raiding Economies: North and South," in Thomas E. Sheridan and Donna J. Guy, eds., *Contested Ground* (Tucson: University of Arizona Press, forthcoming).

23. Molina, *History of Chili*, 95.

24. John Canfield Ewers, *The Horse in Blackfoot Indian Culture, with Comparative Material from other Western Tribes* (Washington, D.C.: U.S. Government Printing Office, 1955); John Canfield Ewers, *The Blackfeet: Raiders on the Northwestern Plains* (Norman: University of Oklahoma Press, 1959), 103–4, 147; John Canfield Ewers, "Horsemen of the Plains," in Jules B. Billard, ed., *The World of the American Indian*, rev. ed. (Washington, D.C.: National Geographic Society, 1989), 255–310; John Canfield Ewers, "The Influence of the Horse on Blackfoot Culture," in Deward E. Walker, Jr., ed., *The Emergent Native Americans* (Boston: Little, Brown, 1972), 252–70; John Canfield Ewers, "Were the Blackfoot Rich in Horses?" *American Anthropologist* n.s., 45 (1943): 602–10; Ernest Wallace, *The Comanches: Lords of the South Plains* (Norman: University of Oklahoma Press, 1952); Stanley Noyes, *Los Comanches: The Horse*

People, 1751–1845 (Albuquerque: University of New Mexico Press, 1993).

25. Haines, "Where Did the Plains Indians Get their Horses?" 117; Alvin M. Josephy, Jr., ed., *The American Heritage Book of Indians* (New York: Simon and Schuster, 1961), 334.

26. On the Cheyenne and the Arapaho, see E. Adamson Hoebel, *The Cheyennes: Indians of the Great Plains* (New York: Holt, 1960); John Stands in Timber, *Cheyenne Memories* (New Haven: Yale University Press, 1967); Donald J. Berthrong, *The Southern Cheyennes* (Norman: University of Oklahoma Press, 1963); and Frank Gilbert Roe, *The Indian and the Horse* (Norman: University of Oklahoma Press, 1955).

27. First quote is from Evelyn Hu-DeHart, *Missionaries, Miners, and Indians: Spanish Contact with the Yaqui Nation of Northwestern New Spain, 1533–1820* (Tucson: University of Arizona Press, 1981), 56; second quote is from Daniel S. Maton and Bernard L. Fontana, eds., *Friar Bringas Reports to the King* (Tucson: University of Arizona Press, 1977), 66; John L. Kessell, "Spanish Exploration in the Western Borderlands," *Montana, The Magazine of Western History* 41, 4 (autumn 1991): 75; Forbes, *Apache, Navajo, and Spaniard*, 41, 74; James E. Officer, *Spanish Arizona, 1536–1856* (Tucson: University of Arizona Press, 1987), 57.

28. Ewers, *Horse in Blackfoot Indian Culture*; Ewers, *The Blackfeet*, 103–04, 147; Ewers, "Horsemen of the Plains," 255–310; Ewers, "Influence of the Horse on Blackfoot Culture," 252–70; Ewers, "Were the Blackfoot Rich in Horses?" 602–10.

29. David G. Mandelbaum, *The Plains Cree* (New York: American Museum of Natural History, 1940), 194–95, 295.

30. On horse-induced changes in plains cultures, see Elizabeth Atwood Lawrence, *Hoofbeats and Society: Studies of Human-Horse Interactions* (Bloomington: Indiana University Press, 1985); Roe, *Indian and the Horse*; Preston Holder, *The Hoe and the Horse on the Plains* (Lincoln: University of Nebraska Press, 1970); and Thomas E. Mails, *The Mystic Warriors of the Plains* (New York: Doubleday, 1972).

31. Hoebel, *The Cheyennes;* Stands in Timber, *Cheyenne Memories*; Berthrong, *Southern Cheyennes*; Berthrong, *The Cheyenne*

and Arapaho Ordeal: Reservation and Agency Life in the Indian Territory, 1875–1907 (Norman: University of Oklahoma Press, 1976); Roe, *Indian and the Horse*; Joseph Jablow, *The Cheyenne in Plains Indian Trade Relations, 1795–1840* (New York: J. J. Augustin, 1951).

32. Spicer, *Cycles of Conquest*, 546; John, *Storms Brewed*, 6, 30; Forbes, *Apache*, 83, 94, 99, 121, 284–85.

33. Document reproduced in Marc Simmons, *Coronado's Land: Essays on Daily Life in Colonial New Mexico* (Albuquerque: University of New Mexico Press, 1991), 171.

34. John, *Storms Brewed*, 89.

35. Simmons, *Coronado's Land*, 133–37, 170.

36. Francis Haines, Sr., "Red Men of the Plains, 1500–1870," *American West* (July 1973): 33; Mails, *Mystic Warriors*, 12.

37. Forbes, *Apache*, 139, 175, 285; Spicer, *Cycles of Conquest*, 26, 463.

38. Julian H. Steward and Louis C. Faron, *Native Peoples of South America* (New York: McGraw Hill, 1959), 392.

39. Jerrod E. Levy, "Is this a System? Comment on Osborn's 'Ecological Aspects of Equestrian Adaptations in Aboriginal North America,'" *American Anthropologist* 86 (1984): 986, 989.

40. Ewers, *The Blackfeet*, 89; Ewers, "Were the Blackfoot Rich in Horses?", 606–7. On the climate debate, see Alan J. Osborn, "Economic Aspects of Equestrian Adaptations in Aboriginal North America," *American Anthropologist* 95 (1983): 563–91; and Levy's critique, "Is this a System?"

41. On the concept of incorporation, see Thomas D. Hall, *Social Change in the Southwest, 1350–1880* (Lawrence: University Press of Kansas, 1989), 18–24, 248–49. On Spanish culture, see Oakah L. Jones, Jr., "Hispanic Traditions and Improvisations on the Frontera Septentrional of New Spain," *New Mexico Historical Review* 56, 4 (1981): 333–47.

42. Richard W. Slatta, *Cowboys of the Americas* (New Haven: Yale University Press, 1990), 11–13, 15, 18–20.

43. See Peter J. Iverson, *When Indians Became Cowboys: Native Peoples and Cattle Ranching in the American West* (Norman: University of Oklahoma Press, 1994); Peter J. Iverson, "Cowboys,

Indians and the Modern West," *Arizona and the West* 28, 2 (1986): 107–24; Peter J. Iverson, ed., *The Plains Indians of the Twentieth Century* (Norman: University of Oklahoma Press, 1985); Harry T. Getty, "San Carlos Apache Cattle Industry," *Human Organization* 20 (1962): 181–86; Harry T. Getty, "The San Carlos Indian Cattle Industry," (Tucson: University of Arizona Anthropological Papers, no. 7, 1963); Donald J. Berthrong, "Cattlemen on the Cheyenne-Arapaho Reservation, 1883–1885," *Arizona and the West* 13 (1971): 5–32; Robert M. Utley, "The Range Cattle Industry in the Big Bend of Texas," *Southwestern Historical Quarterly* 69 (1965): 419–41; Eva Antonia Wilbur-Cruce, "Indian Country," *Journal of Arizona History* 26, 4 (1985): 351–74; Thomas R. Wessel, "Agent of Acculturation: Farming on the Northern Plains Reservations, 1880–1910," *Agricultural History* 60, 2 (1986): 233–45; Gwyneth Harrington Xavier, "The Cattle Industry of the Southern Papago Districts with Some Information on the Reservation Cattle Industry as a Whole," in Robert A. Hackenberg et al., eds., *Papago Indians* (New York: Garland Publishing Inc., 1974), 349–402; Albert L. Hurado and Peter J. Iverson, eds., *Major Problems in American Indian History* (Lexington, Mass.: D. C. Heath, 1994).

3. Extremes of Empire: Spanish Colonial Military Policy in the Pampas of Argentina and the Internal Provinces of New Spain

Portions of this chapter draw upon ideas presented in my essay "Defending Far Frontiers: Spanish Colonial Military Policy in Northern New Spain and the Río de la Plata" in Thomas Sheridan and Donna Guy, eds., *Contested Ground* (Tucson: University of Arizona Press, forthcoming).

1. Evelyn Hu-DeHart, *Missionaries, Miners, and Indians: Spanish Contact with the Yaqui Nation of Northwestern New Spain, 1533–1820* (Tucson: University of Arizona Press, 1981), 8. For recent scholarship on native resistance, see Pilar García Jordán and Miguel Izard, eds., *Conquista y resistencia en la historia de América* (Barcelona: Universidad de Barcelona, 1991).

2. Silvio R. Duncan Baretta and John Markoff, "Civilization and Barbarism: Cattle Frontiers in Latin America," *Comparative Studies in Society and History* 20 (October 1978): 590.

3. On New World frontier definitions, types, and characteristics, see Richard W. Slatta, "Historical Frontier Imagery in the Americas," in Paula Covington, ed., *Latin American Frontiers, Borders, and Hinterlands: Research Needs and Resources* (Albuquerque: SALALM Secretariat, 1990): 5–25. On the concept of incorporation, see Thomas D. Hall, *Social Change in the Southwest, 1350–1880* (Lawrence: University Press of Kansas, 1989), 18–24, 248–49.

4. Alfred Tapson, "Indian Warfare on the Pampa during the Colonial Period," *Hispanic American Historical Review* 42 (February 1962): 5; James Lockhart and Stuart B. Schwartz, *Latin America: A History of Colonial Spanish America and Brazil* (Cambridge: Cambridge University Press, 1983), 56; D. W. Meinig, *Southwest: Three Peoples in Geographical Change, 1600–1970* (New York: Oxford, 1971), 14–15; Jack D. Forbes, *Apache, Navajo, and Spaniard* (Norman: University of Oklahoma Press, 1960), 29–30, 34–35, 73–74, 109; LaVerne Harrell Clark, *They Sang for Horses: The Impact of the Horse on Navajo and Apache Folklore* (Tucson: University of Arizona Press, 1966), 8–9.

5. James Schofield Saeger, "Another View of the Mission as a Frontier Institution: The Guaycuruan Reductions of Santa Fe, 1743–1810," *Hispanic American Historical Review* 65: 3 (1985): 493–517; Carlos Antonio Moncaut, *Los mas remotos origenes de Ranchos* (General Paz, Argentina: Municipalidad de General Paz, 1978), 9.

6. Moncaut, *Ranchos*, 13; Carlos Antonio Moncaut, *Reducción jesuítica de Nuestra Señora de la Concepción de las Pampas, 1740–1753* (n.p.: Ministerio de Economia de la Provincia de Buenos Aires, 1981), 11, 17, 87.

7. Juan Carlos Vedoya et al., *La campaña del desierto y la tecnificación ganadera* (Buenos Aires: EUDEBA, 1979), 15; Roberto H. Marfany, *El indio en la colonización de Buenos Aires* (Buenos Aires: Comisión Nacional de Cultura, 1940), 54–56; Moncaut, *Reducción jesuítica*, 11, 17, 87; Thomas Falkner, *A Description of Patagonia and*

the Adjoining Parts of South America (1774; repr., New York: AMS Press, 1976), v–vi.

8. Quoted in Liberio Justo (Quebracho), *Pampas y lanzas* (Buenos Aires: Editorial Palestra, 1962), 23.

9. Herbert Eugene Bolton, "The Mission as a Frontier Institution in the Spanish American Colonies," in David J. Weber, ed., *New Spain's Far Northern Frontier: Essays on Spain in the American West, 1540–1821* (Albuquerque: University of New Mexico Press, 1979), 56–57.

10. Elizabeth A. H. John, *Storms Brewed in Other Men's Worlds: The Confrontation of Indians, Spanish, and French in the Southwest, 1540–1795* (College Station: Texas A&M University Press, 1975), 65; Bolton, "Mission," 56–57. See also Philip Wayne Powell, "Genesis of the Frontier Presidio in North America," *Western Historical Quarterly* 13, 2 (1982): 124–41.

11. Forbes, *Apache*, 96, 131; Odie B. Faulk, "The Presidio: Fortress or Farce?" in Weber, *New Spain's Far Northern Frontier*, 69, 74.

12. See Forbes, *Apache*, on Spanish-Apache relations, 1540–1700.

13. Antonio Serrano, *Los aborígenes argentinos: síntesis etnográfica* (Buenos Aires: Editorial Nova, 1947), 188, 204; Tapson, "Indian Warfare," 6.

14. Alvar W. Carlson, "Environmental Overview," in Ellwyn R. Stoddard, Richard L. Nostrand, and Jonathan P. West, eds., *Borderlands Sourcebook: A Guide to the Literature on Northern Mexico and the American Southwest* (Norman: University of Oklahoma Press, 1983), 75–78; Walter Prescott Webb, "The American West, Perpetual Mirage," *Harper's Magazine*, May 1957, 26; John, *Storms Brewed*, 12.

15. Thomas H. Naylor and Charles Polzer, eds., *The Presidio and Militia on the Northern Frontier of New Spain, A Documentary History, Volume I: 1570–1700* (Tucson: University of Arizona Press, 1986), 262–64. For more on the region see Oakah L. Jones, *Nueva Vizcaya: Heartland of the Spanish Frontier* (Albuquerque: University of New Mexico Press, 1988).

16. Richard W. Slatta, *Gauchos and the Vanishing Frontier* (Lincoln: University of Nebraska Press, 1983), 17–19, 23–25; Justo, *Pampas y lanzas*, 12–14.

17. Lizárraga and Cattaneo quoted in José Luis Busaniche, ed., *Estampas del pasado: Lecturas de historia argentina* (Buenos Aires: Solar-Hachette, 1971), 65, 120–21; Falkner, *Description of Patagonia*, 38–39.

18. Tapson, "Indian Warfare," 2–6; Marfany, *El indio*, 62–63, 67–68; Madaline Wallace Nichols, "The Spanish Horse of the Pampas," *American Anthropologist* 41 (January 1939): 119–29; Serrano, *Los aborígenes*, 182–184, 189, 201; Ricardo Rodríguez Molas, *Historia social del gaucho* (Buenos Aires: Editorial Marú, 1968), 23–24.

19. Forbes, *Apache*, 7, 12–13, 41.

20. Naylor and Polzer, *Presidio and Militia*, 37–39; Meinig, *Southwest*, 14–15; Forbes, *Apache*, 179.

21. Naylor and Polzer, *Presidio and Militia*, 248–50.

22. Cabildo document of 1608 quoted in Moncaut, *Ranchos*, 8; Marfany, *El indio*, 20–24, 48–49; Mark A. Burkholder and Lyman L. Johnson, *Colonial Latin America*, 2nd ed. (New York: Oxford University Press, 1994), 114–15.

23. Rodríguez Molas, *Historia social*, 169.

24. David Rock, *Argentina, 1516–1987: From Spanish Colonization to Alfonsín*, rev. ed. (Berkeley: University of California Press, 1987), 46–47; Tapson, "Indian Warfare," 8–9; Moncaut, *Reducción Jesuítica*, 16–17.

25. Forbes, *Apache*, 232–33; Clark, *They Sang for Horses*, 147.

26. Oñate letter reproduced in Donald A. Barclay, James H. Maguire, and Peter Wild, eds., *Into the Wilderness: Exploration Narratives of the American West, 1500–1805* (Salt Lake City: University of Utah Press, 1994), 142.

27. Quotation from Falkner, *Description of Patagonia*, 75; Alfred Hasbrouck, "The Conquest of the Desert," *Hispanic American Historical Review* 15 (May 1935): 205; Juan Carlos Walther, *La conquista del desierto*, 2d ed. (Buenos Aires: Círculo Militar, 1964), 118–19.

28. J. Ignatius Molina, *The Geographical, Natural, and Civil History of Chili* (1808; repr., New York: AMS Press, 1973), vol. 2, 65.

29. Marcos de Estrada, *Apuntes sobre el gaucho argentino* (Buenos Aires: Ministerio de Cultura y Educación, 1981), 143–44; Tapson, "Indian Warfare," 6–7; Falkner, *Description of Patagonia*, 128–29.

30. Falkner, *Description of Patagonia*, 129.

31. Chomé quoted in Busaniche, *Estampas*, 77–78.

32. Falkner, *Description of Patagonia*, 122.

33. Forbes, *Apache*, 56–57, 100.

34. Report reproduced in Barclay, Maguire, and Wild, *Into the Wilderness*, 112–13.

35. Constansó narrative reproduced in Barclay, Maguire, and Wild, *Into the Wilderness*, 260.

36. Mark Simmons, *Spanish Government* (Albuquerque: University of New Mexico Press, 1968), 143–46.

37. Simmons, *Spanish Government*, 146–47; Max L. Moorhead, *Presidio: Bastion of the Spanish Borderlands* (Norman: University of Oklahoma Press, 1975), 100–13.

38. Kristine L. Jones, "Indian-Creole Negotiations in the Southern Frontier," in Mark D. Szuchman and Jonathan C. Brown, eds., *Revolution and Restoration: The Rearrangement of Power in Argentina, 1776–1860* (Lincoln: University of Nebraska Press, 1994), 113.

39. Azara quoted in Tapson, "Indian Warfare," 25.

40. Quotation from Vedoya, *Campaña*, 31–32; Walther, *Conquista*, 160–61.

41. Tapson, "Indian Warfare," 26; Jones, "Indian-Creole Negotiations," 109–11.

42. David J. Weber, *The Mexican Frontier, 1821–1846: The Southwest under Mexico* (Albuquerque: University of New Mexico Press, 1982), 93.

43. John, *Storms Brewed*, 37–38, 44, 91.

44. John, *Storms Brewed*, 7.

45. For Spanish policy on the pampas, see Richard W. Slatta, "'Civilization' Battles 'Barbarism': Argentine Frontier Strategies, 1516–1880," *Inter-American Review of Bibliography* 39, 2 (1989): 177–94.

46. Falkner, *Description of Patagonia*, 104–06; Moncaut, *Ranchos*, 10–11.

47. Barclay, Maguire, and Wild, *Into the Wilderness*, 26, 51.

48. Oñate report reproduced in Barclay, Maguire, and Wild, *Into the Wilderness*, 140; Johns, *Storms Brewed*, 6, 30; Forbes, *Apache*, 83, 94, 99, 121, 284–85.

49. Falkner, *Description of Patagonia*, 86; Rodrígues Molas, *Historia social*, 117–18.

50. Forbes, *Apache*, 38–39, 120, 284–85; Clark, *They Sang for Horses*, 86.

51. Marc Simmons, *Coronado's Land: Essays on Daily Life in Colonial New Mexico* (Albuquerque: University of New Mexico Press, 1991), 56–60.

52. S. Thomas Parker, "Peasants, Pastoralists, and *Pax Romana*," *Bulletin of the American Schools of Oriental Research* 265 (1987): 48; S. Thomas Parker, "Exploring the Roman Frontier in Jordan," *Archaeology*, September 1984, 34–35; Thomas D. Hall, "Civilizational Change: The Role of Nomads," *Comparative Civilizations Review* 24 (spring 1991): 38–44.

4. Vaqueros and Charros: Mexico's Horsemen

This chapter, originally appearing in the winter 1994 issue of *Cowboys & Indians*, a popular magazine, lacks full citations. Please refer to the following works, for which full citations appear in the bibliography. My thanks to publishers Reid Slaughter and Robert Hartman, and to editor Charlotte Berney, for reprint permission.

Richard Henry Dana, *Two Years Before the Mast*, describes *californio* life of the 1830s. Joseph J. Mora provides a historical treatment in *Californios: The Saga of the Hard-Riding Vaqueros, America's First Cowboys.*

J. Frank Dobie has written several works, including *A Vaquero of the Brush Country* (1957), "The Mexican Vaquero of the Texas Border" (1927), and "Ranch Mexicans" (1931). More recent treatments of the vaquero include Arnold Rojas, *The Vaquero* and Nora E. Ramírez's 1979 dissertation, "The Vaquero and Ranching in the Southwestern United States, 1600–1970." William D. Wittliff, *Vaquero: Genesis of the Texas Cowboy*, provides a photographic look at Borderlands ranch work.

Manuel A. Machado, Jr., describes the revolutionary destruction and rebirth of *The North Mexican Cattle Industry, 1910–1975*. Michael Moody describes "Rodeo in Mexico: Charros and Charreadas."

James Norman's *Charro: Mexican Horseman* and Kathleen M. Sands, *Charrería Mexicana: An Equestrian Folk Tradition*, are the two major works in English on this colorful figure. Those who can read Spanish should consult Carlos Rincón Gallardo, *El libro del charro mexicano*.

5. Cowboys, Gauchos, and Llaneros

I presented a Spanish version of this essay at a comparative history conference in Tandil, Argentina, in September 1983. The English version originally appeared in *Persimmon Hill* (12, 4 [1983], 8–23), published by the National Cowboy Hall of Fame in Oklahoma City. Thanks to M. J. Van Deventer (a fine writer and editor) for reprint permission. Notes and some new information have been added.

1. Edward Larocque Tinker, *Centaurs of Many Lands* (London: J. A. Allen and Company, 1964), 65.

2. Madaline Wallis Nichols, *The Gaucho: Cattle Hunter, Cavalry-man, Ideal of Romance* (1942; repr., New York: Gordian Press, 1968), 22–35. See also Ricardo Rodríguez Molas, *Historia social del gaucho* (Buenos Aires: Marú, 1968), 13–182.

3. U.S House, *Report on South America*, by Theodore Bland, 15th Cong., 2d sess., 1818–1819, H. Doc. 48; reprinted in William R. Manning, ed., *Diplomatic Correspondence of the United States Concerning the Independence of the Latin-American Nations*, vol. 1, pt. 2 (1925; repr., Ann Arbor: UMI, 1987), 416–17.

4. See Richard W. Slatta, *Gauchos and the Vanishing Frontier* (Lincoln: University of Nebraska Press, 1983).

5. Alexander von Humboldt and Aimé Bonpland, *Personal Narrative of Travels to the Equinoctial Regions of the New Continent, During the Years 1799–1804*, 2d ed. (London: Longman, Hurst, Rees, Orme, Brown, and Green, 1825), vol. 4, 319–20.

6. Edward Laroque Tinker, *Horsemen of the Americas and the Literature They Inspired*, 2d rev. ed. (Austin: University of Texas Press, 1967), 100.

7. Woodbine Parish, *Buenos Ayres and the Provinces of the Rio de la Plata* (1839; repr., London: John Murray, 1852), 122.

8. Ramón Páez, *Wild Scenes in South America; or, Life in the Llanos of Venezuela* (London: Sampson, Low, Son, and Co., 1863), 176–77.

9. Richard W. Slatta, *Cowboys of the Americas* (New Haven: Yale University Press, 1990), 114, 129, 155–56; Richard W. Slatta, "The Demise of the Gaucho and the Rise of Equestrian Sport in Argentina," *Journal of Sport History* 13, 2 (summer 1986): 100, 104.

10. Richard Arthur Seymour, *Pioneering in the Pampas; Or, The First Four Years of a Settler's Experience in the La Plata Camps* (London: Longmans, Green, 1869).

11. Páez, *Wild Scenes*, 47–48.

12. Slatta, *Gauchos*, 73–74.

13. Slatta, *Cowboys of the Americas*, 32–35.

14. Slatta, *Cowboys of the Americas*, 35–39.

15. Slatta, *Cowboys of the Americas*, 45–48.

16. Tinker, *Horsemen of the Americas*, 31–70, 109–22.

17. On cowboy memoirs, see Slatta, "Foreword" to Margot Liberty and Barry Head, *Working Cowboy: Recollections of Ray Holmes* (Norman: University of Oklahoma Press, 1995), xi–xvi.

18. Páez, *Wild Scenes*, 46.

19. John C. Chasteen, "Violence for Show: Knife Dueling on a Nineteenth-Century Cattle Frontier," in Lyman Johnson, ed., *The Problem of Order in Changing Societies: Essays on Crime and Policing in Argentina and Uruguay, 1750–1940* (Albuquerque: University of New Mexico Press, 1990), 47–64.

20. William MacCann, *Two Thousand Miles' Ride through the Argentine Provinces*, 2 vols. (1853; repr., New York: AMS Press, n.d.), vol. 2: 14.

21. Jane M. Loy [Rausch], "Horsemen of the Tropics: A Comparative View of the Llaneros in the History of Venezuela and Colombia," *Boletín Americanista* 31 (1981): 159–71; Jane M. Rausch, *A Tropical Plains Frontier: The Llanos of Colombia, 1531–1831* (Albuquerque: University of New Mexico Press, 1984); Jane M. Rausch, *The Llanos Frontier in Colombian History, 1830–1930* (Albuquerque: University of New Mexico Press, 1993).

22. Slatta, *Cowboys of the Americas*, 220–21.

23. Slatta, *Cowboys of the Americas*, 85–90.
24. Slatta, *Gauchos*, 91–105.
25. Slatta, *Cowboys of the Americas*, 174–77.

6. Frontier Institutions: Western Saloons and Argentine Pulperías

This chapter originally appeared in *Great Plains Quarterly* 7 (summer 1987): 155–65. Thanks to editor Frances W. Kaye for reprint permission, Michael Cummings for research assistance, and the Tinker Foundation of New York for research support.

1. Among recent general treatments of the western saloon are Richard Erdoes, *Saloons of the Old West* (New York: Alfred A. Knopf, 1969); Thomas J. Noel, *The City and the Saloon: Denver, 1858–1916* (Lincoln: University of Nebraska Press, 1982); Elliott West, *The Saloon of the Rocky Mountain Mining Frontier* (Lincoln: University of Nebraska Press, 1979); and Robert L. Brown, *Saloons of the American West* (Silverton, Colo.: Sundance Books, 1978). On the *pulpería*, see Jorge A. Bossio, *Historia de las pulperías* (Buenos Aires: Plus Ultra, 1972); and the less useful León Bouché, *Las pulperías: mojón civilizador* (Buenos Aires: San Telmo, 1970). Although differences exist between them, for stylistic variety, I will use synonymously the terms *barroom*, *tavern*, *saloon*, and *public house*.

2. Quoted from the issue of 3 October 1882, in Clifford P. Westermeier, ed., *Trailing the Cowboy: His Life and Lore as Told by Frontier Journalists* (Caldwell, Idaho: Caxton Printers, 1965), 50; Noel, *City and the Saloon*, 2. Erdoes notes that some journalists in the West had a whiskey allowance in addition to their wages, *Saloons*, 76.

3. Quote from Thomas J. Hutchinson, *Buenos Ayres and Argentine Gleanings* (London: Edward Stanford, 1865), 283. For other unflattering images of pulpería life, see Richard W. Slatta, "Pulperías and Contraband Capitalism in Nineteenth-Century Buenos Aires Province," *The Americas* 38 (January 1982): 352–56.

4. Hugh Talmage Lefler and Albert Roy Newsome, *North Carolina: The History of a Southern State* (1952; repr. Chapel Hill: University of North Carolina Press, 1973), 259–60.

5. Erdoes, *Saloons*, 9; Noel, *City and the Saloon*, 1; Richard Maxwell Brown, "Saloon," in Howard R. Lamar, ed., *The Reader's Encyclopedia of the American West* (New York: Thomas Y. Crowell, 1977), 1061; Walter W. Skeat, *A Concise Etymological Dictionary of the English Language* (1882; repr., New York: Peregee Books, 1980), 461.

6. Ricardo Güiraldes, *Don Segundo Sombra: Shadows on the Pampas*, trans. Harriet de Onis (New York: New American Library, 1966), 51.

7. Richard W. Slatta, *Gauchos and the Vanishing Frontier* (Lincoln: University of Nebraska Press, 1983), 70; Slatta, "Pulperías," 360–61; Ricardo E. Rodríguez Molas, "Variaciones sobre la pulpería ríoplatense," *Revista de la Universidad* 14 (May 1961), 139, 141. See also Ricardo E. Rodríguez Molas, "La pulpería ríoplatense en el siglo XVII: Ensayo de historia social y económica," *Universidad* 49 (1961): 99–134.

8. Richard A. Van Orman, *A Room for the Night: Hotels of the Old West* (Bloomington: University of Indiana Press, 1966), 8, 14–17. Actually Fort Wicked took its name from its proprietor, Holon Godfrey, called "Old Wicked" by the Cheyenne and Sioux because he was one of the few station keepers to withstand repeated Plains Indian attacks on the Overland Trail during the winter of 1865.

9. Erdoes, *Saloons*, 9; Noel, *City and the Saloon*, 14.

10. Richard W. Slatta, "Rural Criminality and Social Conflict in Nineteenth-Century Buenos Aires Province," *Hispanic American Historical Review* 60 (August 1980): 453–61; Bossio, *Historia de las pulperías*, 200–1; Miguel A. Lima, *El estanciero práctico: Manual completo de ganadería* (Buenos Aires: Río de la Plata, 1876), 233; Jonathan C. Brown, *A Socioeconomic History of Argentina, 1776–1860* (Cambridge: Cambridge University Press, 1979), 79, 142–43, 195; Slatta, *Gauchos*, 144.

11. Gastón Gori, *Vagos y mal entretenidos: Aporte al tema hernandiano*, 2d ed. (Santa Fe, Argentina: Colmegna, 1951), 65–68; report by juez de paz de Las Flores, 31 December 1851, doc. 4, X 21–24, Archivo General de la Nación (Buenos Aires); *La Tribuna* (Buenos Aires, 13 December 1853), 2; *La Tribuna*, 22 April 1854, 2;

Buenos Aires Province, Comisión de Hacendados del Estado de Buenos Aires, *Antecedentes y fundamentos del proyecto de código rural* (Buenos Aires, 1864), 69, 170; *La Union del Sud* (Chascomús, Argentina, 25 August 1872), 3.

12. Slatta, *Gauchos*, 87–88, 120–21; Joe B. Frantz and Julian Ernest Choate, Jr., *The American Cowboy: The Myth and the Reality* (Norman: University of Oklahoma Press, 1955), 101–5; Douglas E. Branch, *The Cowboy and His Interpreters* (1926; repr., New York: Cooper Square, 1961), 116–17; Ramon F. Adams, *Western Words: A Dictionary of the American West*, rev. ed. (Norman: University of Oklahoma Press, 1968), 19, 192, 288.

13. Noel, *City and the Saloon*, 90; quote from Darrell W. Bolen, "Gambling: Historical Highlights and Trends and Their Implications for Contemporary Society," in William R. Eadington, ed., *Gambling and Society: Interdisciplinary Studies on the Subject of Gambling* (Springfield, Ill.: Charles C. Thomas, 1976), 17.

14. David G. Mandelbaum, "Alcohol and Culture," in Mac Marshall, ed., *Beliefs, Behaviors, and Alcoholic Beverages: A Cross-Cultural Survey* (Ann Arbor: University of Michigan Press, 1979), 17.

15. See Lionel Tiger, *Men in Groups*, 2d ed. (New York: M. Moyars/Scribner, 1984); and the critique by Rae Lesser Blumberg, *Stratification: Socioeconomic and Sexual Inequality* (Dubuque, Iowa: William C. Brown, 1978), 6–10; Noel, *City and the Saloon*, 91; Sherri Cavan, *Liquor License: An Ethnography of Bar Behavior* (Chicago: Aldine, 1966), 67; William B. Taylor, *Drinking, Homicide, and Rebellion in Colonial Mexican Villages* (Stanford: Stanford University Press, 1979), 65; Robert J. Glynn et al., "Social Contexts and Motives for Drinking in Men," *Journal of Studies on Alcohol* 44 (November 1983): 1021–22.

16. Quote from Adams, *Western Words*, 96; see also 39, 190; Frantz and Choate, *American Cowboy*, 96–97; West, *Saloon*, 19–21.

17. Buenos Aires Province, Comisión de Hacendados, *Antecedentes*, 145, 151; letter from Mauricio Díaz, Bahía Blanca, 6 March 1850, juez de paz de Azul 9-4-4; reports of juez de crimen 1872, 38-4-313; Archivo Histórico de la Provincia de Buenos Aires "Ricardo Levene" (La Plata, Argentina); police reports of March,

June, July 1852, Policía 1852, Archivo Histórico Municipal de Tandil (Tandil, Argentina).

18. Taylor, *Drinking*, 65–66, 156; Michael C. Scardaville, "Alcohol Abuse and Tavern Reform in Late Colonial Mexico City," *Hispanic American Historical Review* 60 (November 1980): 644–45, 670–71; William Madsen and Claudia Madsen, "The Cultural Structure of Mexican Drinking Behavior," in Marshall, *Beliefs, Behaviors, and Alcoholic Beverages*, 49–51. For another Latin American case, see William C. Sayres, "Ritual Drinking, Ethnic Status, and Inebriety in Rural Colombia," *Quarterly Journal of Studies on Alcohol* 17 (March 1956): 53–62.

19. Brown, "Saloon," 1062.

20. Craig MacAndrew and Robert Edgerton, *Drunken Comportment: A Social Explanation* (Chicago: Aldine, 1969), 36, 60, 165; Mandelbaum, "Alcohol and Culture," 17–18; R. O. Pihl, Mark Smith, and Brian Farrell, "Alcohol and Aggression in Men: A Comparison of Brewed and Distilled Beverages," *Journal of Studies on Alcohol* 45 (May 1984): 278, 281.

21. MacAndrew and Edgerton, *Drunken Comportment*, 82, 90–94, 171–73; Taylor, *Drinking*, 66; Slatta, *Gauchos*, 118.

22. Allan M. Winkler, "Drinking on the American Frontier," *Quarterly Journal of Studies on Alcohol* 29 (June 1968): 416; Laurence Ivan Seidman, *Once in the Saddle* (New York: Alfred A. Knopf, 1973), 86; Charles W. Harris and Buck Rainey, eds., *The Cowboys: Six Shooters, Songs, and Sex* (Norman: University of Oklahoma Press, 1976), 87; Edward Charles ("Teddy Blue") Abbott and Helena Huntington Smith, *We Pointed Them North: Recollections of a Cowpuncher* (1939; repr., Norman: University of Oklahoma Press, 1955), 52; Noel, *City and the Saloon*, 30–31.

23. Taylor, *Drinking*, 41; Thomas J. Hutchinson, *The Paraná* (London: Edward Stanford, 1868), 89; quotation from Nathaniel Holmes Bishop, *The Pampas and the Andes: A Thousand Miles' Walk across South America*, 11th ed. (Boston: Lee and Shepard, 1883), 98–99.

24. William MacCann, *Two Thousand Miles' Ride through the Argentine Provinces* (London: Smith, Elder, 1853), vol. 2, 282, 285.

Quotation from Robert B. Cunninghame Graham, "La Pulpería," in John Walker, ed., *The South American Sketches of R. B. Cunninghame Graham* (Norman: University of Oklahoma, 1978), 63.

25. Erdoes, *Saloons*, 25–26; David Dary, *Cowboy Culture: A Saga of Five Centuries* (New York: Alfred A. Knopf, 1981), 211; quote from Adams, *Western Words*, 34, see also 178–79.

26. Noel, *City and the Saloon*, 23–29; Dary, *Cowboy Culture*, 211.

27. Balzac quoted in Bolen, "Gambling," 12; J. Philip Jones, *Gambling Yesterday and Today: A Complete History* (Newton Abbot, England: David and Charles, 1973), 13–14, 64, 84. For a critique of various theories of gambling, see Tomás M. Martínez, *The Gambling Scene: Why People Gamble* (Springfield, Ill.: Charles C. Thomas, 1983), 108–31.

28. Robert K. DeArment, *Knights of the Green Cloth: The Saga of the Frontier Gamblers* (Norman: University of Oklahoma Press, 1982), 227–29; MacCann, *Two Thousand Miles' Ride*, vol. 2, 47; Slatta, "Pulperías," 352; Jorge Paez, *Del truquiflor a la rayuela: Panorama de los juegos y entretenimientos argentinos* (Buenos Aires: Centro Editor de America Latina, 1971), 35–40.

29. Quoted in De Arment, *Knights*, 41; see also 75–85; Brown, "Saloon," 1062; Richard W. Slatta, "Saloon Life in the Old West," *Cowboys & Indians* 2, 3 (fall 1994): 32–42.

30. Dary, *Cowboy Culture*, 214; William H. Forbis, *The Cowboys*, rev. ed. (Alexandria, Va.: Time-Life Books, 1973), 82, 170; quote from John Roderick Craig, *Ranching with Lords and Commons* (1903; repr., New York: AMS, 1971), 89–90, 97; Adams, *Western Words*, 48, 55, 167, 231.

31. Bolen, "Gambling," 16; Hutchinson, *The Paraná*, 91; Madaline Wallis Nichols, *The Gaucho: Cattle Hunter, Cavalryman, Ideal of Romance* (1942; repr., New York: Gordian Press, 1968), 14; Edward Larocque Tinker, *The Horsemen of the Americas and the Literature They Inspired*, 2d ed. (Austin: University of Texas Press, 1967), 24; Paez, *Del truquiflor*, 40–46.

32. Erdoes, *Saloons*, 182; Doten quoted in George M. Blackburn and Sherman L. Richards, "The Prostitutes and Gamblers of Virginia City, Nevada: 1870," *Pacific Historical Review* 48 (May 1979): 241;

Ezequiel Martínez Estrada, *X-Ray of the Pampa*, trans. Alain Swietlicki, (Austin: University of Texas Press, 1971), 205. On the barriers to gaucho family life, see Slatta, *Gauchos*, 58–60.

33. *Rocky Mountain News*, 23 July 1889, quoted in Noel, *City and the Saloon*, 86; Adams, *Western Words*, 51; Erdoes, *Saloons*, 189; Abbott and Smith, *We Pointed Them North*, 108; Paul F. Sharp, *Whoop-Up Country: The Canadian-American West, 1865–1885* (Helena: Historical Society of Montana, 1960), 174; Dary, *Cowboy Culture*, 217. See also Marion S. Goldman, *Gold Diggers and Silver Miners: Prostitution and Social Life on the Comstock Lode* (Ann Arbor: University of Michigan Press, 1981).

34. Slatta, *Gauchos*, 66–67; Tinker, *Horsemen of the Americas*, 27; Bossio, *Historia de las pulperías*, 61.

35. Slatta, *Gauchos*, 114–15, 138–40. One of the most famous pulpería museums is "La Blanqueada," at the Ricardo Güiraldes Park in San Antonio de Areco, Buenos Aires Province. Güiraldes made the site famous in his novel *Don Segundo Sombra*.

36. Quoted in DeArment, *Knights*, 392–93; Herbert Asbury, *The Great Illusion: An Informal History of Prohibition* (Westport, Conn.: Greenwood Press, 1950), 86–87, 94–95; Richard W. Howland and Joe W. Howland, "200 Years of Drinking in the United States: Evolution of the Disease Concept," in John A. Ewing and Beatrice A. Rouse, eds., *Drinking: Alcohol in American Society—Issues and Current Research* (Chicago: Nelson-Hall, 1978), 49–50.

37. Perry Duis, *The Saloon: Public Drinking in Chicago and Boston, 1880–1920* (Urbana: University of Illinois Press, 1983), 293–97; Bossio, *Historia de las pulperías*, 248–50.

7. Turner's Influence in Canada and Latin America

I presented an earlier version of this chapter at the Social Science History Association meeting in Baltimore, November 5, 1993. Thanks to Tom Hall, John Markoff, and Bill Donovan for helpful comments.

1. See Frederick Jackson Turner, "The Significance of the Frontier in American History," reprinted in David J. Weber and Jane

M. Rausch, eds., *Where Cultures Meet: Frontiers in Latin American History* (Wilmington, Del.: Scholarly Resources, 1994), 1–18. This same collection reprints many of the articles discussed below. On changing definitions of the term, see Fulmer Moody, "Notes on the History of the Word Frontier," *Agricultural History* 22, 2 (April 1948); Lucien Febvre, "Frontière: The Word and the Concept," in Peter Burke, ed., *A New Kind of History from the Writings of Lucien Febvre* (London: Routledge and Kegan Paul, 1973); Ray Allen Billington, "Frontier," in C. Vann Woodward, ed., *The Comparative Approach to American History* (New York: Basic Books, 1968), 75–90; David W. Noble, *Historians Against History: The Frontier Thesis and the National Covenant in American Historical Writing Since 1830* (Minneapolis: University of Minnesota Press, 1965); Wilbur R. Jacobs, *On Turner's Trail: 100 Years of Writing Western History* (Lawrence: University Press of Kansas, 1994).

2. Michael S. Cross, ed., *The Turner Thesis and the Canadas: The Debate on the Impact of the Canadian Environment* (Toronto: Copp Clark, 1970) includes reprints of many of the key essays on the topic.

3. Gilman M. Ostrander, "Frederick Jackson Turner's Canadian Frontier Thesis," *Canadian Historical Review* 64, 4 (December 1983): 604–11.

4. Walter N. Sage, "Some Aspects of the Frontier in Canadian History," *Canadian Historical Association Report* 1928, 67–72; Marcus L. Hansen and John B. Brebner, *The Mingling of the Canadian and American Peoples*, vol. 1 (Toronto: Russell and Russell, 1940); J. L. McDougall, "The Frontier School and Canadian History," *Canadian Historical Association Report*, 1929, pp. 121–25.

5. F. H. Underhill, "The Development of National Political Parties in Canada," *Canadian Historical Review* 16, 4 (1935); E. H. Oliver, *The Winning of the Frontier* (Toronto: United Church Publishing House, 1930).

6. A. L. Burt, "The Frontier in the History of New France," *Canadian Historical Association Report* 1940, 93–99.

7. A. R. M. Lower, "Some Neglected Aspects of Canadian History," *Canadian Historical Association Report* 1929; see also A. R.

M. Lower, "The Origins of Democracy in Canada," *Canadian Historical Association Report* 1930, 65–70.

8. A. R. M. Lower quoted in Morris Zaslow, "The Frontier Hypothesis in Recent Historiography," *Canadian Historical Review* 29, 2 (June 1948): 159.

9. George F. G. Stanley, "Western Canada and the Frontier Thesis," *Canadian Historical Association Report* 1940, 104–14.

10. Zaslow, "The Frontier Hypothesis," 153–67.

11. J. M. S. Careless, "Frontierism, Metropolitanism, and Canadian History," *Canadian Historical Review* 35, 1 (March 1954): 1–21, quotation is on page 18.

12. David H. Breen, "The Turner Thesis and the Canadian West," in Lewis H. Thomas, ed., *Essays on Western History in Honour of Lewis Gwynne Thomas* (Edmonton: University of Alberta Press, 1976), 147.

13. Breen, "Turner Thesis," 147–56.

14. Robin W. Winks, "Frontiers, Canada," in Howard R. Lamar, ed., *The Reader's Encyclopedia of the American West* (New York: Crowell, 1977), 416–19.

15. Emilio Daireaux, *Vida y costumbres en La Plata*, 2 vols. (Buenos Aires: Lajouane, 1888), 2, 197–202.

16. Mary Lombardi, "The Frontier in Brazilian History: An Historiographical Essay," *Pacific Historical Review* 44, 4 (November 1975): 444–46.

17. Victor Andrés Belaúnde, "The Frontier in Hispanic America," *Rice Institute Pamphlet* 10, 4 (October 1923): 202–13. Reprinted in Weber and Rausch, *Where Cultures Meet*, 33–41.

18. Silvio Zavala, "The Frontiers of Hispanic America" in Walker D. Wyman and Clifton B. Kroeber, eds., *The Frontier in Perspective* (Madison: University of Wisconsin Press, 1957), 35–58.

19. Arthur S. Aiton, "Latin-American Frontiers," *Canadian Historical Association Report* 1940, 100–4. Reprinted in Weber and Rausch, *Where Cultures Meet*, 19–25.

20. Lombardi, "Frontier in Brazilian History," 447–48.

21. Hebe Clementi, "National Identity and the Frontier," *American Studies International* 18, 3–4 (1981): 36–44. Reprinted in Weber and Rausch, *Where Cultures Meet*, 141–50.

22. Clementi, "National Identity," 42.

23. Clodomir Vianna Moog, *Bandeirantes and Pioneers* (Portuguese, 1954; English trans. by L. L. Barrett, New York: G. Braziller, 1964). Extract reprinted in Weber and Rausch, *Where Cultures Meet*, 166.

24. For an excellent summary of the historiographical issues, see David J. Weber, "Turner, the Boltonians, and the Borderlands," *American Historical Review* 91, 1 (February 1986): 66–81. On Bolton, see Albert L. Hurtado, "Parkmanizing the Spanish Borderlands: Bolton, Turner, and the Historians' World," *Western Historical Quarterly* 26, 2 (summer 1995): 149–68.

25. Weber, "Turner," 69.

26. Weber, "Turner," 77.

27. Weber, "Turner," 80.

28. Domingo F. Sarmiento, *Life in the Argentine Republic in the Days of the Tyrants; or, Civilization and Barbarism*, trans. Mrs. Horace [Mary] Mann (1845; repr., New York: Hafner, 1971); Domingo F. Sarmiento, "Frontier Barbarism," reprinted in Weber and Rausch, *Where Cultures Meet*, 26–32; Euclides da Cunha, *Rebellion in the Backlands (Os Sertões)* trans. Samuel Putnam (1902; repr., Chicago: University of Chicago Press, 1944). For a summary and critique of Sarmiento's thought see Richard W. Slatta, *Gauchos and the Vanishing Frontier* (Lincoln: University of Nebraska Press, 1983), 180–84.

29. Silvio R. Duncan Baretta and John Markoff, "Civilization and Barbarism: Cattle Frontiers in Latin America," *Comparative Studies in Society and History* 20 (October 1978), 611.

30. For a summary see "The Great Frontier." Reprinted in Weber and Rausch, *Where Cultures Meet*, 51–63.

31. Thomas D. Hall, *Social Change in the Southwest, 1350–1880* (Lawrence: University Press of Kansas, 1989), 20.

32. Hall, *Social Change*, 24; Christopher Chase-Dunn and Thomas D. Hall, "Epilogue," in Christopher Chase-Dunn and Thomas D. Hall, eds., *Core/Periphery Relations in Precapitalist Worlds* (Boulder: Westview Press, 1991), 285.

33. Martin Ridge, "Frederick Jackson Turner, Ray Allen Billington, and American Frontier History," *Western Historical Quarterly* 19, 1

(January 1988): 20. See also Martin Ridge, "The Life of an Idea: The Significance of Frederick Jackson Turner's Frontier Thesis," *Montana, The Magazine of Western History* 41, 1 (winter 1991): 2–13; and Frederic L. Paxon, "A Generation of the Frontier Hypothesis: 1893–1932," *Pacific Historical Review* 2, 1 (March 1933): 34–51.

34. Richard Maxwell Brown, "Western Violence: Structure, Values, Myth," *Western Historical Quarterly* 25, 1 (February 1993): 6.

35. Brown, "Western Violence," 13. Brown draws upon Richard W. Slatta, ed., *Bandidos: The Varieties of Latin American Banditry* (Westport, Conn.: Greenwood Press, 1987) and Richard W. Slatta, *Cowboys of the Americas* (New Haven: Yale University Press, 1990).

8. Gaúcho and Gaucho: Comparative Socioeconomic Change in Rio Grande do Sul and Buenos Aires Province, 1869–1920

This chapter originally appeared in *Estudos Ibero-Americanos* 6, 2 (December 1980): 191–202. The journal is published in Pôrto Alegre, Rio Grande do Sul, Brazil. This version contains corrections and some editorial changes.

1. In *Brazil South: Its Conquest and Settlement* (New York: Knopf, 1968), Moysés Vellinho argues unconvincingly against the similarities between the gaúcho and gaucho. For a critique of the concept of modernity, see Alejandro Portes, "Modernity and Development: A Critique," *Studies in Comparative International Development* 9, 2 (spring 1974): 247–79. On the relationship between modernization and demographic change, see Calvin Goldscheider, *Population, Modernization, and Social Structure* (Boston: Little, Brown, 1971), 70–101, esp. 93–98. On Rio Grande's political marginality, see Joseph L. Love, *Rio Grande do Sul and Brazilian Regionalism, 1882–1930* (Stanford: Stanford University Press, 1971); Spencer Leitman, "Socio-Economic Roots of the Ragamuffin War: A Chapter in Early Brazilian History," (Ph.D. diss., University of Texas, 1972); and John C. Chasteen, *Heroes on Horseback: A Life and Times of the Last Gaucho Caudillos* (Albuquerque: University of New Mexico Press, 1995). In *Politics and Beef in Argentina: Patterns of Conflict and Change* (New York: Columbia University Press,

1969), Peter H. Smith details the political dominance of the cattle industry.

2. Fernando O. Assunção, *El gaucho* (Montevideo: Imprenta Nacional, 1963), 365–66; Madaline Wallis Nichols, *The Gaucho: Cattle Hunter, Cavalryman, Ideal of Romance* (1942; repr., New York: Gordian Press, 1968), 23; A. Tenorio D'Albuquerque, "Gaúcho: O Discutidissimo Etimo de Vocábulo," *Revista Brasileira* 9, 21 (January 1958): 215–43.

3. Fernando L. Osorio, *Sociogêneses do pampa brasileiro* (Pelotas, Rio Grande do Sul: Livraria Comercial, 1927), 39; José A. Goulart, *Brasil: do bio e do couro* (Rio de Janeiro: Edições GRD, 1965), 1, 152; Aristides de Moraes Gomes, *Fundação e evolução das estâncias serranas* (Cruz Alta, Rio Grande do Sul: Livraria Liderança, 1966), 148; F. J. Oliveira Vianna, *Populações meridionais do Brasil: O campeador rio-grandense* (Rio de Janeiro: José Olympio, 1952), 2, 289–91, 298, 338–39.

4. Assunção, *El gaucho*, 182, 188, 196, 202; Eduardo B. Gomez, "El gaucho y su pampa," *Boletim do Centro Rio-grandense de Estudos Historicos* 1, 1 (1939): 5; on Argentine nationalism, see Richard W. Slatta, "The Gaucho in Argentina's Quest for National Identity," *Canadian Review of Studies in Nationalism* 12, 1 (1985): 99–122.

5. Love, *Rio Grande*, 16, 264–65.

6. Love, *Rio Grande*, 6; Brasil, Directoria Geral de Estatística, *Recenseamento do Brasil realizado em 1 de setembro de 1920* (Rio de Janeiro: Typ. da Estatística, 1923), vol. 3, pt. 1, xxii, lxxv, lxxvi, lxxviii.

7. On ranching in Buenos Aires Province, see Richard W. Slatta, *Gauchos and the Vanishing Frontier* (Lincoln: University of Nebraska Press, 1983); Horacio C. E. Giberti, *Historia económica de la ganadería argentina* (Buenos Aires: Solar-Hachette, 1970).

8. Love, *Rio Grande*, 16; Richard Graham, *Britain and the Onset of Modernization in Brazil, 1850–1914* (Cambridge: Cambridge University Press, 1968); Roberto Cortés Conde and Ezequiel Gallo, *La formación de la Argentina moderna* (Buenos Aires: Paídos, 1967).

9. Cortés Conde and Gallo, *La formación*, 55–56, 101–3; Slatta, *Gauchos*, 91–125.

10. Leitman, "Socio-Economic Roots," 98, 117, 181, 185.

11. Argentine Republic, Comisión Nacional del Censo, *Tercer censo nacional*, 10 vols. (Buenos Aires: L. J. Rosso, 1917), 8, 34–35.

12. Felipe Arana, *Historia económica y social argentina* (Buenos Aires: El Coloquio, 1969), 216, 219–20; James R. Scobie, *Revolution on the Pampas: A Social History of Argentine Wheat, 1860–1910* (Austin: University of Texas Press, 1967).

13. Florencio C. de Abreu e Silva, "Retrospecto economico y financeiro de Rio Grande do Sul, 1822–1922," *Revista do Archivo Público de Rio Grande do Sul* 8 (December 1922): 240–45, 248–49; Wolfgang Hoffmann-Harnisch, *O Rio Grande do Sul: a terra e o homen*, 2d ed. (Pôrto Alegre, Brazil: Globo, 1952), 160–61, 167; Agustín Ruano Fournier, *Estudio económico de la producción de las carnes del Río de la Plata* (Montevideo: Peña, 1936), 364.

14. Love, *Rio Grande*, 55; Nilo Ruschel, *O gaúcho a pé* (Pôrto Alegre, Brazil: Sulina, 1959), 47; Slatta, *Gauchos*, 141–60.

15. Jacinto Oddone, *La burguesía terrateniente argentina*, 2d ed. (Buenos Aires: n.p., 1936), 65, 68–69; Argentine Republic, *Tercer censo nacional*, 6, 523–35, 679–97; Slatta, *Gauchos*, 92, 104.

16. Brasil, Directora Geral de Estatística, *Synopse do recenseamento realizado em 1 de setembro de 1920: População pecuaria* (Rio de Janeiro: Typ. da Estatística, 1922), 19, 30–31.

17. Vicente Vásquez-Presedo, *Estadísticas históricas argentinas comparadas: Primera parte, 1875–1914* (Buenos Aires: Macchi, 1971), 26; Centro de Estudios Urbanos y Regionales, *Diagnóstico preliminar del area sud este de la Provincia de Buenos Aires* (Buenos Aires: Instituto Torcuato Di Tella, 1967), 17.

18. Brazil, Instituto Brasileiro de Geografia e Estatística, *Recenseamento geral do Brasil: Censo demografico* (Rio de Janeiro: Instituto Brasileiro de Geografia e Estatística, 1950), vol. 1, pt. 20, 1. See Michael G. Mulhall, *Rio Grande do Sul and its German Colonies* (London: Longmans, Green, 1873), for a nineteenth-century description of the agricultural settlements.

19. Aldo Ferrer, *The Argentine Economy*, trans. Marjory M. Urquidi (Berkeley: University of California Press, 1967), 116–17; Hoffmann-Harnisch, *O Rio Grande do Sul*, 150; Roberto Cortés Conde,

"Tendencias en la evolución de los salarios reales en Argentina, 1880–1910: Resultados preliminares," (Buenos Aires: Instituto Torcuato Di Tella, 1975, working paper).

20. Argentine Republic, *Tercer censo nacional*, 3, 43, 45; Brasil, *Recenseamento de 1920*, vol. 4, pt. 2, 21.

21. Warren S. Thompson, "Population," *American Journal of Sociology* 29 (1929): 959–75; Donald O. Cowgill, "Transition Theory as General Population Theory," *Social Forces* 41 (1963): 270–74.

22. Giogio Mortara, "A Riddle Solved: Brazil's Population," *Estadística: Journal of the Inter-American Statistical Institute* 1 (March 1943): 143; Tânia Pütten Velloso, *Demografia e desenvolvimento do Rio Grande do Sul* (Pôrto Alegre, Brazil: PUCRGS, 1971), table A; U.S. Bureau of the Census, *Argentina: Summary of Biostatistics* (Washington, D.C.: Government Printing Office, 1945), 80–83, 102–5.

23. Brasil, Directoria Geral de Estatística, *Synopse do recenseamento realizado em 1 de setembro de 1920* (Rio de Janeiro: Typ. da Estatística, 1924), 84–85.

24. O. Andrew Collver, *Birth Rates in Latin America: New Estimates of Historical Trends and Fluctuations* (Berkeley: Institute of Population and Urban Research, 1965), 58; Jorge Somoza and Alfredo Lattes, *Muestras de los dos primeros censos nacionales de población, 1869 y 1895* (Buenos Aires: Instituto Torcuato Di Tella, 1967), 17–18; Brasil, *Recenseamento de 1920*, vol. 4, pt. 2, 21; Argentine Republic, *Tercer censo nacional*, 3, 28–29, 42–43.

25. Pütten Velloso, *Demografia*, table A; Collver, *Birth Rates*, 31.

26. Pütten Velloso, *Demografia*, table A; U.S. Bureau of the Census, *Argentina*, 80–83, 102–5.

27. João Damesceno Vieira Fernandes, *A travez do Rio da Prata* (Pôrto Alegre, Brazil: Jornal do Comercio, 1890), 149–52; Argentine description quoted by José Arena et al., *Ensayo histórico del partido de Olavarría* (Olavarría, Argentina: Municipalidad de Olavarría, 1967), 320.

28. Ernesto A. Lassance Cunha, *O Rio Grande do Sul: Contribução para o estudo de suas condições economicas* (Rio de Janeiro: Imprensa Nacional, 1908), 100–39; Love, *Rio Grande*, 6; Centro de Estudios

Urbanos y Regionales, *Diagnóstico*, 16; Argentine Republic, *Tercer censo nacional*, 4, 469-75; Zulma Recchini de Lattes and Alfredo Lattes, *La población de Argentina* (Buenos Aires: CICRED, 1975), 205.

29. David M. Heer, *Society and Population*, 2d ed. (Englewood Cliffs: Prentice-Hall, 1975), 56-58, 116-17.

30. Goldscheider, *Population*, 244-49.

31. Edward A. Wrigley, *Population and History* (New York: McGraw-Hill, 1969), 183; Heer, *Society*, 97-98. On the Tandil massacre, see Hugo Nario, *Tata Dios: El mesías de la última montonera* (Buenos Aires: Plus Ultra, 1967).

32. Cowgill, "Transition Theory," 270-74; Goldscheider, *Population*, 93-98; Heer, *Society*, 94-95.

33. Antonio J. Pérez Amuchástegui, *Mentalidades argentinas, 1860-1930* (Buenos Aires: EUDEBA, 1965), 378-79. Quote from Walter Larden, *Estancia Life: Agricultural, Economic, and Cultural Aspects of Argentina* (1911; repr., Detroit: B. Ethridge, 1974), 62-63. For a description of ranch labor in Rio Grande do Sul, see Dante de Laytano, *A estância gaúcha* (Rio de Janeiro: Ministerio de Agricultura, 1952), 39-46.

34. María Teresa Villafañe Casal, *La mujer en la pampa, siglos XVIII y XIX* (La Plata: Domínguez e Hijo, 1958), 59-62, 69; Ann M. Pescatello, *Power and Pawn: The Female in Iberian Families, Societies, and Cultures* (Westport, Conn.: Greenwood Press, 1976), 163-65; Slatta, *Gauchos*, 57-68.

35. Wrigley, *Population*, 28.

9. Social History in the Saddle: Trailing Cowboys of the Americas

This chapter draws upon the eleventh annual Charles Wood Lecture which I delivered at Texas Tech University in Lubbock on February 17, 1995. My thanks to Dr. Idris Traylor and the Wood Lecture Committee for their hospitality during my stay.

1. For descriptions of these and other Western Hemisphere cowboys, see Richard W. Slatta, *Cowboys of the Americas* (New Haven: Yale University Press, 1990), and Richard W. Slatta, *The Cowboy Encyclopedia* (Santa Barbara: ABC-CLIO Press, 1994).

2. Quoted in Darrell Arnold, "Cowboy Pride," *Cowboy Magazine* 5, 1 (summer 1994): 4.

3. Glenn R. Vernam, *Man on Horseback: The Story of the Mounted Man from the Scythians to the American Cowboy* (Lincoln: University of Nebraska Press, 1964), 154–55; Terry G. Jordan, *North American Cattle-Ranching Frontiers: Origins, Diffusion, and Differentiation* (Albuquerque: University of New Mexico Press, 1993), 23.

4. Vernam, *Man on Horseback*, 199–92. See chapter 2.

5. On memoirs by real, working cowboys, see Richard W. Slatta, "In Their Own Words: Cowboy Memoirs," *Cowboys & Indians* 2, 1 (spring 1994): 45–50; Jeanne Ronda and Richard W. Slatta, "Cowboying at the Chapman-Barnard Ranch," *Persimmon Hill* 21, 3 (spring 1993): 36–41.

6. Richard W. Slatta, *Gauchos and the Vanishing Frontier* (Lincoln: University of Nebraska Press, 1983), 127.

7. Jack Weston, *The Real American Cowboy* (New York: Schocken Books, 1985), documents some attempts by cowboys to strike for better wages.

8. From "After the Roundup," an 1893 poem by D. J. O'Malley, arranged by Michael Martin Murphey, *Cowboy Songs* (Secaucus, N.J.: Warner Brothers, 1991), 70.

9. Charles Darbyshire, *My Life in the Argentine Republic* (London: Frederick Warne, 1918), 78.

10. Edmond Temple, *Travels in Various Parts of Peru: Including a Year's Residence in Potosí*, 2 vols. (1833; repr., New York: AMS Press, 1971), 1, 60.

11. Guy Logsdon, *"The Whorehouse Bells were Ringing" and Other Songs Cowboys Sing* (Urbana: University of Illinois Press, 1989), 300.

12. Edward Charles ("Teddy Blue") Abbott and Helena Huntington Smith, *We Pointed Them North: Recollections of a Cowpuncher* (1939; repr., Norman: University of Oklahoma Press, 1955).

13. For cautions on interpreting such documents, see Mary Louise Pratt, *Imperial Eyes: Travel Writing and Transculturation* (London and New York: Routledge, 1992).

14. Alexander von Humboldt and Aimé Bonpland, *"Personal Narrative" of Travels to the Equinoctial Regions of the New Continent,*

During the Years 1799–1804, 2d ed., trans. Helen María Williams (London: Longman, Hurst, Rees, Orme, Brown, and Green, 1825), 319–20; Alexander von Humboldt, *Political Essay on the Kingdom of New Spain*, 2 vols., trans. John Black (New York: I. Riley, 1811).

15. Charles Darwin, *The Correspondence of Charles Darwin, vol. 1, 1821–1836* (Cambridge: Cambridge University Press, 1985), 276.

16. Darwin, *Correspondence*, 277.

17. Darwin, *Correspondence*, 370.

18. Charles Darwin, *Journal of Researches into the Geology and Natural History of the various countries visited by H. M. S. Beagle* (1839; facsimile repr., New York: Hafner, 1952), 49–50.

19. Slatta, *Gauchos*, 73–75.

20. Erwin E. Smith, *Life on the Texas Range* (Austin: University of Texas Press, 1952); W. S. Perryman, *Indian Territory: A Frontier Photographic Record* (Norman: University of Oklahoma Press, 1957). See also David Phillips and Robert Weinstein, *The Taming of the West: A Photographic Perspective* (Chicago: Henry Regnery, 1974).

21. Michael Rutherford, *The American Cowboy: Tribute to a Vanishing Breed* (New York: Gallery Books 1990); Dudley Witney, *The Spirit of the West* (Secaucus, N.J.: Chartwell Books, 1987); Elizabeth Clair Flood, "Barbara Van Cleve: A Ranch Woman's Vision of the West," *Cowboys & Indians* 2, 4 (winter 1994): 56–62; Richard Pearce-Moses, comp., *Photographic Collections in Texas: A Union Guide* (College Station: Texas Historical Foundation/Texas A&M University Press, 1987).

22. George Reid Andrews, *The Afro-Argentines of Buenos Aires, 1800–1900* (Madison: University of Wisconsin Press, 1980), 47–48, 56–57.

23. See police documents for Buenos Aires Province, Archivo General de la Nación, Buenos Aires, Argentina, X 26-8-3, Policía 1849; X 21-2-4, X 21-1-1, Policía 1851, cited in Slatta, *Gauchos*, 217–18.

24. William F. Cochrane, "Letterbook," Glenbow Archives, Calgary, Alberta, Canada, M 234.

25. Letter, Cross Correspondence, Glenbow Archives, Calgary, Alberta, M 289 f6. See also Henry C. Klassen, "Entrepreneurship in

the Canadian West: The Enterprises of A. E. Cross, 1886–1920,"
Western Historical Quarterly 22, 3 (August 1991): 313–34.

26. Patricia Nelson Limerick, *The Legacy of Conquest: The
Unbroken Past of the American West* (New York: Norton, 1987),
50, 52.

27. J. Frank Dobie, *Guide to Life and Literature of the Southwest* rev.
ed. (Dallas: Southern Methodist University Press, 1952), 99.

28. Jordan, *North American Cattle-Ranching Frontiers*, 127,
140–41, 161–63.

29. Definition from *Webster's Third International Dictionary*
quoted in Thomas J. Schlerth, "Teaching History with Material
Culture Evidence," *The International Journal of Social Education* 1, 1
(Spring 1986): 6. See also Tyler Beard, *100 Years of Western Wear*
(Salt Lake City: Peregrine Smith Books, 1993); Tyler Beard, *The
Cowboy Boot Book* (Salt Lake City: Peregrine Smith Books, 1992);
Vernam, *Man on Horseback*; David Dary, *Cowboy Culture: A Saga of
Five Centuries* (New York: Knopf, 1981); William Foster-Harris, *The
Look of the Old West* (New York: Bonanza Books, 1955).

30. Ramon F. Adams, *Western Words: A Dictionary of the American
West* rev. ed. (Norman: University of Oklahoma Press, 1968) and
Winfred Blevins, *Dictionary of the American West* (New York: Facts
on File, 1993) well document the West's tremendous linguistic debt
to Spanish.

31. Helen Simons and Cathryn A. Hoyt, eds., *Hispanic Texas: A
Historical Guide* (Austin: University of Texas Press, 1992), 25–75,
442.

32. José Hernández, *The Gaucho Martín Fierro*, trans. Walter
Owen (1872, 1879; repr., Buenos Aires: Editorial Pampa, 1960), 12.

33. Hernández, *Martín Fierro*, 13.

34. Slatta, *Cowboys of the Americas*, 43.

35. For a sampling of traditional and modern poetry, see Hal
Cannon, ed., *Cowboy Poetry: A Gathering* (Salt Lake City: Peregrine
Smith Books, 1985); Hal Cannon, ed., *New Cowboy Poetry: A
Contemporary Gathering* (Salt Lake City: Peregrine Smith Books,
1990); Phil Martin, comp., *Coolin' Down: An Anthology of Con-
temporary Cowboy Poetry* (Tulsa: Guy Logsdon Books, 1992); John C.

Dofflemyer, ed., *Maverick Western Verse* (Salt Lake City: Peregrine Smith Books, 1994); Teresa Jordan, ed., *Graining the Mare: The Poetry of Ranch Women* (Salt Lake City: Peregrine Smith Books, 1994).

36. Richard W. Slatta, "Modern Cowboy Minstrel: Michael Martin Murphey," *Western Styles* 2, 4 (August 1994), 28-34; Don Edwards, *Classic Cowboy Songs* (Salt Lake City: Peregrine Smith Books, 1994); Guy Logsdon, Mary Rogers, and William Jacobson, *Cowboy Serenaders* (Salt Lake City: Peregrine Smith Books, 1994).

37. Jim Lewis, "Red Steagall Corners Cowboy Market," United Press International *Arts & Entertainment*, May 5, 1994 (downloaded from CompuServe); Rosemary Kent, *Genuine Texas Handbook* (New York: Workman, 1981), 164-65; Country Joe Flint and Judy Nelson, *The Insider's Country Music Handbook* (Salt Lake City: Peregrine Smith Books, 1993); Cecilia Tichi, ed., *Readin' Country Music: Steel Guitars, Opry Stars, and Honky Tonk Bars* (Durham: Duke University Press, 1995).

38. For examples of oral history interviews to illuminate cowboy life, see Ronda and Slatta, "Cowboying at the Chapman-Barnard Ranch"; Thomas Lee Charlton, *Oral History for Texans*, 2d ed. (Austin: Texas Historical Commission, 1985); Julie Jones-Eddy, *Homesteading Women: An Oral History of Colorado, 1890-1950* (New York: Twayne/Maxwell Macmillan, 1992); Richard W. Slatta, "Foreword," in Margot Liberty and Barry Head, *Working Cowboy: Recollections of Ray Holmes* (Norman: University of Oklahoma Press, 1995).

39. On methods and problems in oral history, see Elizabeth Tonkin, *Narrating our Pasts: The Social Construction of Oral History* (Cambridge: Cambridge University Press, 1992); Willa K. Baum, *Transcribing and Editing Oral History*, 2d ed. (Nashville: American Association for State and Local History, 1981); Paul Thompson, *The Voice of the Past: Oral History*, 2d ed. (Oxford: Oxford University Press, 1988); Michael Frisch, *A Shared Authority: Essays on the Craft and Meaning of Oral and Public History* (Albany: State University of New York Press, 1990).

40. See John F. Garganigo, *Javier de Viana* (New York: Twayne, 1972).

41. The quoted phrase comes from Limerick, *The Legacy of Conquest*, 18–19. See also David M. Emmons, "Constructed Province: History and the Making of the Last American West," *Western Historical Quarterly* 25, 4 (winter 1994): 451–52; Edward L. Ayres, "The South, the West, and the Rest," *Western Historical Quarterly* 25, 4 (winter 1994): 473–76.

42. Sincere thanks to John David Smith, Graduate Alumni Distinguished Professor of History at North Carolina State University, for guidance on the topic of southern mythology. For a full analysis, see Patrick Gerster and Nicholas Cords, eds., *Myth and Southern History*, 2 vols., 2d ed. (Urbana: University of Illinois Press, 1989); F. Garvin Davenport, Jr., *The Myth of Southern History: Historical Consciousness in Twentieth-Century Southern Literature* (Nashville: Vanderbilt University Press, 1970); Emmons, "Constructed Province," 338–41, 352; Charles Reagan Wilson, "In Search of the True West: Looking for Answers in the South," *Western Historical Quarterly* 25, 4 (winter 1994): 470–73; Ayers, "The South, the West, and the Rest," 473–76.

43. Michael P. Malone, "Beyond the Last Frontier: Toward a New Approach to Western American History," in Patricia Nelson Limerick, Clyde Milner II, and Charles E. Rankin, eds., *Trails: Toward a New Western History* (Lawrence: University Press of Kansas, 1991), 148–50; Warren A. Beck and Ynez D. Haase, *Historical Atlas of the American West* (Norman: University of Oklahoma Press, 1989), 24–25, 34, 37–38, 46, 56–60.

44. Ron Tyler, *Prints of the West: Prints from the Library of Congress* (Golden, Colo.: Fulcrum Publishing, 1994), 5; Richard White, *"It's Your Misfortune and None of My Own": A New History of the American West* (Norman: University of Oklahoma Press, 1991), 119–35.

45. For a sample of revisionist historiography, see William Cronon, George Miles, and Jay Gitlin, eds., *Under an Open Sky: Rethinking America's Western Past* (New York: Norton, 1992).

46. A. B. McCullough, "Eastern Capital and Managerial Contributions to Canadian Ranching" (paper presented at the Canadian Historical Association, Calgary, Alberta, June 1994), 7, 9, 18.

47. On Native American equestrian and ranch culture, see Peter J. Iverson, *When Indians Became Cowboys: Native Peoples and Cattle Ranching in the American West* (Norman: University of Oklahoma Press, 1994); Peter J. Iverson, "Cowboys, Indians, and the Modern West," *Arizona and the West* 28, 2 (1986): 107–24; Peter J. Iverson, ed., *The Plains Indians of the Twentieth Century* (Norman: University of Oklahoma Press, 1985); Harry T. Getty, "San Carlos Apache Cattle Industry," *Human Organization* 20 (1962): 181–86; Harry T. Getty, *The San Carlos Indian Cattle Industry* (Anthropological Papers, no. 7, Tucson: University of Arizona, 1963); Donald J. Berthrong, "Cattlemen on the Cheyenne-Arapaho Reservation, 1883–1885," *Arizona and the West* 13 (1971): 5–32; Robert M. Utley, "The Range Cattle Industry in the Big Bend of Texas," *Southwestern Historical Quarterly* 69 (1965): 419–41; Eva Antonia Wilbur-Cruce, "Indian Country," *Journal of Arizona History* 26, 4 (1985): 351–74; Thomas R. Wessel, "Agent of Acculturation: Farming on the Northern Plains Reservations, 1880–1910," *Agricultural History* 60, 2 (1986): 233–45; Gwyneth Harrington Xavier, "The Cattle Industry of the Southern Papago Districts with Some Information on the Reservation Cattle Industry as a Whole," in Robert A. Hackenberg et al., eds., *Papago Indians* (New York: Garland Publishing, 1974), 349–402; Albert L. Hurtado and Peter J. Iverson, eds., *Major Problems in American Indian History* (Lexington, Mass.: D. C. Heath, 1994).

48. Bailey C. Hanes, *Bill Pickett, Bulldogger: The Biography of a Black Cowboy* (Norman: University of Oklahoma Press, 1977); J. W. G. MacEwan, *John Ware's Cattle Country* (Saskatoon: Western Producer Prairie Books, 1974); Franklin Folsom, *Black Cowboy: The Life and Legend of George McJunkin* (Niwot, Colo.: Roberts Rinehart, 1992).

49. Harriet Rochlin and Fred Rochlin, *Pioneer Jews: A New Life in the Far West* (Boston: Houghton Mifflin, 1984), 73–77. See also press and letter excerpts on Jewish experiences in the West in Kenneth Libo and Irving Howe, *We Lived There Too* (New York: St. Martin's/Marek, 1984), 153–206; Ed Cray, *Levi's* (Boston: Houghton Mifflin, 1978).

50. On the regional and national differences see entries under various cowboy types in Richard W. Slatta, *The Cowboy Encyclopedia* (Santa Barbara: ABC-CLIO Press, 1994).

51. Slatta, *Cowboys of the Americas*, 220–21.

52. Donald E. Worster, *Cowboy Ecology: A New Look at the Old West* (Lubbock: Texas Tech University, International Center for Arid and Semiarid Land Studies, 1991), 6.

53. Slatta, *Cowboys of the Americas*, 16–18.

54. Quoted in Florence B. Hughes, "Listening-in at the Old Timers' Hut," *Canadian Cattlemen* 4, 1 (June 1941): 32.

55. John Tosh, *The Pursuit of History: Aims, Methods, and New Directions in the Study of Modern History*, 2d ed. (London and New York: Longman, 1991), 230–31.

56. Slatta, *Cowboys of the Americas*, 231. For a good sampling of western fiction, see Martin H. Greenberg, ed., *Great Stories of the American West* (New York: Donald I. Fine, 1994).

10. Dangers of Frontier Overrevisionism: Cautionary Notes from Alberta to Abilene to Argentina

This chapter derives from several sources. The South American material comes from my paper titled "Argentina's Livestock Frontier: Myth and Overrevisionism," delivered to the Canadian Historical Association, in Calgary, Alberta, Canada, June 1994. The material on the American West comes from "Social History in the Saddle: Trailing the Cowboys of the Americas," the eleventh annual Charles Wood Lecture delivered at Texas Tech University in Lubbock on February 17, 1995. The information on Canada comes primarily from my commentary on a panel titled "Some Canadian Perspectives on the Ranching Frontier," at the Canadian Historical Association meeting, Calgary, Alberta, Canada, June 1994.

1. This introduction draws upon my review of several western books in the *News and Observer* (Raleigh, N.C., 8 January 1995).

2. See Elizabeth Maret, *Women of the Range: Women's Roles in the Texas Beef Cattle Industry* (College Station: Texas A&M University Press, 1993).

3. Terry G. Jordan, "Cowboys," in Randall M. Miller and John David Smith, eds., *Dictionary of Afro-American Slavery* (Westport, Conn.: Greenwood Press, 1988), 152; Terry G. Jordan, *North American Cattle-Ranching Frontiers*, 153, 256. His earlier *Trails to Texas: Southern Roots of Western Cattle Ranching* (Lincoln: University of Nebraska Press, 1981), 14–15, contains similar linguistic errors and seriously underestimates Hispanic influences.

4. William of Ockham (or Occam, circa 1280–1349) probably did not originate the idea that bears his name. He repeated it enough, however, to have his name attached to it. David L. Sills and Robert K. Merton, eds., *The Macmillan Book of Social Science Quotations: Who Said What, When, and Where* (New York: Macmillan, 1991), 175.

5. Jordan, *North American Cattle-Ranching Frontiers*, 55, 63, 311.

6. Terry G. Jordan, *The Overemphasis of Texas as a Source of Western Cattle Ranching* (Lubbock: Texas Tech University, International Center for Arid and Semiarid Land Studies, 1992); Jordan, *North American Cattle-Ranching Frontiers*, 153, 256.

7. Andrew Gulliford, "Visitors Respond: Selections from 'The West as America' Comment Books," *Montana, The Magazine of Western History* 42, 3 (summer 1992): 79.

8. Vincent Leitch, "Deconstruction," *The Software Toolworks Multimedia Encyclopedia*, CD-ROM edition (Novato, Calif.: Grolier, 1992). See also John Ellis, *Against Deconstruction* (Princeton: Princeton University Press, 1989) and Pauline Marie Rosenau, *Post-Modernism and the Social Sciences: The Insights, Inroads, and Intrusions* (Princeton: Princeton University Press, 1992).

9. Ben Yagoda, "After years of theory, educators return to the fact of the matter," (Raleigh, N.C.) *News and Observer* 11 September 1994, 17A, 20A.

10. Yagoda, "After years of theory," 20A.

11. Blake Allmendinger, *The Cowboy: Representations of Labor in an American Work Culture* (New York: Oxford University Press, 1992). These comments build on my review of Allmendinger, *Journal of Arizona History* 35, 4 (winter 1994): 449–50. See also Alvin G. Davis's rhymed review of Allmendinger, *Montana, The Magazine of Western History* 44, 3 (summer 1994): 74–75.

12. David A. Zonderman, "Labor History and the Language of Work," *American Literary History* 7 (1996): 341–49.

13. Zonderman, "Labor History"; Leitch, "Deconstructionism."

14. See Gilbert Joseph, "On the Trail of Latin American Bandits: A Reexamination of Peasant Resistance," *Latin American Research Review* 25, 3 (1990): 7–54; Richard W. Slatta, "Banditry and Rural Social History: A Comment on Joseph," *Latin American Research Review* 26, 1 (1991): 145–51; Richard W. Slatta, "Banditry as Political Participation in Latin America," *Criminal Justice History: An International Review* 11 (1990): 171–87.

15. Erick Langer, "Andean Banditry and Peasant Community Organization," in Richard W. Slatta, ed., *Bandidos: The Varieties of Latin American Banditry* (Westport, Conn.: Greenwood Press, 1987), 124.

16. Jeff Dykes, "Afterword," in Robert F. Kadlec, ed., *They "Knew" Billy the Kid: Interviews with Old-Time New Mexicans* (Santa Fe: Ancient City Press, 1987), 109–11; Stephen Tatum, *Inventing Billy the Kid: Visions of the Outlaw in America, 1881–1981* (Albuquerque: University of New Mexico Press, 1982), 5–8, 168; Robert M. Utley, *Billy the Kid: A Short and Violent Life* (Lincoln: University of Nebraska Press, 1989). Larry McMurtry added yet another telling of the tale in *Anything for Billy* (New York: Simon and Schuster, 1988).

17. Richard White, "'Far West. See also frontier': The 'New Western History,' Textbooks, and the U.S. History Survey Course," *Perspectives* 30, 6 (September 1992): 10; Patricia Nelson Limerick, *The Legacy of Conquest: The Unbroken Past of the American West* (New York: Norton, 1987), 25.

18. Patricia Nelson Limerick, "The Adventure of the Frontier in the Twentieth Century," in James R. Grossman, ed., *The Frontier in American Culture* (Chicago: The Newberry Library; Berkeley: University of California Press, 1994), 94.

19. Domingo F. Sarmiento, *Life in the Argentine Republic in the Days of the Tyrants; or, Civilization and Barbarism*, trans. Mrs. Horace [Mary] Mann (1845; repr., New York: Hafner, 1971); Ricardo Levene, *A History of Argentina* (Chapel Hill: University of North Carolina Press, 1937). On the historiographical debates, see Rómulo D.

Carbia, *Historia crítica de la historiografía argentina* (Buenos Aires: Coni, 1940); Jaime Perriaux, *Las generaciones argentinas* (Buenos Aires: EUDEBA, 1970); Ataúlfo Pérez Aznar, *Temas de historia y política argentina* (Buenos Aires: Librería Editorial Platero, 1975); Horacio Juan Cuccorese, *Historia crítica de la historiografía socio-económica argentina del siglo XX* (La Plata: Universidad Nacional de la Plata, 1975); Héctor José Tanzi, *Historiografía argentina contemporanea* (Caracas: Instituto Panamericano de Geografía e Historia, 1976); Miguel Angel Scenna, *Los que escribieron nuestra historia* (Buenos Aires: Ediciones La Bastilla, 1976); Jorge A. Bossio, *Argentina: La historiografía en crisis* (Buenos Aires: Ediciones CICHAL, 1977); Eduardo Segovia Guerrero, *La historiografía argentina del romanticismo* (Madrid: Universidad Complutense de Madrid, 1980). Aware that many of you do not read Spanish, I am focusing my remarks on readily available English-language studies.

20. Roberto Etchepareborda, *Rosas: Controvertida historiografía* (Buenos Aires: Editorial Pleamar, 1972); Arturo Jauretche, *Política national y revisionismo histórico* (Buenos Aires: Editorial A. Peña Lillo, 1959); Clifton B. Kroeber, *Rosas y la revisión de la historia argentina*, trans. J. L. Muñoz Azpiri (Buenos Aires: Fundo Editor Argentino, 1964); Ernesto Palacio, *La historia falsificada* (Buenos Aires: Editorial A. Peña Lillo, 1960); José María Rosa, *Historia del revisionismo y otros ensayos* (Buenos Aires: Editorial Merlin, 1968).

21. Fred Russell Murphy, "Post-Independence State Formation in Argentina: Explaining the Shift from Caudillismo to Parliamentarism" (paper presented at the Latin American Studies Association meeting, Atlanta, Ga., March 1994, 6.

22. Richard W. Slatta, *Gauchos and the Vanishing Frontier*, rev. ed. (Lincoln: University of Nebraska Press, 1992), 96.

23. María Sáenz Quesada, *Los estancieros* (Buenos Aires: Editorial de Belgrano, 1980); John Lynch, *Argentine Dictator: Juan Manuel de Rosas, 1829–1852* (Oxford: Clarendon Press, 1981); David Rock, *Argentina, 1516–1987: From Spanish Colonization to Alfonsín* (Berkeley: University of California Press, 1987), 113–20; Mark D. Szuchman, *Order, Family, and Community in Buenos Aires, 1810–1860* (Stanford: Stanford University Press, 1988); Richard W. Slatta and Karla

Robinson, "Continuities in Crime and Punishment: Buenos Aires, 1820–50," in Lyman Johnson, ed., *The Problem of Order in Changing Societies: Essays on Crime and Policing in Argentina and Uruguay* (Albuquerque: University of New Mexico Press, 1990), 19–45; Richard W. Slatta, "'Civilization' Battles 'Barbarism': Argentine Frontier Strategies, 1516–1880," *Inter-American Review of Bibliography* 39, 2 (1989): 177–94.

24. Jonathan C. Brown, *A Socioeconomic History of Argentina, 1776–1860* (Cambridge: Cambridge University Press, 1979).

25. Lyman Johnson, "Wealth Inequality in Argentina's Livestock Frontier: Buenos Aires Province, 1800–1900" (paper presented at the Canadian Historical Association meeting, Calgary, Alberta, June 1994).

26. Ricardo Rodríguez Molas, *Historia social del gaucho* (Buenos Aires: Editorial Marú, 1968); Gastón Gori, *Vagos y mal entretenidos: Aporte al tema hernandiano*, 2d ed. (Santa Fe, Argentina: Colmegna, 1965); Slatta, *Gauchos*, 106–40; Richard W. Slatta, "The Demise of the Gaucho and the Rise of Equestrian Sport in Argentina," *Journal of Sport History* 13, 2 (summer 1986): 97–110.

27. Jonathan C. Brown, "Revival of the Rural Economy and Society in Buenos Aires," in Mark D. Szuchman and Jonathan C. Brown, eds., *Revolution and Restoration: The Rearrangement of Power in Argentina, 1776–1860* (Lincoln: University of Nebraska Press, 1994), 241.

28. Lynch, *Argentine Dictator*, 68–69; Brown, *Socioeconomic History*, 162.

29. See maps of Buenos Aires Province in *Contribución directa: Registro catastral de la provincia de Buenos Aires con esclusión de la capital, año 1863* (Buenos Aires: Provincia de Buenos Aires, 1863).

30. Brown, "Revival of the Rural Economy," 255; Mark D. Szuchman, "From Imperial Hinterland to Growth Pole: Revolution, Change, and Restoration in the Río de la Plata," in Szuchman and Brown, *Revolution and Restoration*, 19.

31. Mario Dotta, Duaner Freire, and Nelson Rodríguez, *El Uruguay ganadero: De la explotación primitiva a la crisis actual* (Montevideo: Banda Oriental, 1972); Enrique Mendez Vives,

Historia uruguaya, vol. 5: *El Uruguay de la modernización, 1876–1904* (Montevideo: Banda Oriental, 1975); José Pedro Barrán and Benjamín Nahum, *Historia rural del Uruguay moderno*, 7 vols. (Montevideo: Ediciones de la Banda Oriental, 1967–1978); José Pedro Barrán and Benjamín Nahum, "Uruguayan Rural History," *Hispanic American Historical Review* 64, 4 (November 1984): 655–74; Juan Rial and Jaime Klaczko, "Historiography and Historical Studies in Uruguay," *Latin American Research Review* 17, 3 (1982): 231.

32. Carlos A. Mayo, "Landed but not Powerful: The Colonial Estancieros of Buenos Aires (1750–1810)," *Hispanic American Historical Review* 71, 4 (November 1991): 761–79; John Chasteen, "Background to Civil War: The Process of Land Tenure in Brazil's Southern Borderland, 1801–1893," *Hispanic American Historical Review* 71, 4 (November 1991): 737–60.

33. Eduardo Azcuy Ameghino, "Economía y sociedad colonial en el ámbito rural bonaerense," in *Economía y historia: Contribuciones a la historia económica argentina*, comp. Mario Rapoport (Buenos Aires: Editorial Tesis, 1988), 23; Eduardo Azcuy Ameghino and Garbriela Martínez Dougnac, *Tierra y ganado en la campaña de Buenos Aires (según los censos de hacendados de 1789)* (Buenos Aires: IIHHES, 1989).

34. Ricardo Salvatore and Jonathan C. Brown, "Trade and Proletarianization in Late Colonial Banda Oriental: Evidence from the Estancia de las Vacas, 1791–1805," *Hispanic American Historical Review* 67, 3 (August 1987): 457.

35. Jorge Gelman, "New Perspectives on the Old Problem and the Same Source: The Gaucho and Rural History of the Colonial Río de la Plata," *Hispanic American Historical Review* 69, 4 (November 1989): 715–31.

36. Richard W. Slatta, "Images of Social Banditry in the Argentina Pampa," in Slatta, *Bandidos*, 49–65; Slatta, "Banditry as Political Participation"; Slatta, "Banditry and Rural Society History"; Richard W. Slatta, "Pulperías and Contraband Capitalism in Nineteenth-Century Buenos Aires Province," *The Americas* 38, 3 (January 1982): 347–62.

37. Brown, "Revival of the Rural Economy," 265. On post-1850s repression and marginalization, see Slatta, *Gauchos*, 37, 49–50, 87–89, 114–17, 133–38.

38. Brown, "Revival of the Rural Economy," 255.

39. Miguel Izard, "Ni cuatreros ni montoneros: Llaneros," *Boletín Americanista* 31 (1981): 83–142; Miguel Izard, "Mi coronel, hasta aquí le llegaron las matemáticas: Los llaneros del Apure," in Miguel Izard, ed., *Marginados, fronterizos, rebeldes y oprimidos*, vol. 2 (Barcelona: Ediciones del Serbal, 1985), 38–55; David McCreery, "Debt Servitude in Rural Guatemala, 1867–1936," *Hispanic American Historical Review* 63, 4 (November 1983); 735–59; Barrán and Nahum, *Historia rural del Uruguay moderno*; Barrán and Nahum, "Uruguayan Rural History"; Michael J. Gonzalez, "Planters and Politics in Peru, 1895–1919," *Journal of Latin American Studies* 23, 3 (October 1991): 515–41.

40. David H. Breen, *The Canadian Prairie West and the Ranching Frontier, 1874–1924* (Toronto: University of Toronto Press, 1983); David H. Breen, "The Ranching Frontier in Canada, 1875–1905," in Lewis G. Thomas, ed., *The Prairie West to 1905: A Canadian Sourcebook* (Toronto: Oxford University Press, 1975).

41. Simon Evans, "The Origins of Ranching in Western Canada: American Diffusion or Victorian Transplant?" *Great Plains Quarterly* 3, 2 (spring 1983): 79–91; Simon Evans, "American Cattlemen on the Canadian Range, 1874–1914," *Prairie Forum* 4, 1 (1979): 121–35; Simon Evans, "Some Observations on the Labour Force of the Canadian Ranching Frontier During its Golden Age, 1882–1901" (paper presented at the Canadian Historical Association meeting, Calgary, Alberta, June 1994); Warren M. Elofson, "Adapting to the Frontier Environment: The Ranching Industry in Western Canada, 1881–1914," *Canadian Papers in Rural History* 8 (Gananoque, Ont.: Langdale Press, 1992), 307–27; Warren M. Elofson, "The Myth of Ranching in Southern Alberta" (paper presented at the Canadian Historical Association meeting, Calgary, Alberta, June 1994.

Other studies of Canadian ranching include Austin A. Lupton, "Cattle Ranching in Alberta, 1874–1910," *Albertan Geographer* 3 (1966–67): 48–58; Patrick A. Dunae, ed., *Ranchers' Legacy: Alberta*

Essays by Lewis G. Thomas (Edmonton: University of Alberta Press, 1986); Edward Brado, *Cattle Kingdom: Early Ranches in Alberta* (Vancouver: Douglas and MacIntyre, 1984); Simon Evans, "The Passing of a Frontier: Ranching in the Canadian West, 1882–1912" (Ph.D. diss., University of Calgary, 1976); Simon Evans, *Prince Charming Goes West: The Story of the E. P. (Edward Prince) Ranch* (Calgary: University of Calgary Press, 1993); R. Douglas Francis, *Images of the West: Responses to the Canadian Prairies* (Saskatoon: Western Producer Prairie Books, 1989); R. Douglas Francis, "Changing Images of the West," *Journal of Canadian Studies* 17 (fall 1982); R. Douglas Francis, "From Wasteland to Utopia: Changing Images of the Canadian West in the Nineteenth Century," *Great Plains Quarterly* 7, 3 (summer 1987): 179–81; Henry C. Klassen, "The Conrads in the Alberta Cattle Business, 1875–1911," *Agricultural History* 64, 3 (1990): 31–59; Carl E. Solberg, *The Prairies and the Pampas: Agrarian Policy in Canada and Argentina, 1880–1930* (Stanford: Stanford University Press, 1987); Sherm Ewing, *The Range* (Missoula, Mont.: Mountain Press, 1990).

42. Thomas D. Hall, *Social Change in the Southwest, 1350–1880* (Lawrence: University Press of Kansas, 1989); Christopher Chase-Dunn and Thomas D. Hall, eds., *Core/Periphery Relations in Precapitalist Worlds* (Boulder: Westview Press, 1991).

43. Brian W. Dippie, "American Wests: Historiographical Perspectives," in Limerick et al., *Trails*, 136.

Glossary

acción. License to hunt wild cattle in the colonial Río de la Plata.

alpargatas. Sandals (in Chile, **ojotas**; in Mexico, **huaraches**).

amansador. Horse tamer.

amo. Master.

apartar. To separate or sort cattle.

apple. Saddle horn or pommel of the saddle (from the Spanish *manzana*).

Araucanians. Indians of southern Chile and western Argentina.

Arbuckle's. Brand of coffee favored by the American cowboy.

arepa. Filled corn cakes eaten in Venezuela.

argentinidad. "Argentinity," the essence of Argentine national character.

armas. Large, stiff protective leather skirts hanging off the saddle.

asado. Río de la Plata barbecue; beef quick-roasted over an open fire.

avestruz. Rhea or ostrich of the pampa, often hunted by gauchos for its feathers.

bagual. Gaucho term for wild horse.

Banda Oriental. "Eastern Bank," modern-day Uruguay.

bandeirante. Slave hunter and explorer from colonial São Paulo, Brazil.

bit. Metal portion of a bridle that fits through the horse's mouth.

blandengue. Argentine gaucho militia man of the colonial era.

bolas. Also **boleadoras**, weapon used by gauchos and Indians of the Río de la Plata to entangle the feet of rheas (ostriches), horses, or cattle.

bombachas. Baggy, bloused trousers adopted by the gaucho to replace the traditional diaper-like chiripá.

bombilla. Hollow tube tipped with an infuser used to sip *mate.*

botas de potro. Supple gaucho boots made from the legskin of a calf.

broncobusting. Taming a wild horse to be saddled and ridden.

buckaroo. Northwestern term for a cowboy; probably from the Spanish *vaquero.*

bulldogging. Steer wrestling; a major rodeo event.

campanha. Rolling plains of Rio Grande do Sul, in southern Brazil.

caña. Rum, sugar cane liquor.

capataz. Ranch foreman who works under the manager (*mayordomo*).

caporal. Range boss in charge of seasonal roundup (rodeo).

castas. Nonwhite, lower classes of colonial Spanish America.

caudillo. Local or regional military chieftain in Spanish America.

changador. Cattle thief; early derogatory term applied to the gaucho.

chaparejos. Also **chaparreras**; chaps, usually leather, worn to protect the legs.

charango. Small guitar-like instrument fashioned from an armadillo shell.

charque. Portuguese term for dried beef; usually rendered *charqui* in Spanish, hence the English word *jerky.*

charrería. Also **charreada**; charro rodeo competition and riding exhibition.

charro. Gentleman rider of Mexico.

Chichimecs. Indians of northern New Spain (Mexico).

chiripá. Large diaper-like cloth worn by gauchos in lieu of trousers.

cinchada. Gaucho tug-of-war on horseback.

cobija. Poncho or cape worn on the llanos.

colear. To throw a bull or cow to the ground by grasping the tail.

correr el gallo. "Chicken pull" or "chicken race," Mexican equestrian game.

corrido. Mexican folk song.

cowpen. Enclosure to hold cattle in the colonial Carolinas.

criollo. Creole, American-born, applied to people, cattle, and horses.

criollismo. Also **costumbrismo**, romanticized literature celebrating idyllic rural life and customs.

cuatra de cordón. Riding whip, Anglicized to *quirt*.

curandero. Folk healer, medicine man.

dally. To wrap the end of the rope around the saddle horn when roping a cow; from the Spanish phrase *dar la vuelta*.

desgracia. Gaucho term for an unfortunate accident, such as a death in a knife fight.

desjarretadera. Hocking knife used to down cattle in colonial Spanish America.

domador. Gaucho broncobuster.

encomienda. Royal grant of Indian labor made to Spanish conquerors.

estancia. Cattle or sheep ranch in the Río de la Plata.

estanciero. Rancher in the Río de la Plata.

facón. Gaucho's long, swordlike knife.

fazenda. Brazilian term for ranch or rural estate, owned by a **fazendeiro**.

filiación. Physical description of a person found on government documents.

fundo. Cattle ranch or estate in Chile.

gachupín. Derogatory term for Spaniard.

garrocha. Pike used to prod cattle in colonial Spanish America.

gauchesco. Literary genre that uses gaucho themes and/or dialect.

gaucho. Horseman/ranch worker of Argentina and Uruguay.

gaúcho. Horseman/ranch worker of the campanha region of Rio Grande do Sul, Brazil.

gauderio. Eighteenth-century pejorative term for gaucho.

greaser. Derogatory Anglo term for Mexican.
gringo. Term for foreigner in Spanish America.

hatero. Ranch owner on the llanos.
hato. Cattle ranch on the llanos.
hierra. Also **yerra**, branding season in the Río de la Plata.
huaraches. See **alpargatas**.
huaso. Chilean horseman, sometimes rendered **guaso**.

jáquima. Rope placed over a horse's head; Anglicized to *hackamore*.
jinetea. Short-stirruped riding style passed by the Moors to the Spaniards and thence to Spanish America.
juego de cañas. Equestrian joust with canes.
juez de campo. Roundup judge or overseer in Spanish America.

latifundia. Large, landed estates that dominate the Latin American countryside.
llanero. Horseman of the llanos.
Llano Estacado. High, dry plains of north and west Texas.
llanos. Tropical inland plains of Venezuela and Colombia.
longhorn. Semiwild, rangy cattle of northern Mexico and Texas.

macana. Wooden battle ax used by Indians of the Americas.
machismo. Ideal type of extreme, sometimes violent behavior to prove manliness in Latin America.
maestre de campo. Frontier military commander.
malón. Indian raid.
manta. More costly, finely made poncho used on the llanos.
maroma. Gaucho game in which a man drops from a corral gate onto the back of a charging bull.
matadero. Slaughterhouse.
matanza. Slaughter of wild cattle for their hides and tallow.
mate. Highly caffeinated tea made from leaves of the holly-like *Ilex paraguariensis*.
matrero. Gaucho outlaw, fugitive, murderer.
mayordomo. Ranch manager in Spanish America.

mecate. Fine, horsehair rope, Anglicized to *McCarty*.

mercachifle. Itinerant peddler of the pampas, often an immigrant.

mescal. Alcoholic beverage distilled from the maguey plant.

Mesta. Rancher's organization and lobby in Spain and New Spain.

mesteño. Translated as *mustang*, wild Spanish cattle in New Spain.

mestizo. Racially mixed, Indian and Spanish heritage.

montonera. Popular uprising against the government led by a caudillo.

municipio. Term for county in Brazil.

mustang. See **mesteño**.

ñandú. Rhea or ostrich of the pampas hunted by gauchos for its feathers.

nighthawk. Rider who watches the horses on a trail drive at night.

ojotas. See **alpargatas**.

ombú. Large, twisted tree-like shrub of the pampas.

Palliser's Triangle. Canadian region thought to be uninhabitable by whites; bounded on the east by the Souris River in the Turtle Mountains and on the south by the forty-ninth parallel.

pampa. Fertile, grassy plains of the Río de la Plata.

paniolo. Also **paniola**. Horseman of Hawaii, from *español*.

partido. Term for county in Argentina.

paso de muerte. Bareback wild-horse ride performed at the Mexican charrería.

pato. Equestrian gaucho game in which riders contest the possession of a duck sewn into a hide.

patrón. Boss, ranch owner.

payador. Gaucho troubadour, folk singer.

pechando. "Breasting," equestrian gaucho game in which riders run their horses into one another.

peón. Worker, generally landless.

pialar. Gaucho equestrian game.

pingo. Gaucho term for his horse.

porteño. Resident of Buenos Aires, capital of Argentina.

presidio. Frontier fort.

pulpería. Combination tavern and general store.

pulpero. Tavern keeper, operator, sometimes owner, of a pulpería.

pulquería. Mexican tavern selling corn liquor (*pulque*).

reata. Rawhide rope, Anglicized to *lariat*.

recado. Soft, multilayered gaucho saddle.

resero. Also **tropero**, trail driver, man who moves cattle.

retobado. Someone who, according to gaucho superstition, could not be injured by firearms.

rhea. Pampas ostrich hunted by gauchos for its feathers.

riña de gallos. Cockfight.

Río de la Plata. The region drained by the river of that name in southern South America.

riograndense. Native of Rio Grande do Sul, southernmost state of Brazil.

road ranching. Raising cattle along emigration routes in the American West.

rodeo. Roundup of cattle, usually for branding.

rustler. A cattle or horse thief; **good rustler**, an animal skilled at finding grass.

saladero. Meat-salting plant.

serape. Mantle or cape worn in Mexico.

sertão. "Backlands," dry inland plains of northeastern Brazil.

"slow elk." Beef poached by an unemployed cowboy; also called **"big antelope."**

sombrero. Wide-brimmed Mexican hat.

sortija. Equestrian ring race.

swampers. Wild cattle of the east Texas Gulf coast.

taba. Dice-like game of throwing the knuckle bone of a cow.

tapaderas. Long, pointed leather coverings that hang from the stirrups of a Mexican saddle.

tasajo. Jerky, dried meat, also **charqui** or **carne seca**.

terrateniente. Member of the landed elite in Spanish America.

tienda de raya. Company store of a large Mexican estate.
tirador. Broad, leather belt worn by gauchos and vaqueros.
toldería. Mobile Indian camp on the pampas.
topeo. Huaso game of pushing each other's horse along a rail.
tres Marías. "The three Marys," gaucho term for **boleadoras**.
tropilla. Gaucho's herd of remounts.

umbu. Portuguese term for the ombú tree.

vago y mal entretenido. "Vagrant and ne'er-do-well," legal classification imposed on the unemployed gaucho.
vaqueiro. Horseman of Northeastern Brazil.
vaquería. Wild cattle hunt (called **rebuque** in Chile).
vaquero. Working cowboy of Mexico.
vizcacha. Prairie dog of the pampas.

wrangler. Man or boy in charge of extra mounts on a trail drive.

Selected Bibliography

This bibliography does not include every source cited in the book. Rather, it focuses on the most important and relevant books and articles written about frontiers in the Americas. See the notes to each article for full citations to works not included herein.

Abbott, Edward Charles ("Teddy Blue"), and Helena Huntington Smith. *We Pointed Them North: Recollections of a Cowpuncher.* 1939. Reprint, Norman: University of Oklahoma Press, 1955.

Adams, Andy. *The Log of the Cowboy: A Narrative of the Old Trail Days.* 1903. Reprint, Lincoln: University of Nebraska Press, 1964.

Adams, Ramon Frederick. *Come an' Get It: The Story of the Old Cowboy Cook.* Norman: University of Oklahoma Press, 1952.

———. *Western Words: A Dictionary of the Range, Cowcamp, and Trail.* 1945. Reprint, Norman: University of Oklahoma Press, 1968.

———. *The Rampaging Herd: A Bibliography of Books and Pamphlets on Men and Events in the Cattle Industry.* Norman: University of Oklahoma Press, 1959.

Ahlborn, Richard E. "The Hispanic Horseman." *El Palacio* 89, 2 (summer 1983): 12–21.

————, ed. *Man Made Mobile: Early Saddles of Western North America*. Washington, D.C.: Smithsonian Institution Press, 1980.

Alexander, Hartley B. "The Horse in American Culture." In *So Live the Works of Men: Essays in Honor of Edgar Lee Hewett*. Albuquerque: University of New Mexico Press, 1939.

Allard, William A. *Vanishing Breed: Photographs of the Cowboy and the West*. New York: Little, Brown, 1982.

Allen, Jules Verne. *Cowboy Lore*. San Antonio: Naylor, 1933.

Allmendinger, Blake. *The Cowboy: Representations of Labor in an American Work Culture*. New York: Oxford University Press, 1992.

Almaráz, Félix D., Jr. *The San Antonio Missions and Their System of Land Tenure*. Austin: University of Texas Press, 1989.

Alvarez de Villar, José. *Men and Horses of Mexico: History and Practice of Charrería*. Mexico City: Ediciones Lara, 1979.

Amaral, Anthony A. *Will James: The Last Cowboy Legend*. Reno: University of Nevada Press, 1980.

Appun, Karl Ferdinand. "Los llanos de El Baúl." Translated by Federica de Ritter. *Anales de la Universidad Central de Venezuela* 32 (January 1953): 155–242.

Armas, Julio de. "Nacimiento de la ganadería venezolana." *Revista Shell* 3, 11 (June 1954): 26–35.

————. *La ganadería en Venezuela: Ensayo histórico*. Caracas: Congreso de la República, 1974.

Armas Chitty, José Antonio de. *Tucupido: Formación de un pueblo del llano*. Caracas: Universidad Central de Venezuela, 1961.

————. *Vocabulario del hato*. Caracas: Universidad Central de Venezuela, 1966.

Armitage, Susan. "Women and Men in Western History: A Stereoptical Vision." *Western Historical Quarterly* 16, 4 (October 1985): 381–96.

Armitage, Susan, and Elizabeth Jameson, eds. *The Women's West*. Norman: University of Oklahoma Press, 1987.

Armitage, Susan, et al. *Women in the West: A Guide to Manuscript Sources*. New York: Garland, 1991.

Ashford, Gerald. *Spanish Texas: Yesterday and Today.* Austin: Jenkins Publishing, 1971.

Assunção, Fernando. *El gaucho.* Montevideo: Imprenta Nacional, 1963.

————. *El gaucho: Estudio socio-cultural.* 2 vols. Montevideo: Dirección General de Extensión Universitaria, 1978–1979.

————. *Pilchas criollas: Usos y costumbres del gaucho.* Rev. ed. Montevideo: Master Fer, 1979.

Athearn, Robert G. *The Mythic West in Twentieth-Century America.* Lawrence: University Press of Kansas, 1986.

Atherton, Lewis E. *The Cattle Kings.* Bloomington: Indiana University Press, 1961.

Bader, Thomas M. "A 'Second Field' for Historians of Latin America: An Application of the Theories of Bolton, Turner, and Webb." *Journal of Inter-American Studies and World Affairs* 12 (1970): 47–54.

Baigell, Matthew. *The Western Art of Frederic Remington.* New York: Ballantine Books, 1976.

Baldwin, Gordon Curtis. *Games of the American Indian.* New York: Norton, 1969.

Ball, Charles E. *The Finishing Touch.* Amarillo: Texas Cattle Breeders' Association, 1988.

Ballesteros, José Ramón. *Oríigen y evolución del charro mexicano.* Mexico City: Manuel Porrúa, 1972.

Baretta, Silvio Duncan, and John Markoff. "Civilization and Barbarism: Cattle Frontiers in Latin America." *Comparative Studies in Society and History* 20 (October 1978): 587–620.

Barnes, William Croft. *Apaches and Longhorns.* Los Angeles: Ward Ritchie, 1941.

Barnett, Louise K. *The Ignoble Savage: American Literary Racism, 1790–1890.* Westport, Conn.: Greenwood Press, 1975.

Barrán, José Pedro. "Uruguayan Rural History." *Hispanic American Historical Review* 64, 4 (November 1984): 655–74.

Barrán, José Pedro, and Benjamín Nahum. *Historia rural del Uruguay moderno.* 7 vols. Montevideo: Ediciones de la Banda Oriental, 1967–1978.

Beard, Tyler. *The Cowboy Boot Book.* Salt Lake City: Peregrine Smith Books, 1992.

―――. *100 Years of Western Wear.* Salt Lake City: Peregrine Smith Books, 1993.

Beatie, Russell H. *Saddles.* Norman: University of Oklahoma Press, 1982.

Becco, Horacio Jorge. "La poesía gauchesca en el Río de la Plata." *Inter-American Review of Bibliography* 24, 2 (April 1974): 135–46.

―――, ed. *Antología de la poesía gauchesca.* Madrid: Aguilar, 1972.

Belaúnde, Victor Andrés. "The Frontier in Hispanic America." *Rice Institute Pamphlet* 10, 4 (October 1923): 202–13.

Berger, Carl. *The Writing of Canadian History: Aspects of English-Canadian Writing, 1900–1970.* Toronto: Oxford University Press, 1976.

Berthrong, Donald J. *The Southern Cheyennes.* Norman: University of Oklahoma Press, 1963.

―――. "Cattlemen on the Cheyenne-Arapaho Reservation, 1883–1885." *Arizona and the West* 13 (1971): 5–32.

―――. *The Cheyenne and Arapaho Ordeal: Reservation and Agency Life in the Indian Territory, 1875–1907.* Norman: University of Oklahoma Press, 1976.

Billard, Jules B., ed. *The World of the American Indian.* Rev. ed. Washington, D.C.: National Geographic Society, 1974.

Billington, Ray Allen. *America's Frontier Heritage.* New York: Holt, Rinehart and Winston, 1966.

―――. *Frederick Jackson Turner: Historian, Scholar, Teacher.* New York: Oxford University Press, 1973.

―――. "The American Frontier." In Paul Bohannan and Fred Plog, eds., *Beyond the Frontier: Social Process and Cultural Change.* Garden City: Natural History Press, 1976.

―――. *Land of Savagery, Land of Promise: The European Image of the American Frontier in the Nineteenth Century.* Norman: University of Oklahoma Press, 1981.

―――, ed. *The Frontier Thesis: Valid Interpretation of American History?* New York: Krieger, 1966.

Bishko, Charles J. "The Peninsular Background of Latin American Cattle Ranching." *Hispanic American Historical Review* 32, 4 (November 1952): 491–515.

Blackstone, Sarah J. *Buckskins, Bullets, and Business: A History of Buffalo Bill's Wild West.* Westport, Conn.: Greenwood Press, 1986.

Blasingame, Ike. *Dakota Cowboy: My life in the Old Days.* New York: Putnam, 1958.

Blevins, Winfred. *Dictionary of the American West.* New York: Facts on File, 1993.

Blouet, Brian W., and Merlin P. Lawson, eds. *Images of the Plains: The Role of Human Nature in Settlement.* Lincoln: University of Nebraska Press, 1975.

Bold, Christine. *Selling the Wild West: Popular Western Fiction, 1860–1960.* Bloomington: Indiana University Press, 1987.

Bolton, Herbert Eugene. "The Epic of Greater America." *American Historical Review* 38, 3 (April 1933): 448–74.

Borges, Jorge Luis, and Adolfo Bioy Casares, eds. *Poesía gauchesca.* 2 vols. Mexico City: Fondo de Cultura Económica, 1955.

Borne, Lawrence R. *Dude Ranching: A Complete History.* Albuquerque: University of New Mexico Press, 1983.

Bowden, Martyn J. "The Great American Desert and the American Frontier, 1800–1882: Popular Images of the Plains." In Tamara K. Hareven, ed., *Anonymous Americans: Explorations in Nineteenth-Century Social History.* Englewood Cliffs: Prentice-Hall, 1971.

Bowman, Isaiah. *The Pioneer Fringe.* New York: American Geographical Society, 1931.

Brado, Edward. *Cattle Kingdom: Early Ranching in Alberta.* Vancouver and Toronto: Douglas and MacIntyre, 1984.

Bramlett, Jim. *Ride the High Points: The Real Story of Will James.* Missoula, Mont.: Mountain Press Publishing, 1987.

Branch, E. Douglas. *The Cowboy and His Interpreters.* 1926. Reprint, New York: D. Appleton, 1961.

Brand, Donald D. "The Early History of the Range Cattle Industry in Northern Mexico." *Agricultural History* 35, 3 (July 1961): 132–39.

Breen, David H. "The Ranching Frontier in Canada, 1875–1905." In Lewis G. Thomas, ed., *The Prairie West to 1905: A Canadian Sourcebook*. Toronto: Oxford University Press, 1975.

———. "The Turner Thesis and the Canadian West: A Closer Look at the Ranching Frontier." In Lewis H. Thomas, ed., *Essays on Western History in Honour of Lewis Gwynne Thomas*. Edmonton: University of Alberta Press, 1976.

———. *The Canadian Prairie West and the Ranching Frontier, 1874–1924*. Toronto: University of Toronto Press, 1983.

Briceño, Tarcila. *La ganadería en los llanos centro-occidentales venezolanos, 1900–1935*. Caracas: Biblioteca de la Academia Nacional de la Historia, 1985.

Brown, Jonathan C. *A Socioeconomic History of Argentina, 1776–1860*. Cambridge: Cambridge University Press, 1979.

———. "Revival of the Rural Economy and Society in Buenos Aires." In Mark D. Szuchman and Jonathan C. Brown, eds., *Revolution and Restoration: The Rearrangement of Power in Argentina, 1776–1860*. Lincoln: University of Nebraska Press, 1994.

Brown, Richard Maxwell. *No Duty to Retreat: Violence and Values in American History and Society*. Norman: University of Oklahoma Press, 1991.

———. "Western Violence: Structure, Values, Myth." *Western Historical Quarterly* 24, 1 (February 1993): 5–20.

Burchan, L. T. "Cattle and Range Forage in California, 1770–1880." *Agricultural History* 35, 3 (July 1961): 140–49.

Burroughs, John Rolfe. *Where the Old West Stayed Young*. New York: Morrow, 1962.

Busaniche, José Luis, ed. *Estampas del pasado: Lecturas de historia argentina*. 1959. Reprint, Buenos Aires: Solar-Hachette, 1971.

Butler, Anne E. *Daughters of Joy, Sisters of Misery: Prostitutes in the American West, 1865–90*. Urbana: University of Illinois Press, 1985.

Byam, George. *Wanderings in Some of the Western Republics of America*. London: John W. Parker, 1850.

Calzadilla Valdés, Fernando. *Por los llanos de Apure*. Santiago: Imprenta Universitaria, 1940.

Campo L., Carlos del, and Luis Durand. *Huasos chilenos: Folklore campesino*. Santiago: Leblanc, 1939.

Cannon, Hal, ed. *Cowboy Poetry: A Gathering*. Salt Lake City: Peregrine Smith Books, 1985.

———. *New Cowboy Poetry: A Contemporary Gathering*. Salt Lake City: Peregrine Smith Books, 1990.

Cannon, Hal and Thomas West, eds. *Buckaroo: Visions and Voices of the American Cowboy*. New York: Simon and Schuster, 1993.

Cárcano, Miguel Angel. *Evolución histórica del régimen de la tierra pública, 1810–1916*. 1917. Reprint, Buenos Aires: EUDEBA, 1972.

Carvallo, Gastón. *El hato venezolano, 1900–1980*. Caracas: Fondo Editorial Tropykos, 1985.

Catlin, George. *Episodes from Life Among the Indians and Last Rambles*. 1868. Reprint, Norman: University of Oklahoma Press, 1959.

Cawalti, John G. *The Six-Gun Mystique*. 2d ed. Bowling Green: Bowling Green University Popular Press, 1984.

Chasteen, John C. "Violence for Show: Knife Dueling on a Nineteenth-Century Cattle Frontier." In Lyman L. Johnson, ed., *The Problem of Order in Changing Societies: Essays on Crime and Policing in Argentina and Uruguay, 1750–1940*. Albuquerque: University of New Mexico Press, 1990.

———. *Heroes on Horseback: A Life and Times of the Last Gaucho Caudillos*. Albuquerque: University of New Mexico Press, 1995.

Chenevix Trench, Charles P. *A History of Horsemanship*. Garden City: Doubleday, 1970.

Chrisman, Harry E. *The Ladder of Rivers: The Story of I. P. (Print) Olive*. Denver: Sage Books, 1962.

Christianson, C. J. *My Life on the Range*. Lethbridge, Alberta: Southern Publishing, 1968.

Christopher, A. J. "Southern Africa and the United States: A Comparison of Pastoral Frontiers." *Journal of the West* 20, 1 (1981): 52–59.

Cisneros, José. *Riders Across the Centuries: Horsemen of the Spanish Borderlands.* El Paso: Texas Western Press, 1984.

Clark, LaVerne Harrell. *They Sang for Horses: The Impact of the Horse on Navajo and Apache Folklore.* Tucson: University of Arizona Press, 1966.

Cleaveland, Agnes Morley. *No Life for a Lady.* Lincoln: University of Nebraska Press, 1941.

Clementi, Hebe. "National Identity and the Frontier." *American Studies International* 19, 3–4 (1981): 36–44.

————. *La frontera en América.* 4 vols. Buenos Aires: Editorial Leviatan, 1986–1988.

Coel, Margaret. *Chief Left Hand, Southern Arapaho.* Norman: University of Oklahoma Press, 1981.

Cole, D. C. *The Chiricahua Apache, 1846–1876: From War to Reservation.* Albuquerque: University of New Mexico Press, 1988.

Collier, John. *The Indians of the Americas.* New York: Norton, 1947.

Collins, Michael L. *That Damned Cowboy: Theodore Roosevelt and the American West, 1883–1898.* New York: Peter Lang, 1989.

Coluccio, Félix. *Diccionario folklórico argentino.* 2 vols. Buenos Aires: Lasserre, 1964.

Craig, John R. *Ranching with Lords and Commons; or Twenty Years on the Range.* 1903. Reprint, New York: AMS Press, 1971.

Cray, Ed. *Levi's.* Boston: Houghton Mifflin, 1978.

Cronon, William. "Revisiting the Vanishing Frontier: The Legacy of Frederick Jackson Turner." *Western Historical Quarterly* 18, 2 (April 1987): 157–76.

Cronon, William, George Miles, and Jay Gitlin, eds. *Under an Open Sky: Rethinking America's Western Past.* New York: Norton, 1992.

Cross, Michael S., ed. *The Turner Thesis and the Canadas: The Debate on the Impact of the Canadian Environment.* Toronto: Copp Clark, 1970.

Curtain, Philip D. "Depth, Span, and Relevance," *American Historical Review* 89, 1 (February 1984): 1–9.

Da Cunha, Euclides. *Rebellion in the Backlands (Os Sertões)*. Translated by Samuel Putnam. 1902. Reprint, Chicago: University of Chicago Press, 1944.

Daireaux, Emilio. *Vida y costumbres en La Plata*. 2 vols. Buenos Aires: Lajouane, 1888.

Dale, Edward Everett. *The Range Cattle Industry: Ranching on the Great Plains from 1865 to 1925*. 1930. Reprint, Norman: University of Oklahoma Press, 1960.

———. *Cow Country*. Norman: University of Oklahoma Press, 1965.

Dana, Richard Henry. *Two Years Before the Mast*. 1840. Reprint, New York: New American Library, 1964.

Daniels, George G., ed. *The Spanish West*. Alexandria, Va.: Time-Life Books, 1976.

Dary, David. *Cowboy Culture*. New York: Knopf, 1981.

Davidson, Arnold E. *Coyote Country: Fictions of the Canadian West*. Durham: Duke University Press, 1994.

Davis, Robert Murray. *Playing Cowboys: Low Culture and High Art in the Western*. Norman: University of Oklahoma Press, 1992.

DeArment, Robert K. *Knights of the Green Cloth: The Saga of the Frontier Gamblers*. Norman: University of Oklahoma Press, 1982.

DeLeon, Arnoldo. *They Called Them Greasers: Anglo Attitudes toward Mexicans in Texas, 1821–1900*. Austin: University of Texas Press, 1983.

Deloria, Jr., Vine. *Red Earth, White Lies: Native Americans and the Myth of Scientific Fact*. New York: Scribner, 1995.

Dempsey, Hugh A. "Calgary's First Stampede." *Alberta Historical Review* 3, 3 (summer 1955): 3–13.

Denhardt, Robert Moorman. *The Horse of the Americas*. Rev. ed. Norman: University of Oklahoma Press, 1947.

———. "The Chilean Horse." *Agricultural History* 24, 3 (July 1950): 161–65.

———. *The King Ranch Quarter Horses, and Something of the Ranch and the Men that Bred Them*. Norman: University of Oklahoma Press, 1970.

Denoon, Donald. *Settler Capitalism: The Dynamics of Dependent Development in the Southern Hemisphere*. New York: Oxford University Press, 1982.

Depons, Francisco. *Viaje a la parte oriental de Tierra Firme*. 2 vols. Translated by Enrique Planchart. 1806. Reprint, Caracas: Tipografía Americana, 1930.

Deverell, William. "Fighting Words: The Significance of the American West in the History of the United States." *Western Historical Quarterly* 25, 2 (summer 1994): 185–206.

Díaz, José Antonio. *El agricultor venezolano ó lecciones de agricultura práctica nacional*. 2 vols. Caracas: Rojas Brothers, 1877.

Dickason, Olive Patricia. *The Myth of the Savage and the Beginnings of French Colonialism in the Americas*. Edmonton: University of Alberta Press, 1984.

Dinsmore, Wayne. *The Horses of the Americas*. Norman: University of Oklahoma Press, 1978.

Dippie, Brian W. *The Vanishing American: White Attitudes and U.S. Indian Policy*. Lawrence: University Press of Kansas, 1982.

Dobie, J. Frank. "The Mexican Vaquero of the Texas Border." *Southwestern Political and Social Science Quarterly* 8, 1 (June 1927): 1–12.

———. "Ranch Mexicans." *Survey* 66 (May 1, 1931), 167–70.

———. *The Longhorns*. New York: Grosset and Dunlap, 1941.

———. "Indian Horses and Horsemanship." *Southwest Review* 35 (autumn 1950): 265–75.

———. *Guide to Life and Literature of the Southwest*. Rev. ed. Dallas: Southern Methodist University Press, 1952.

———. *The Mustangs*. Boston: Little, Brown, 1952.

———. *A Vaquero of the Brush Country*. Austin: University of Texas Press, 1957.

———. *Cow People*. Boston: Little, Brown, 1964.

———, ed. *Texas and Southwestern Lore*. Austin: Texas Folklore Society, 1927.

Donahue, John. *Don Segundo Sombra y El Virginiano: Gaucho y cowboy*. Madrid: Editorial Pliegos, 1988.

Downs, James F. *Animal Husbandry in Navajo Society and Culture.* Berkeley: University of California Press, 1964.

————. *The Navajo.* New York: Holt, Rinehart, and Winston, 1972.

Doyle, James. "American Literary Images of the Canadian Prairies, 1860–1910." *Great Plains Quarterly* 6 (winter 1983), 3–20.

Drinnon, Richard. *Facing West: The Metaphysics of Indian-Hating and Empire-Building.* Minneapolis: University of Minnesota Press, 1980.

Durham, Philip, and Everett L. Jones. *The Negro Cowboys.* Lincoln: University of Nebraska Press, 1965.

Dusard, Jay. *The North American Cowboy: A Portrait.* Prescott, Arizona: Consortium, 1983.

Dusenberry, William H. *The Mexican Mesta.* Urbana: University of Illinois Press, 1963.

Dyal, Donald H. *Sun, Sod, and Wind: A Bibliography of Ranch House Architecture.* Monticello: Vance Bibliographies, 1982.

Dykstra, Robert R. *The Cattle Towns.* New York: Atheneum, 1976.

Echaiz, René León. *Interpretación histórica del huaso chileno.* Santiago: Editorial Universitaria, 1955.

Edwards, Elwyn Hartley. *Horses: Their Role in the History of Man.* London: Willow Books, 1987.

Ellis, John. *Against Deconstruction.* Princeton: Princeton University Press, 1989.

Ellison, Glenn R. *Cowboys Under the Mogollon Rim.* Tucson: University of Aridona Press, 1968.

————. *More Tales from Slim Ellison.* Tucson: University of Arizona Press, 1981.

Elofson, Warren M. "Adapting to the Frontier Environment: The Ranching Industry in Western Canada, 1881–1914." *Canadian Papers in Rural History* 8, (1992): 307–27.

————. "The Myth of Ranching in Southern Alberta." Paper presented to the Canadian Historical Association, Calgary, June 1994.

Emmons, David M. *Garden in the Grasslands: Boomer Literature of the Central Great Plains.* Lincoln: University of Nebraska Press, 1971.

———. "Social Myth and Social Reality." *Montana, The Magazine of Western History* 39,4 (autumn 1989): 2–9.

———. "Constructed Province: History and the Making of the Last American West." *Western Historical Quarterly* 24, 4 (winter 1994): 437–60.

Erdoes, Richard. *Saloons of the Old West.* New York: Knopf, 1969.

Erickson, John R. *Panhandle Cowboy.* Lincoln: University of Nebraska Press, 1980.

———. *The Modern Cowboy.* Lincoln: University of Nebraska Press, 1981.

Etulain, Richard W. "Frontier, Region, and Myth: Changing Interpretations of Western American Culture." *Journal of American Culture* 3, 2 (summer 1980): 268–84.

———. "Changing Images: The Cowboy in Western Films." *Colorado Heritage* 1 (1981): 36–55.

———. "Frontier, Region, and Border: Cultural Current in the Recent Southwest." *Montana, The Magazine of Western History* 44, 1 (winter 1994): 64–70.

———, ed. *The American Literary West.* Manhattan: Sunflower University Press, 1980.

———, ed. "Western Films: A Brief History." *Journal of the West* 22, 4 (October 1983): 3–81.

———, ed. *The American West in the Twentieth Century: A Bibliography.* Norman: University of Oklahoma Press, 1994.

Evans, Simon M. "The Passing of a Frontier: Ranching in the Canadian West, 1882–1912." Ph.D. diss., University of Calgary, 1976.

———. "American Cattlemen on the Canadian Range, 1874–1914." *Prairie Forum* 4, 1 (1979): 121–35.

———. "The Origins of Ranching in Western Canada: American Diffusion or Victorian Transplant?" *Great Plains Quarterly* 3, 2 (spring 1983): 79–91.

———. *Prince Charming Goes West: The Story of the E. P. (Edward Prince) Ranch.* Calgary: University of Calgary Press, 1993.

———. "Some Observations on the Labour Force of the Canadian Ranching Frontier During its Golden Age, 1882–1901."

Paper presented to the Canadian Historical Association, Calgary, June 1994.

Ewers, John Canfield. *The Horse in Blackfoot Indian Culture, with Comparative Material from other Western Tribes*. Washington, D.C.: U.S. Government Printing Office, 1955.

Ewing, Sherm. *The Range*. Missoula, Mont.: Mountain Press Publishing, 1990.

———. *The Ranch: A Modern History of the North American Cattle Industry*. Missoula, Mont.: Mountain Press Publishing, 1995.

Fagan, Brian M. *Clash of Cultures*. New York: W. H. Freeman, 1984.

Faragher, John Mack. "Clint Eastwood's *Unforgiven*: The Western is Back." *Montana, The Magazine of Western History* 43, 1 (winter 1993): 74–78.

———. "The Frontier Trail: Rethinking Turner and Reimagining the West." *American Historical Review* 98, 1 (February 1993): 109–17.

Faulk, Odie B. "Ranching in Spanish Texas." *Hispanic American Historical Review* 45, 2 (May 1965): 257–66.

Febvre, Lucien. "Frontière: The Word and the Concept." In Peter Burke, ed., *A New Kind of History from the Writings of Lucien Febvre*. Translated by K. Folca. London: Routledge and Kegan Paul, 1973.

Findlay, John M. *People of Chance: Gambling in American Society from Jamestown to Las Vegas*. New York: Oxford University Press, 1986.

Fishwick, Marshall W. "The Cowboy: America's Contribution to the World's Mythology." *Western Folklore* 11, 2 (April 1952): 77–92.

Flood, Elizabeth Clair. "Dude Ranches: Where East Meets West." *Cowboys & Indians* 1, 3 (winter 1993): 36–40.

Folsom, James K. *The American Western Novel*. New Haven: Yale University Press, 1966.

———, ed. *The Western: A Collection of Critical Essays*. Englewood Cliffs: Prentice-Hall, 1979.

Foote, Cheryl J. "Changing Images of Women in the Western Film." *Journal of the West* 22, 4 (1983): 64–71.

Forbes, Douglas. "The Appearance of the Mounted Indian in Northern Mexico and the Southwest to 1680." *Southwestern Journal of Anthropology* 15 (1959): 189–212.

Forbes, Jack D. *Apache, Navajo, and Spaniard.* 2d ed. Norman: University of Oklahoma Press, 1960.

———. "Frontiers in American History." *Journal of the West* 1, 1 and 2 (1962): 63–74.

———. "Frontiers in American History and the Role of the Frontier Historian." *Ethnohistory* 15 (spring 1968): 203–35.

Forbis, William H. *The Cowboys.* Rev. ed. Alexandria, Va.: Time-Life Books, 1978.

Foster-Harris, William. *The Look of the Old West.* New York: Bonanza Books, 1955.

Fox, William L, ed. *TumbleWords: Writers Reading the West.* Reno: University of Nevada Press, 1995.

Francis, R. Douglas. "Changing Images of the West." *Journal of Canadian Studies* 17, 3 (fall 1982): 5–19.

———. "From Wasteland to Utopia: Changing Images of the Canadian West in the Nineteenth Century." *Great Plains Quarterly* 7, 3 (summer 1987): 178–94.

———. *Images of the West: Responses to the Canadian Prairies.* Saskatoon: Western Producer Prairie Books, 1989.

Frantz, Joe B., and Julian E. Choate, Jr. *The American Cowboy: The Myth and the Reality.* Norman: University of Oklahoma Press, 1955.

Fredriksson, Kristine. *American Rodeo: From Buffalo Bill to Big Business.* College Station: Texas A&M University Press, 1984.

Freedman, Russell. *Cowboys of the Wild West.* New York: Clarion Books, 1985.

French, Giles. *Cattle Country of Peter French.* Portland, Ore.: Binsford and Mort, 1964.

Friend, John B. *Cattle of the World.* Poole, England: Blandford Press, 1978.

Frink, Maurice W., Turrentine Jackson, and Agnes Wright Spring. *When Grass Was King.* Boulder: University of Colorado Press, 1956.

Fritz, Henry E. "The Cattlemen's Frontier in the Trans-Mississippi West: An Annotated Bibliography." *Arizona and the West* 14, 1 and 2 (spring and summer 1972): 45–70, 169–90.

Fugate, Francis L. "Origins of the Range Cattle Era in South Texas." *Agricultural History* 35, 3 (July 1961): 155–58.

Furlong, Charles Wellington. *Let 'er Buck: A Story of the Passing of the Old West.* 3d ed. New York: G. P. Putnam's Sons, 1923.

Gallegos, Rómulo. *Doña Bárbara.* Translated by Robert Malloy. New York: Peter Smith, 1948.

Garavaglia, Louis, and Charles G. Worman. *Firearms of the American West, 1803–1865.* Albuquerque: University of New Mexico Press, 1984.

Gard, Wayne. *Frontier Justice.* Norman: University of Oklahoma Press, 1949.

———. *The Chisholm Trail.* Norman: University of Oklahoma Press, 1954.

Gardiner, Allen Francis. *A Visit to the Indians on the Frontiers of Chili.* London: Seeley and Burnside, 1841.

Garfield, Brian. *Western Films: A Complete Guide.* New York: Da Capo, 1982.

Garganigo, John F. *Javier de Viana.* New York: Twayne, 1972.

Garry, Jim. *This Ol' Drought Ain't Broke Us Yet (But We're All Bent Pretty Bad): Stories of the American West.* New York: Orion Books, 1992.

Gerhard, Dietrich. "The Frontier in Comparative View." *Comparative Studies in Society and History* 1, 3 (1959): 205–29.

Getty, Harry T. *The San Carlos Indian Cattle Industry.* Tucson: University of Arizona Press, 1963.

Giberti, Horacio. *Historia económica de la ganadería argentina.* Buenos Aires: Solar-Hachette, 1954.

Gipson, Fred. *Fabulous Empire: Colonel Zack Miller's Story.* Boston: Houghton Mifflin, 1946.

Goldstein, Kenneth S. "Bowdlerization and Expurgation: Academic and Folk." *Journal of American Folklore* 80 (1967): 374–86.

Góngora, Mario. *Vagabundaje y sociedad fronteriza en Chile, siglos XVII a XIX.* Santiago: Universidad de Chile, 1966.

Goodrich, Samuel Griswold. *The Manners, Customs, and Antiquities of the Indians of North and South America*. Boston: Bradbury, Soden, 1844.

Gori, Gastón. *Vagos y mal entretenidos: Aporte al tema hernandiano*. 2d ed. Santa Fe, Argentina: Colmegna, 1965.

Gould, Ed. *Ranching: Ranching in Western Canada*. Saanichton, B.C.: Hancock House, 1978.

Graham, Don. *Cowboys and Cadillacs: How Hollywood Looks at Texas*. Austin: Texas Monthly Press, 1983.

Graham, Robert Bontine Cunninghame. *José Antonio Páez*. London: Heinemann, 1929.

———. *The Horses of the Conquest*. 1930. Reprint, Norman: University of Oklahoma Press, 1949.

———. *Rodeo: A Collection of Tales and Sketches*. Edited by A. F. Tschiffely. Garden City: Doubleday, Doran and Co., 1936.

———. *The South American Tales and Sketches of Robert B. Cunninghame Graham*. Edited by John Walker. Norman: University of Oklahoma Press, 1978.

Grant, Bruce. *The Cowboy Encyclopedia: The Old and the New West from the Open Range to the Dude Ranch*. Chicago: Rand McNally, 1951.

Grant, Ted, and Andy Russell. *Men in the Saddle: Working Cowboys of Canada*. Toronto and New York: Van Nostrand Reinhold, 1978.

Griffith, James S. "The Cowboy Poetry of Everett Brisendine: A Response to Cultural Change." *Western Folklore* 42, 1 (1983): 38–45.

Grinnell, George Bird. *The Cheyenne Indians: Their History and Way of Life*. Lincoln: University of Nebraska Press, 1972.

Griswold del Castillo, Richard. "New Perspectives on the Mexican and American Borderlands." *Latin American Research Review* 19, 1 (1984): 199–209.

Grossman, James R., ed. *The Frontier in American Culture*. Berkeley: University of California Press, 1994.

Guarda, Gabriel. *La sociedad en Chile astral antes de la colonización alemana, 1645–1845*. Santiago: Andrés Bello, 1979.

Guice, John D. W. "Cattle Raisers of the Old Southwest: A Reinterpretation." *Western Historical Quarterly* 8, 2 (April 1977): 167–87.

Guichard du Plessis, Jean, and Jo Mora. *Cowboys et gauchos des Amériques*. Paris: André Bonne, 1968.

Güiraldes, Ricardo. *Don Segundo Sombra: Shadows on the Pampas*. Translated by Harriet de Onís. 1935. Reprint, New York: Signet, 1966.

Gump, James. "The Subjugation of the Zulus and Sioux: A Comparative Study." *Western Historical Quarterly* 19, 1 (January 1988): 21–36.

———. *The Dust Rose Like Smoke: The Subjugation of the Zulu and the Sioux*. Lincoln: University of Nebraska Press, 1994.

Guy, Donna J. *Sex and Danger in Buenos Aires: Prostitution, Family, and Nation in Argentina*. Lincoln: University of Nebraska Press, 1991.

Hadley-Garcia, George. *Hispanic Hollywood: The Latins in Motion Pictures*. New York: Citadel Press, 1990.

Haines, Francis D. "How Did the Indians Get Their Horses?" *American Anthropologist*, n.s., 40, 1 (1938): 112–17.

———. "The Northward Spread of Horses among The Plains Indians." *American Anthropologist*, n.s., 40 (1938): 429–37.

———. *Horses in America*. New York: Crowell, 1971.

Haley, J. Evetts. *The XIT Ranch of Texas and the Early Days of the Llano Estacado*. Norman: University of Oklahoma Press, 1929.

———. *Charles Goodnight: Cowman and Plainsman*. Norman: University of Oklahoma Press, 1936.

Hall, Thomas D. *Social Change in the Southwest, 1350–1880*. Lawrence: University Press of Kansas, 1989.

Hanes, Bailey C. *Bill Pickett, Bulldogger: The Biography of a Black Cowboy*. Norman: University of Oklahoma Press, 1977.

Hanke, Lewis, ed. *Do the Americas Have a Common History? A Critique of the Bolton Theory*. New York: Knopf, 1964.

Harris, Charles W., and Buck Rainey, eds. *The Cowboy: Six-shooters, Songs, and Sex*. Norman: University of Oklahoma Press, 1976.

Harrod, Howard L. *Renewing the World: Plains Indian Religion and Morality*. Tucson: University of Arizona Press, 1987.

Hassrick, Peter. *The Way West: Art of Frontier America*. New York: Abrams, 1977.

———. *History of Western American Art*. New York: Exeter Press, 1987.

Hatch, Alden. *Remington Arms in American History*. New York: Holt, Rinehart, 1956.

Havinghurst, Walter. *Annie Oakley of the Wild West*. Lincoln: University of Nebraska Press, 1954.

Hayes, M. Horace. *Points of the Horse: A Treatise on the Conformation, Movements, and Evolution of the Horse*. New York: Scribners, 1969.

Heaton, Herbert. "Other Wests than Ours." *Journal of Economic History* 6 (supplement 1946): 50–62.

Hennessy, Alistair. *The Frontier in Latin American History*. Albuquerque: University of New Mexico Press, 1978.

Hernández, José. *The Gaucho Martín Fierro*. Translated by Walter Owen. 1872, 1879. Reprint. Buenos Aires: Editorial Pampa, 1960.

Hilzheimer, Max. "The Evolution of the Domestic Horse." *Antiquity* 9 (1935): 133–39.

Hinton, Harwood P., Jr. "John Simpson Chisum, 1877–84," *New Mexico Historical Review* 31, 3 (July 1956): 177–205; 31, 4 (October 1956): 310–37; 32, 1 (January 1957): 53–65.

Hodge, William. *A Bibliography of Contemporary North American Indians*. New York: Interland Publishing, 1976.

Hoebel, E. Adamson. *The Cheyennes: Indians of the Great Plains*. New York: Holt, 1960.

Hofstadter, Richard, and Seymour Martin Lipset, eds. *Turner and the Sociology of the Frontier*. New York: Basic Books, 1968.

Hogarth, Paul. *Artists on Horseback: The Old West in Illustrated Journalism, 1857–1900*. New York: Watson-Guptill, 1972.

Hoig, Stan. *The Humor of the American Cowboy*. Lincoln: University of Nebraska Press, 1958.

Holden, William C. *The Espuela Land and Cattle Company: A Study of a Foreign-Owned Ranch in Texas.* 1934. Reprint, Austin: Texas State Historical Association, 1970.

Holder, Preston. *The Hoe and the Horse on the Plains.* Lincoln: University of Nebraska Press, 1970.

Hollon, William Eugene. *The Great American Desert Then and Now.* New York: Oxford University Press, 1966.

———. *Frontier Violence: Another Look.* New York: Oxford University Press, 1974.

Hornung, Clarence P. *The Way it Was in the West.* New York: Smithmark, 1978.

Hough, Emerson. *The Story of the Cowboy.* New York: D. Appleton, 1897.

———. *Getting a Wrong Start: A Truthful Autobiography.* New York: Macmillan, 1915.

———. *North of 36.* New York: D. Appleton, 1923.

Howey, M. Oldfield. *The Horse in Magic and Myth.* London: Rider and Son, 1923.

Hoy, Jim. *Cowboys and Kansas: Stories from the Tallgrass Prairie.* Norman: University of Oklahoma Press, 1995.

Hughes, Stella. *Chuck Wagon Cookin'.* Tucson: University of Arizona Press, 1974.

———. *Hashknife Cowboy: Recollections of Mack Hughes.* Tucson: University of Arizona Press, 1984.

Humboldt, Alexander von, and Aimé Bonpland. *"Personal Narrative" of Travels to the Equinoctial Regions of the New Continent, During the Years 1799–1804.* 2d ed. Translated by Helen María Williams. London: Longman, Hurst, Rees, Orme, Brown, and Green, 1825.

Hunt, Frazier. *Horses and Heroes: The Story of the Horse in America for 450 Years.* New York: Scribner's Sons, 1949.

Hurtado, Albert L. "Parkmanizing the Spanish Borderlands: Bolton, Turner, and the Historians' World." *Western Historical Quarterly* 26, 2 (summer 1995): 149–68.

Hurtado, Albert L., and Peter J. Iverson, eds. *Major Problems in American Indian History.* Lexington, Mass.: D. C. Heath, 1994.

Hutchinson, William H. *The Life and Personal Writings of Eugene Manlove Rhodes, a Bar Cross Man.* Norman: University of Oklahoma Press, 1956.

Hutton, Paul Andrew. "Showdown at the Hollywood Corral: Wyatt Earp and the Movies." *Montana, The Magazine of Western History* 45, 3 (summer 1995): 2–31.

Ings, Frederick W. *Before the Fences: Tales from the Midway Ranch.* Calgary: McAra Printing, 1980.

Irons, William, and Neville Dyson-Hudson, eds. *Perspectives on Nomadism.* Leiden, England: Brill, 1972.

Isern, Thomas D. "Farmers, Ranchers, and Stockmen of the Flint Hills." *Western Historical Quarterly* 16, 3 (July 1985): 253–64.

Iverson, Peter. *The Navajos: A Critical Bibliography.* Bloomington: Indiana University Press, 1976.

———. "The Emerging Navajo Nation." In Alfonso Ortiz, ed., *Handbook of North American Indians. Vol. 10. Southwest.* Washington, D.C.: Smithsonian Institution, 1983.

———. *The Navajo Nation.* Westport, Conn.: Greenwood Press, 1981; Albuquerque: University of New Mexico Press, 1983.

———. *When Indians Became Cowboys: Native Peoples and Cattle Ranching in the American West.* Norman: University of Oklahoma Press, 1994.

———, ed. *The Plains Indians of the Twentieth Century.* Norman: University of Oklahoma Press, 1985.

Izard, Miguel. "Ni cuatreros ni montoneros: Llaneros." *Boletín Americanista* 31 (1981): 83–142.

———. "Oligarcas temblad, viva la libertad: Los llaneros de Apure y la Guerra Federal." *Boletín Americanista* 32 (1982): 227–77.

———. "Sin domicilio fijo, senda segura, ni destino conocido: Los llaneros del Apure a finales del período colonial." *Boletín Americanista* 33 (1983): 13–83.

———. "Mi coronel, hasta aquí le llegaron las matemáticas: Los llaneros del Apure." In Miguel Izard, comp., *Marginados, fronterizos, rebeldes y oprimidos.* 2 vols. Barcelona: Ediciones del Serbal, 1985.

Jablow, Joseph. *The Cheyenne in Plains Indian Trade Relations, 1795–1840*. New York: J. J. Augustin, 1951.

Jackson, Jack. *Los Mesteños: Spanish Ranching in Texas, 1721–1821*. College Station: Texas A&M University Press, 1986.

Jacobs, Wilbur R. *On Turner's Trail: 100 Years of Writing Western History*. Lawrence: University Press of Kansas, 1994.

James, Will. *Cowboys North and South*. 1924. Reprint, Missoula, Mont.: Mountain Press Publishing, 1995.

———. *The Drifting Cowboy*. 1925. Reprint, Missoula, Mont.: Mountain Press Publishing, 1995.

———. *Cow Country*. New York: Scribner's, 1927.

———. *Lone Cowboy: My Life Story*. New York: Scribner's Sons, 1930.

———. *Will James: The Spirit of the Cowboy*, ed. J. M. Neil. Casper, Wyo.: Nicolaysen Art Museum, 1985.

Jameson, Sheilagh. *Ranches, Cowboys, and Characters: The Birth of Alberta's Western Heritage*. Calgary: Glenbow Museum, 1987.

Jaques, Mary J. *Texan Ranch Life: With Three Months through Mexico in a Prairie Schooner*. 1896. Reprint, College Station: Texas A&M University Press, 1989.

Jennings, Francis. *The Invasion of America*. Chapel Hill: University of North Carolina Press, 1975.

Johnson, Michael L. *The New Westers: The West in Contemporary American Culture*. Lawrence: University Press of Kansas, 1996.

Johnston, Moira. *Ranch: Portrait of a Surviving Dream*. Garden City: Doubleday, 1983.

Johnstone, Iain. *Clint Eastwood: The Man With No Name*. New York: Quill/William Morrow, 1981.

Jones, J. Philip. *Gambling Yesterday and Today: A Complete History*. Newton Abbot, England: David and Charles, 1973.

Jones, Kristine L. "Indian-Creole Negotiations in the Southern Frontier." In Mark D. Szuchman and Jonathan C. Brown, eds., *Revolution and Restoration: The Rearrangement of Power in Argentina, 1776–1860*. Lincoln: University of Nebraska Press, 1994.

Jones, Oakah L., Jr. "Hispanic Traditions and Improvisations on the Frontera Septentrional of New Spain." *New Mexico Historical Review* 56, 4 (1981): 333–47.

———. *Nueva Vizcaya: Heartland of the Spanish Frontier.* Albuquerque: University of New Mexico Press, 1988.

Jones, Peter d'A. *Since Columbus: Pluralism and Poverty in the History of the Americas.* London: Heinemann, 1975.

Jordan, Roy A., and Tim R. Miller. "The Politics of a Cowboy Culture." *Annals of Wyoming* 52, 1 (spring 1980): 40–45.

Jordan, Teresa. *Cowgirls: Women of the American West.* New York: Anchor Books, 1982.

———, ed. *Graining the Mare: The Poetry of Ranch Women.* Salt Lake City: Peregrine Smith Books, 1994.

Jordan, Terry G. "The Origin of Anglo-American Cattle Ranching in Texas: A Documentation of Diffusion from the Lower South." *Economic Geography* 45 (January 1969): 63–87.

———. *Trails to Texas: Southern Roots of Western Cattle Ranching.* Lincoln: University of Nebraska Press, 1981.

———. *North American Cattle-Ranching Frontiers: Origins, Diffusion, and Differentiation.* Albuquerque: University of New Mexico Press, 1993.

Karr, Charles Lee, Jr., and Carol Robbins Karr. *Remington Handguns.* New York: Bonanza Books, 1960.

Katz, William Loren. *Black People Who Made the Old West.* New York: Crowell, 1977.

Katzman, Martin T. "The Brazilian Frontier in Comparative Perspective." *Comparative Studies in Society and History* 17, 3 (July 1975): 266–85.

Kelly, Leroy Victor. *The Range Men: The Story of the Ranchers and Indians of Alberta.* 1913. Reprint, New York: Argonaut Press, 1965.

Kelton, Elmer. *The Day the Cowboys Quit.* New York: Bantam, 1971.

Kesey, Ken. *Last Go Round.* New York: Viking, 1994.

Kiskaddon, Bruce. *Rhymes of the Ranges.* Edited by Hal Cannon. Salt Lake City: Peregrine Smith Books, 1987.

Klassen, Henry C. "The Conrads in the Alberta Cattle Business, 1875–1911." *Agricultural History* 64 (summer 1990): 31–59.

———. "Entrepreneurship in the Canadian West: The Enterprises of A. E. Cross, 1886–1920." *Western Historical Quarterly* 22, 3 (August 1991): 313–34.

Kristof, Ladis K. D. "The Nature of Frontiers and Boundaries." *Annals of the American Association of Geographers* 49, 3, pt. 1 (1959): 269–82.

Kroeber, Alfred L. *The Arapaho.* Lincoln: University of Nebraska Press, 1983.

Lago, Tomás. *El huaso.* Santiago: Universidad de Chile, 1953.

Lamar, Howard R. "Much to Celebrate: The Western History Association's Twenty-Fifth Birthday." *Western Historical Quarterly* 17, 4 (October 1986): 397–416.

———, ed. *The Reader's Encyclopedia of the American West.* New York: Crowell, 1977.

Lamar, Howard R., and Leonard Thompson, eds. *The Frontier in History: North America and South Africa Compared.* New Haven: Yale University Press, 1981.

Lamb, Gene. *Rodeo: Back of the Chutes.* Denver: Bell Press, 1956.

L'Amour, Louis. "The Cowboy: Reflections of a Western Writer." *Colorado Heritage* 1 (1981): 1–6.

Larkin, Margaret. *Singing Cowboy: A Book of Western Songs.* 1931. Reprint, New York: Da Capo Press, 1979.

Larson, T. A., comp. *Bill Nye's Western Humor.* Lincoln: University of Nebraska Press, 1968.

Lattimore, Owen. *Studies in Frontier History: Collected Papers, 1928–1958.* London: Oxford University Press, 1958.

Laune, Paul. *America's Quarter Horses.* Garden City: Doubleday, 1973.

Lavington, H. Dude. *Nine Lives of a Cowboy.* Victoria, B.C.: Sono Nis Press, 1982.

Lawrence, Elizabeth Atwood. *Rodeo: An Anthropologist Looks at the Wild and Tame.* Chicago: University of Chicago Press, 1984.

———. *Hoofbeats and Society: Studies of Human-Horse Interactions.* Bloomington: Indiana University Press, 1985.

Laxalt, Robert. "The Gauchos: Last of a Breed." *National Geographic* 158, 4 (October 1980): 478–501.

Lea, Tom. *The King Ranch*. Boston: Little, Brown, 1957.

LeCompte, Mary Lou. "The Hispanic Influence on the History of Rodeo, 1823–1922." *Journal of Sport History* 12, 1 (spring 1985): 21–38.

———. *Cowgirls of the Rodeo: Pioneer Professional Athletes*. Bloomington: Indiana University Press, 1993.

LeCompte, Mary Lou, and William H. Beezley. "Any Sunday in April: The Rise of Sport in San Antonio and the Hispanic Borderlands." *Journal of Sport History* 13, 2 (summer 1986): 128–46.

Lee, Katie. *Ten Thousand Goddam Cattle: A History of the American Cowboy in Song, Story, and Verse*. Rev. ed. Jerome, Arizona: Katydid Books and Records, 1985.

Lee, Lawrence B. *Reclaiming the American West: A Historiography and Guide*. Santa Barbara: ABC-CLIO Press, 1980.

LeGrand, Catherine. *Frontier Expansion and Peasant Protest in Colombia, 1850–1936*. Albuquerque: Qniversity of New Mexico Press, 1986.

Lenihan, John H. *Showdown: Confronting Modern America in the Western Film*. Urbana: University of Illinois Press, 1980.

Lewis, Archibald R., and Thomas F. McGann, eds. *The New World Looks at Its History*. Austin: University of Texas Press, 1966.

Lichtblau, Myron I. *The Argentine Novel in the Nineteenth Century*. New York: Hispanic Institute in the United States, 1959.

Limerick, Patricia Nelson. *The Legacy of Conquest: The Unbroken Past of the American West*. New York: W. W. Norton, 1987.

———. "Turnerians All: The Dream of a Helpful History in an Intelligible World." *American Historical Review* 100, 3 (June 1995): 697–716.

Limerick, Patricia Nelson, Clyde A. Milner II, and Charles E. Rankin, eds. *Trails: Toward a New Western History*. Lawrence: University Press of Kansas, 1991.

Lincoln, John. *Rich Grass and Sweet Water: Ranch Life with the Koch Matador Cattle Company*. College Station: Texas A&M University Press, 1989.

Liscano, Juan. *Rómulo Gallegos.* 2d ed. Mexico: Novano, 1970.

Logsdon, Guy. "Cowboy Poets." In Francis Edward Abernethy, ed., *Hoein' the Short Rows.* Fort Worth: South Methodist University Press, 1988.

———. *"The Whorehouse Bells Were Ringing" and Other Songs Cowboys Sing.* Urbana: University of Illinois Press, 1989.

Lomax, John Avery. *Songs of the Cattle Trail and Cow Camp.* London: T. F. Unwin, 1920.

Lomax, John Avery, and Alan Lomax, comps. *Cowboy Songs and Other Frontier Ballads.* New York: Macmillan, 1938.

Lombardi, Mary. "The Frontier in Brazilian History: An Historiographical Essay." *Pacific Historical Review* 44, 4 (November 1975): 437–57.

Long, Philip Sheridan. *The Great Canadian Range.* Toronto: Ryerson Press, 1963.

Loomis, Noel M. "Early Cattle Trails in Southern Arizona." *Arizoniana* 3, 4 (1962): 18–24.

Lopez, David E. "Cowboy Strikes and Unions." *Labor History* 18, 3 (summer 1977): 325–40.

Loveman, Brian. *Struggle in the Countryside: Politics and Rural Labor in Chile, 1919–1973.* Bloomington: Indiana University Press, 1976.

———. *Chile: The Legacy of Hispanic Capitalism.* 2d ed. New York: Oxford University Press, 1988.

Loy, Jane M. "Horsemen of the Tropics: A Comparative View of the Llaneros in the History of Venezuela and Colombia." *Boletín Americanista* 31 (1981): 159–71.

Luccetti, Cathy, and Carol Olwell. *Women of the West.* New York: Orion Books, 1982.

Lugones, Leopoldo. *El payador.* 4th ed. Buenos Aires: Huemul, 1972.

Lupton, Austin A. "Cattle Ranching in Alberta, 1874–1910: Its Evolution and Migration." *Albertan Geographer* 3 (1966): 48–58.

McCallum, Henry D., and Frances T. McCallum. *The Wire That Fenced the West.* Norman: University of Oklahoma Press, 1965.

McCoy, Joseph G. *Cattle Trade of the West and Southwest.* 1874. Reprint, n.p.: Readex Microprint, 1966.

McCracken, Harold. *Frederic Remington, Artist of the Old West.* Philadelphia: J. B. Lippincott, 1947.

———. *Great Painters and Illustrators of the Old West.* 1952. Reprint, New York: Dover, 1988.

———. *The Charles M. Russell Book.* Garden City: Doubleday, 1957.

———. *The Frederic Remington Book: A Pictorial History of the West.* Garden City: Doubleday, 1966.

———. *The American Cowboy.* Garden City: Doubleday, 1973.

McDonald, Archie P., ed. *Shooting Stars: Heroes and Heroines of Western Film.* Bloomington: Indiana University Press, 1987.

McDowell, Bart. *The American Cowboy in Life and Legend.* Washington, D.C.: National Geographic Society, 1972.

McDowell, R. Bruce. *Evolution of the Winchester.* Tacoma, Washington: Armory Publications, 1985.

MacEwan, John Walter Grant. *Blazing the Old Cattle Trail.* 1952. Reprint, Saskatoon: Western Producer Prairie Books, 1975.

———. *John Ware's Cattle Country.* Saskatoon: Western Producer Prairie Books, 1974.

McFadden, Cyra. *Rain or Shine : A Family Memoir.* New York: Knopf, 1986.

McGrath, Roger D. *Gunfighters, Highwaymen, and Vigilantes: Violence on the Frontier.* Berkeley: University of California Press, 1984.

Machado, Manuel A., Jr. *The North Mexican Cattle Industry, 1910–1975: Ideology, Conflict, and Change.* College Station: Texas A&M University Press, 1981.

Mackin, Bill. *Cowboy and Gunfighter Collectibles: A Photographic Encyclopedia with Price Guide and Markers Index.* Missoula, Mont.: Mountain Press Publishing, 1989.

McLoughlin, Denis. *Wild and Woolly: An Encyclopedia of the Old West.* Garden City: Doubleday, 1975.

McMurtry, Larry. *Lonesome Dove.* New York: Simon and Schuster, 1985.

McNeill, William. *The Great Frontier: Freedom and Hierarchy in Modern Times.* Princeton: Princeton University Press, 1983.

Macoun, John, ed. *Manitoba and the Great North West*. Guelph, Ont.: World Publishing, 1882.

McRae, Wallace. *Cowboy Curmudgeon and Other Poems*. Salt Lake City: Peregrine Smith Books, 1992.

Mails, Thomas E. *The Mystic Warriors of the Plains*. Garden City: Doubleday, 1972.

Malone, Michael P. "Beyond the Last Frontier: Toward a New Approach to Western American History." *Western Historical Quarterly* 20, 4 (November 1989): 409–28.

————, ed. *Historians and the American West*. Lincoln: University of Nebraska Press, 1983.

Mantilla Trejos, Eduardo. *Sobre los llanos*. Caracas: Fotomecánica Industrial, 1988.

Marks, Paula Mitchell. *Turn Your Eyes Toward Texas: Pioneers Sam and Mary Maverick*. College Station: Texas A&M University Press, 1989.

Markus, Kurt. *Buckaroo: Images from the Sagebrush Basin*. Boston: Little, Brown, 1987.

Marrin, Albert. *Cowboys, Indians, and Gunfighters: The Story of the Cattle Kingdom*. New York: Atheneum, 1993.

Marriott, Alice Lee. *Hell on Horses and Women*. 1953. Reprint, Norman: University of Oklahoma Press, 1993.

Marshall, Howard W., and Richard E. Ahlborn. *Buckaroos in Paradise: Cowboy Life in Northern Nevada*. Lincoln: University of Nebraska Press, 1981.

Martin, Phil, comp. *Coolin' Down: An Anthology of Contemporary Cowboy Poetry*. Tulsa: Guy Logsdon Books, 1992.

Martin, Russell. *Cowboy: The Enduring Myth of the Wild West*. New York: Stewart, Tabori, and Chang, 1983.

Martínez Estrada, Ezequiel. *Muerte y transfiguración de Martín Fierro*. 2 vols. Mexico City: Fonda de Cultura Económica, 1948.

————. *X-Ray of the Pampa*. Translated by Alain Swietlicki. Austin: University of Texas Press, 1971.

Matthews, Robert Paul. *Violencia rural en Venezuela, 1840–1858: Antecedentes socioeconómicas de la Guerra Federal*. Caracas: Monte Avila, 1977.

Mayer, John. "El llanero." *Atlantic Monthly* 3 (February 1859): 174–88.

Medicine Crow, Joseph. *From the Heart of the Crow Country: The Crow Indians' Own Stories*. New York: Orion Books, 1992.

Meinig, D. W. *Southwest: Three Peoples in Geographical Change, 1600–1970*. New York: Oxford, 1971.

Meldrum, Barbara Howard, ed. *Under the Sun: Myth and Realism in Western American Literature*. Troy, N.Y.: Whitson, 1985.

————. *Old West—New West: Centennial Essays*. Moscow: University of Idaho Press, 1993.

Mellen, Joan. *Big Bad Wolves: Masculinity in the American Film*. New York: Pantheon, 1977.

Mikesell, Marvin W. "Comparative Studies in Frontier History." *Annals of the Association of American Geographers* 50, 1 (1960): 62–74.

Miller, David Harry, and Jerome Steffen, eds. *The Frontier: Comparative Studies, Volume 1*. Norman: University of Oklahoma Press, 1977.

Miller, Leo O. *The Great Cowboy Stars of Movies and Television*. Westport, Conn.: Arlington House, 1979.

Miller, Nathan. *TR: A Life*. New York: William Morrow, 1992.

Miller, Robert Henry. *Reflections of a Black Cowboy*. Englewood Cliffs: Silver Burdett Press, 1991.

Milton, John R. *The Novel of the American West*. Lincoln: University of Nebraska Press, 1980.

Molinari, Ricardo Luis. *Biografía de la pampa: Cuatro siglos de historia del campo argentino*. Buenos Aires: Arte Gaglianone, 1988.

Monaghan, Jay, ed. *The Book of the American West*. New York: Bonanza Books, 1963.

Monroy, Douglas. *Thrown Among Strangers: The Making of Mexican Culture in Frontier California*. Berkeley: University of California Press, 1990.

Moody, Michael. "La fiesta huasa." *Américas* 38, 1 (January 1986): 20–24, 46.

————. "Rodeo is Hot—in Chile." *Persimmon Hill* 15, 3 (autumn 1987): 5–17.

———. "Rodeo in Mexico: Charros and Charreadas." *Persimmon Hill* 17, 1 (spring 1989): 49–55.

Moore, Arthur K. *The Frontier Mind.* Lexington: University of Kentucky Press, 1957.

Moore, Daniel G. *Log of a Twentieth-Century Cowboy.* Tucson: University of Arizona Press, 1965.

Moore, Ethel, and Chauncey O. Moore. *Ballads and Folk Songs of the Southwest: More than 600 Titles, Melodies, and Texts Collected in Oklahoma.* Norman: University of Oklahoma Press, 1964.

Mora, Carl J. *Mexican Cinema: Reflections of a Society, 1896–1980.* Berkeley: University of California Press, 1982.

Mora, Joseph J. *Trail Dust and Saddle Leather.* 1946. Reprint, Lincoln: University of Nebraska Press, 1973.

———. *Californios: The Saga of the Hard-Riding Vaqueros, America's First Cowboys.* Garden City: Doubleday, 1949.

Morrisey, Richard J. "The Early Range Cattle Industry in Arizona." *Agricultural History* 24, 3 (July 1950): 151–56.

———. "The Shaping of Two Frontiers." *Americas* 3, 1 (January 1951): 3–6, 41–42.

———. "The Northward Expansion of Cattle Raising in New Spain, 1550–1600." *Agricultural History* 25, 3 (July 1951): 115–21.

Morse, Richard, ed. *The Bandeirantes: The Historical Role of the Brazilian Pathfinders.* New York: Knopf, 1967.

Motolinia, Toribio. *History of the Indians of New Spain.* Washington, D.C.: Academy of American Franciscan History, 1951.

Mueller, Ellen Crago. *Calamity Jane.* Laramie, Wyo.: Jelm Mountain Press Publishing, 1981.

Mulroy, Kevin. *Freedom on the Border: The Seminole Maroons in Florida, the Indian Territory, Coahuila, and Texas.* Lubbock: Texas Tech University Press, 1993.

Murphey, Michael Martin. "How I Became a Singing Cowboy." *Cowboys & Indians* 2, 1 (spring 1994): 77–78.

———, comp. *Cowboys Songs.* Secaucus, N.J.: Warner Brothers, 1991.

Myres, Sandra L. "The Spanish Cattle Kingdom in the Province of Texas." *Texana* 4, 3 (fall 1966): 233–46.

————. *The Ranch in Spanish Texas, 1691–1800.* El Paso: Texas Western Press, 1969.

Nagler, Barney. *The American Horse.* New York: Macmillan, 1966.

Nash, Gerald D. *Creating the West: Historical Interpretations, 1890–1990.* Albuquerque: University of New Mexico Press, 1991.

————. "The Great Adventure: Western History, 1890–1990." *Western Historical Quarterly* 22, 1 (February 1991): 5–18.

Neel, Susan Rhoades. "A Place of Extremes: Nature, History, and the American West." *Western Historical Quarterly* 24, 4 (winter 1994): 489–506.

Nichols, David A. "Civilization over Savage: Frederick Jackson Turner and the Indian." *South Dakota History* 2 (fall 1972).

Nichols, Madaline Wallis. "The Spanish Horse of the Pampas." *American Anthropologist* 41 (1939): 119–29.

————. *The Gaucho: Cattle Hunter, Cavalryman, Ideal of Romance.* 1942. Reprint, New York: Gordian Press, 1968.

Noel, Thomas J. *The City and the Saloon: Denver, 1858–1916.* Lincoln: University of Nebraska Press, 1982.

Nolan, Frederick. *The Lincoln Country War: A Documentary History.* Norman: University of Oklahoma Press, 1992.

Nordyke, Lewis. *Cattle Empire: The Fabulous Story of the 3,000,000 Acre XIT.* New York: Morrow, 1949.

————. *Great Roundup: the Story of Texas and Southwestern Cowmen.* New York: Morrow, 1955.

Norman, James. *Charro: Mexican Horseman.* New York: Putnam's, 1969.

Nugent, Walter. "Frontiers and Empires in the Late Nineteenth Century." *Western Historical Quarterly* 20, 4 (November 1989): 393–408.

————. "Where is the American West? Report on a Survey." *Montana, The Magazine of Western History* 42, 3 (summer 1992): 2–23.

Null, Gary. *Black Hollywood: The Negro in Motion Pictures.* New York: Carol Publishing Group, 1975.

Nunis, Doyce B., Jr. *The Life of Tom Horn Revisited.* Arcadia, Calif.: The Westerners Los Angles Corral, 1992.

Ohrlin, Glenn. *The Hell-Bound Train: A Cowboy Songbook.* Urbana: University of Illinois Press, 1973.

Oliphant, J. Orin. *On the Cattle Ranges of the Oregon Country.* Seattle: University of Washington Press, 1968.

O'Neal, Bill. *Encyclopedia of Western Gunfighters.* Norman: University of Oklahoma Press, 1979.

O'Neil, Paul. *The End and the Myth.* Alexandria, Va.: Time-Life Books, 1979.

Ovalles, Victor Manuel. *El llanero: Estudio sobre su vida, sus costumbres, su carácter, y su poesía.* Caracas: Herrera Irigoyen, 1905.

Páez, Ramón. *Wild Scenes in South America, or Life in the Llanos of Venezuela.* New York: Charles Scribner, 1862.

Paladino Giménez, José M. *El gaucho: Reseña fotográfica, 1860–1930.* Buenos Aires: Palsa, 1971.

Paredes, Américo. *Folktales of Mexico.* University of Chicago Press, 1970.

———, ed. *A Texas-Mexican Cancionero: Folksongs of the Lower Border.* Urbana: University of Illinois Press, 1976.

Pattie, Jane. *Cowboy Spurs and Their Makers.* College Station: Texas A&M University Press, 1991.

Paul, Rodman W. *The Far West and the Great Plains in Transition.* New York: Harper and Row, 1988.

Paullada, Stephen. *Rawhide and Song: A Comparative Study of the Cattle Cultures of the Argentinian Pampa and North American Great Plains.* New York: Vantage Press, 1963.

Paxon, Frederic L. "A Generation of the Frontier Hypothesis: 1893–1932." *Pacific Historical Review* 2, 1 (March 1933): 34–51.

Payne, Darwin. *Owen Wister: Chronicler of the West, Gentleman of the East.* Dallas: Southern Methodist University Press, 1985.

Pearce, Ray Harvey. *The Savages of America: A Study of the Indian and the Idea of Civilization.* Baltimore: Johns Hopkins University Press, 1965.

Pendley, William Perry. *War on the West: Government Tyranny on America's Great Frontier.* Washington, D.C.: Regnery Publishing, 1995.

Pereira Salas, Eugenio. *Juegos y alegrías coloniales en Chile.* Santiago: Zig-Zag, 1947.

Perkins, David, and Norman Tanis. *Native Americans of North America: A Bibliography.* Metuchen, N.J.: Scarecrow Press, 1975.

Perry, Kenneth D., and Luanne Cullen. "The Cowboy: Balancing Fact and Fantasy in a Museum Project." *Curator* 25, 3 (1982): 213–22.

Petersen, Gwen. "Git Along Li'l Doggerels: Cowboys and Poetry." *Persimmon Hill* 16, 1 (spring 1988): 28–37.

Pevoto, Charlotte Wren. *Cattle Barons and the Mansions They Built in Texas, 1870–1905.* Monticello: Vance Bibliographies, 1984.

Phillips, David, and Robert Weinstein. *The Taming of the West: A Photographic Perspective.* Chicago: Henry Regnery, 1974.

Pike, Frederick B. *The United States and Latin America: Myths and Stereotypes of Civilization and Nature.* Austin: University of Texas Press, 1992.

Pingenot, Ben E. *Siringo: The True Story of Charles A. Siringo.* College Station: Texas A&M University Press, 1989.

Pinto, Luis C. *El gaucho y sus detractores: Defensa de las tradiciones argentinas; reivindicación del gaucho.* Buenos Aires: Ateneo, 1943.

———. *El gaucho rioplatense, frente a los malos historiadores.* Buenos Aires: Ciordia y Rodríguez, 1944.

Platt, D. C. M., and Guido Di Tella, eds. *Argentina, Australia, and Canada: Studies in Comparative Development, 1870–1965.* London: Macmillan, 1985.

Pointer, Larry. *Rodeo Champions: Eight Memorable Moments of Riding, Wrestling, and Roping.* Albuquerque: University of New Mexico Press, 1985.

Porter, Robert Ker. *Sir Robert Ker Porter's Caracas Diary, 1825–1842: A British Diplomat in a Newborn Nation.* Edited by Walter Dupuoy. Caracas: Dupuoy, 1966.

Powers, Bob. *Cowboy Country.* Glendale, Calif.: Arthur H. Clark, 1987.

Prado, Caio, Jr. *The Colonial Background of Modern Brazil.* Translated by Suzette Macedo. Berkeley: University of California Press, 1967.

Prado P., Uldaricio. *El caballo chileno, 1541 a 1914: Estudio zootécnico e histórico hípico.* Santiago: Imprenta Santiago, 1914.

Prettyman, W. S. *Indian Territory: A Frontier Photographic Record.* Norman: University of Oklahoma Press, 1957.

Rainbolt, Jo. *The Last Cowboy: Twilight Era of the Horseback Cowhand, 1900–1940.* Helena, Mont.: America and World Geographic Publications, 1992.

Ramírez, Nora E. "The Vaquero and Ranching in the Southwestern United States, 1600–1970." Ph.D. diss., Indiana University, 1979.

Randolph, Edmond. *Beef, Leather, and Grass.* Norman: University of Oklahoma Press, 1981.

Randolph, J. Ralph. *British Travelers among the Southern Indians, 1660–1763.* Norman: University of Oklahoma Press, 1973.

Rapoport, Mario, comp. *Economía e historia: Contribuciones a la historia económica argentina.* Buenos Aires: Editorial Tesis, 1988.

Rattenbury, Richard. *Packing Iron: Gunleather of the Frontier West.* Springfield, Ohio: Zon International Publishing, 1993.

Rausch, Jane M. *A Tropical Plains Frontier: The Llanos of Colombia, 1531–1831.* Albuquerque: University of New Mexico Press, 1984.

———. "Frontiers in Crisis: The Breakdown of the Missions in Far Northern Mexico and New Granada, 1821–1849." *Comparative Studies in Society and History* 29, 2 (1987): 340–59.

———. *The Llanos Frontier in Colombian History, 1830–1930.* Albuquerque: University of New Mexico Press, 1993.

Rector, Ray. *Cowboy Life on the Texas Plains: The Photographs of Ray Rector.* Edited by Margaret L. Rector. College Station: Texas A&M University Press, 1982.

Reese, William S. *Six Score: The 120 Best Books on the Range Cattle Industry.* Austin: Jenkins Publishing, 1976.

Reiter, Joan Swallow. *The Women*. Alexandria, Va.: Time-Life Books, 1978.

Remington, Frederic. *Pony Tracks*. 1895. Reprint, Norman: University of Oklahoma Press, 1961.

———. *Frederic Remington's Own West*. Edited by Harold McCracken. New York: Dial Press, 1960.

Remley, David. *Bell Ranch: Cattle Ranching in the Southwest, 1824–1947*. Albuquerque: University of New Mexico Press, 1993.

Reynolds, James. *A World of Horses*. New York: Creative Age Press, 1947.

Rhodes, Eugene Manlove. *Pasó Por Aquí*. Norman: University of Oklahoma Press, 1973.

———. *The Rhodes Reader: Stories of Virgins, Villains, and Varmints*. 2d ed. Selected by W. H. Hutchinson. Norman: University of Oklahoma Press, 1975.

Ridge, Martin. "Frederick Jackson Turner, Ray Allen Billington, and American Frontier History." *Western Historical Quarterly* 19, 1 (January 1988): 5–20.

———. "Frederick Jackson Turner and His Ghost: The Writing of Western History." In George Miles, ed. *Writing the History of the American West*. Worcester, Mass.: American Antiquarian Society, 1991.

———. "The Life of an Idea: The Significance of Frederick Jackson Turner's Frontier Thesis." *Montana, The Magazine of Western History* 41, 1 (winter 1991): 2–13.

———. *Atlas of American Frontiers*. Chicago: Rand McNally, 1993.

———. "Turner the Historian: A Long Shadow." *Journal of the Early Republic* 13, 2 (summer 1993): 133–44.

———. "Frederick Jackson Turner: His Broader Legacy." Paper presented to the State Historical Society of Wisconsin, Madison, November 12, 1993.

Rifkin, Jeremy. *Beyond Beef: The Rise and Fall of the Cattle Culture*. New York: Dutton, 1992.

Riley, Glenda. "Women in the West." *Journal of American Culture* 3, 2 (summer 1980): 311–29.

————. *A Place to Grow: Women in the American West*. Arlington Heights, Ill.: Harlan Davidson, 1992.

————. *The Life and Legacy of Annie Oakley*. Norman: University of Oklahoma Press, 1994.

————. "Annie Oakley: Creating the Cowgirl." *Montana, The Magazine of Western History* 45, 3 (summer 1995): 32–6.

Rincón Gallardo, Carlos. *El libro del charro mexicano*. 3d ed. Mexico City: Porrúa, 1960.

Rivas Sosa, Alejandro. *Nuestro ganado vacuno: La ganadería como fuente potential de requeza nacional*. Caracas: Elite, 1938.

Roach, Joyce Gibson. *The Cowgirls*. 2d ed. Denton: University of North Texas Press, 1990.

Robb, John Donald, ed. *Hispanic Folk Music of New Mexico and the Southwest*. Norman: University of Oklahoma, 1980.

Robbins, William G. "Western History: A Dialectic on the Modern Condition." *Western Historical Quarterly* 20, 4 (November 1989): 429–50.

————. *Colony and Empire: The Capitalist Transformation of the American West*. Lawrence: University Press of Kansas, 1994.

Rodríguez Molas, Ricardo. *Historia social del gaucho*. Buenos Aires: Marú, 1968.

Roe, Frank Gilbert. "Remittance Men." *Alberta Historical Review* 2, 1 (January 1954): 3–12.

————. *The Indian and the Horse*. Norman: University of Oklahoma Press, 1955.

Rogin, Michael P. *Ronald Reagan, the Movie and Other Episodes in Political Demonology*. Berkeley: University of California Press, 1987.

Rojas, Arnold R. *The Vaquero*. Charlotte, N.C.: McNally and Loftin, 1964.

Rojas, Ricardo. *Historia de la literatura argentina: Ensayo filosófico sobre la evolución de la cultura en el Plata*. 4 vols. Buenos Aires: Coni, 1917–1922.

Rollins, Philip Ashton. *The Cowboy: An Unconventional History of Civilization on the Old-Time Range*. 1922. Reprint, Albuquerque: University of New Mexico Press, 1979.

————. *Jinglebob: A True Story of a Real Cowboy*. New York: Grosset and Dunlap, 1927.

Rollinson, John K. *Wyoming Cattle Trails: History of the Migration of Oregon-Raised Herds to Mid-Western Markets*. Caldwell, Idaho: Caxton Printers, 1948.

Ronda, Jeanne, and Richard W. Slatta. "Cowboying at the Chapman-Barnard Ranch." *Persimmon Hill* 21, 1 (spring 1993): 36–41.

Roosevelt, Theodore. *Ranch Life and the Hunting-Trail*. New York: St. Martin's Press, 1985.

Rosa, Joseph G. *The Gunfighter: Man or Myth?* Norman: University of Oklahoma Press, 1969.

Rosa, Joseph G., and Robin May. *Buffalo Bill and His Wild West: A Pictorial Biography*. Lawrence: University Press of Kansas, 1989.

Rosenau, Pauline Marie. *Post-Modernism and the Social Sciences: The Insights, Inroads, and Intrusions*. Princeton: Princeton University Press, 1992.

Rosenberg, Bruce A. *The Code of the West*. Bloomington: Indiana University Press, 1982.

Rosti, Pál. *Memorias de un viaje por Amé*rica. Translated by Judith Sarosi. 1861. Reprint, Caracas: Universidad Central de Venezuela, 1968.

Rouse, John E. *World Cattle*. Norman: University of Oklahoma Press, 1970.

Russell, Charles Marion. *Trails Plowed Under*. Garden City: Doubleday, 1927.

————. *Good Medicine: The Illustrated Letters of Charles M. Russell*. Garden City: Doubleday, 1929.

Russell, Don. *The Lives and Legends of Buffalo Bill*. Norman: University of Oklahoma Press, 1960.

————. *The Wild West: A History of the Wild West Shows*. Fort Worth: Amon Carter Museum, 1970.

Ruth, Kent. *Landmarks of the West: A Guide to Historic Sites*. 1963. Reprint, Lincoln: University of Nebraska Press, 1986.

Rutherford, Michael. *The American Cowboy: Tribute to a Vanishing Breed*. New York: Gallery Books, 1990.

Ryan, Kathleen Jo. *Ranching Traditions: Legacy of the American West.* New York: Abbeville Press, 1990.

Sachs, Karl. *De los llanos: Descripción de un viaje de ciencias naturales a Venezuela.* Translated by José Izquierdo. 1878. Reprint, Caracas and Madrid: Edime, 1955.

Sackett, Samuel John. *Cowboys and the Songs They Sang.* New York: William R. Scott, 1967.

Saeger, James Schofield. "Another View of the Mission as a Frontier Institution: The Guaycuruan Reductions of Santa Fe, 1743–1810." *Hispanic American Historical Review* 65, 3 (1985): 493–517.

Sáenz Quesada, María. *Los estancieros.* Buenos Aires: Belgrano, 1980.

St. John, Bob. *On Down the Road: The World of the Rodeo Cowboy.* Englewood Cliffs: Prentice-Hall, 1977.

Sambrano Urdaneta, Oscar. *El llanero: Un problema de crítica literaria.* Caracas: Cuadernos Literarios, 1952.

Samper, José María. *Ensayo sobre las revoluciones políticas y la condición social de las repúblicas colombianos.* Paris: Thurnot, 1861.

Samuels, Peggy, and Harold Samuels. *Frederic Remington: A Biography.* Garden City: Doubleday, 1982.

San Diego Museum of Art. *The Cowboy.* San Diego: San Diego Museum of Art, 1981.

Sandoz, Mari. *Old Jules.* Boston: Little, Brown, 1935.

———. *The Cattlemen from the Rio Grande Across the Far Marias.* 1958. Reprint, Lincoln: University of Nebraska Press, 1978.

Sands, Kathleen M. *Charrería Mexicana: An Equestrian Folk Tradition.* Tucson: University of Arizona Press, 1993.

Santee, Ross. *Men and Horses.* 1926. Reprint, Lincoln: University of Nebraska Press, 1977.

———. *Cowboy.* 1928. Reprint, Lincoln: University of Nebraska Press, 1977.

———. *Lost Pony Tracks.* New York: Scribner's, 1953.

Sarmiento, Domingo F. *Life in the Argentine Republic in the Days of the Tyrants; or, Civilization and Barbarism.* Translated by Mrs. Horace [Mary] Mann. 1845. Reprint, New York: Hafner, 1971.

Saubidet, Tito. *Vocabulario y refranero criollo*. 7th ed. Buenos Aires: Rafael Palumbo, 1975.

Savage, W. Sherman. *Blacks in the West*. Westport, Conn.: Greenwood Press, 1976.

Savage, William W., Jr. *The Cowboy Hero: His Image in American History and Culture*. Norman: University of Oklahoma Press, 1979.

———. "What You'd Like the World to Be: The West and the American Mind." *Journal of American Culture* 3, 2 (summer 1980): 302–10.

———, ed. *Cowboy Life: Reconstructing an American Myth*. Norman: University of Oklahoma Press, 1975.

———, ed. *Indian Life: Transforming an American Myth*. Norman: University of Oklahoma Press, 1977.

Savage, William W., Jr., and Stephen I. Thompson, eds. *The Frontier: Comparative Studies, Volume 2*. Norman: University of Oklahoma Press, 1979.

Savitt, Sam. *Rodeo: Cowboys, Bulls, and Broncs*. Garden City: Doubleday, 1963.

Sawey, Orlan. *Charles A. Siringo*. Boston: Twayne Publishers, 1981.

Seemann, Charlie, prod. *Back in the Saddle Again*. New York: New World Records, 1983. Sound recording NW314, 315.

Seidman, Laurence Ivan. *Once in the Saddle: The Cowboy's Frontier, 1866–1896*. New York: Knopf, 1973.

Sell, Henry Blackman, and Victor Weybright. *Buffalo Bill and the Wild West*. New York: Oxford University Press, 1955.

Serven, James E. *Conquering the Frontiers: Stories of American Pioneers and the Guns Which Helped Them Establish a New Life*. La Habra, Calif.: Foundation Press, 1974.

———. *200 Years of American Firearms*. Chicago: Follett Publishing, 1975.

———. *Colt Firearms Since 1836*. Harrisburg, Pa.: Stackpole Books, 1979.

Sharp, Paul F. "The American Farmer and the 'Last Best West,'" *Agricultural History* 21, 2 (April 1947): 65–75.

———. "Three Frontiers: Some Comparative Studies of Canadian, American, and Australian Settlement." *Pacific Historical Review* 24, 4 (1955): 369–77.

———. *Whoop-Up Country: The Canadian-American West, 1865–1885*. Helena, Mont.: Historical Society of Montana, 1962.

Shirley, Glen. *Pawnee Bill: A Biography of Major Gordon W. Lillie*. Albuquerque: University of New Mexico, 1958.

Simons, Helen, and Cathryn A. Hoyt, eds. *Hispanic Texas: A Historical Guide*. Austin: University of Texas Press, 1992.

Siringo, Charles A. *A Texas Cowboy: or, Fifteen Years on the Hurricane Deck of a Spanish Pony, Taken from Real Life*. 1885. Reprint, Lincoln: University of Nebraska Press, 1950.

Skaggs, Jimmy M. *The Cattle-Trailing Industry: Between Supply and Demand, 1866–1890*. 1973. Norman: University of Oklahoma Press, 1991.

———. *Prime Cut: Livestock Raising and Meatpacking in the United States, 1607–1983*. College Station: Texas A&M University Press, 1986.

Slatta, Richard W. *Gauchos and the Vanishing Frontier*. Lincoln: University of Nebraska Press, 1983. Rev. ed., 1992.

———. "The Gaucho in Argentina's Quest for National Identity." *Canadian Review of Studies in Nationalism* 12, 1 (1985): 99–122. Reprinted in David J. Weber and Jane M. Rausch, eds. *Where Cultures Meet: Frontiers in Latin American History*. Wilmington, Del.: Scholarly Resources, 1994.

———. "The Demise of the Gaucho and the Rise of Equestrian Sport in Argentina." *Journal of Sport History* 13, 2 (summer 1986): 97–110.

———. "'Civilization' Battles 'Barbarism': Argentine Frontier Strategies, 1516–1880." *Inter-American Review of Bibliography* 39, 2 (1989): 177–94.

———. *Cowboys of the Americas*. New Haven: Yale University Press, 1990.

———. *The Cowboy Encyclopedia*. Santa Barbara: ABC-CLIO Press, 1994; New York: W. W. Norton, 1996.

————. "In Their Own Words: Cowboy Memoirs." *Cowboys & Indians* 2, 1 (spring 1994): 45–50.

————. "Roots of Rodeo." *Cowboys & Indians* 2, 1 (spring 1994): 18–22.

————. "Modern Cowboy Minstrel: Michael Martin Murphey." *Western Styles* 2, 4 (August 1994): 28–34.

————. "Saloon Life in the Old West." *Cowboys & Indians* 2, 3 (fall 1994): 32–42.

————. "America's Breed: The Quarter Horse." *Cowboys & Indians* 3, 1 (spring 1995): 20–27.

————. "Regulators of the Old West." *Cowboys & Indians* 3, 1 (spring 1995): 10–18.

————. Foreword to *Working Cowboy: Recollections of Ray Holmes*, by Margot Liberty and Barry Head. Norman: University of Oklahoma Press, 1995.

————, ed. *Bandidos: The Varieties of Latin American Banditry*. Westport, Conn.: Greenwood Press, 1987.

Slatta, Richard W., and Arturo Alvarez d'Armas. "El llanero y el hato venezolano: Aportes bibliográficos." *South Eastern Latin Americanist* 29, 2–3 (September 1985): 33–41.

Slatta, Richard W., and Corinne Frist Glover. "The Indian and the Horse." *Cowboys & Indians* 2, 2 (summer 1994): 48–54.

Slatta, Richard W., and Mark Mayer. "The Sound of the West: A Cowboy's Spurs." *Cowboys & Indians* 3, 2 (summer 1995): 10–18.

Slotkin, Richard. *The Fatal Environment: The Myth of the Frontier in the Age of Industrialization, 1800–1890*. New York: Atheneum, 1985.

————. *Gunfighter Nation: The Myth of the West in Twentieth-Century America*. New York: Atheneum, 1992.

Smith, Dwight L., ed. *The American and Canadian West: A Bibliography*. Santa Barbara: ABC-CLIO Press, 1979.

Smith, Erwin Evans. *Life on the Texas Range*. Austin: University of Texas Press, 1952.

Solberg, Carl E. "A Discriminatory Frontier Land Policy: Chile, 1870–1914." *The Americas* 26, 2 (October 1969): 115–33.

————. *Immigration and Nationalism: Argentina and Chile, 1890–1914*. Austin: University of Texas Press, 1970.

————. *The Pampas and the Prairies: Agrarian Policy in Canada and Argentina, 1880–1930*. Stanford: Stanford University Press, 1987.

Somora, Julian, Joe Bernal, and Albert Peña. *Gunpowder Justice: A Reassessment of the Texas Rangers*. Notre Dame: University of Notre Dame Press, 1979.

Spicer, Edward H. *Cycles of Conquest: The Impact of Spain, Mexico, and the United States on the Indians of the Southwest, 1533–1960*. Tucson: University of Arizona Press, 1962.

Stands in Timber, John. *Cheyenne Memories*. New Haven: Yale University Press, 1967.

Stearns, Peter N., ed. *Encyclopedia of Social History*. New York: Garland, 1994.

Steffen, Jerome O. *Comparative Frontiers: A Proposal for Studying the American West*. Norman: University of Oklahoma Press, 1980.

————, ed. *The American West: New Perspectives, New Dimensions*. Norman: University of Oklahoma Press, 1979.

Stegner, Wallace. *Wolf Willow: A History, a Story, and a Memory of the Last Plains Frontier*. 1955. Reprint, Toronto: Macmillan, 1977.

Stegner, Wallace, and Richard W. Etulain. *Conversations with Wallace Stegner on Western History and Literature*. Salt Lake City: University of Utah Press, 1990.

Stern, Peter, and Robert H. Jackson. "*Vagabundaje* and Settlement in Colonial Northern Sonora." *The Americas* 44, 4 (1988): 461–81.

Stewart, Elinore Pruitt. *Letters of a Woman Homesteader*. Boston: Houghton Mifflin, 1942.

Stewart, Janet Ann. *Arizona Ranch Houses: Southern Territorial Styles, 1867–1900*. Tucson: University of Arizona Press, 1974; Arizona Historical Society, 1987.

Stoeltje, Beverly J. "Rodeo: From Custom to Ritual." *Western Folklore* 48, 3 (1989): 244–55.

Stong, Philip Duffield. *Horses and Americans*. New York: Frederick A. Stokes, 1939.

Stuart, Granville. *Forty Years on the Frontier*, vol. 2 of *Pioneering in Montana: The Making of a State, 1864–1887*. 1925. Reprint, Lincoln: University of Nebraska Press, 1977.

Sullivan, Tom R. *Cowboys and Caudillos: Frontier Ideology of the Americas*. Bowling Green: Bowling Green State University Popular Press, 1990.

Szuchman, Mark D. "From Imperial Hinterland to Growth Pole: Revolution, Change, and Restoration in the Río de la Plata." In Mark D. Szuchman and Jonathan C. Brown, eds., *Revolution and Restoration: The Rearrangement of Power in Argentina, 1776–1860*. Lincoln: University of Nebraska Press, 1994.

Taft, Robert. *Artists and Illustrators of the Old West, 1850–1900*. 1953. Reprint, Princeton: Princeton University Press, 1982.

Tanner, Ogden. *The Ranchers*. Alexandria, Va.: Time-Life Books, 1977.

Tapson, Alfred J. "Indian Warfare on the Pampa During the Colonial Period." *Hispanic American Historical Review* 42 (February 1962): 1–28.

Taylor, Lonn, and Ingrid Maar. *The American Cowboy*. New York: Harper and Row, 1983.

Taylor, Louis. *The Horse America Made: The Story of the American Saddle Horse*. New York: Harper, 1961.

———. *Harper's Encyclopedia for Horsemen: The Complete Book of the Horse*. New York: Harper and Row, 1973.

Tenenbaum, Barbara A., ed. *Encyclopedia of Latin American History*. 5 vols. New York: Scribners, 1995.

Texas Cowboy Artists Association. *The Texas Cowboy*. Fort Worth: Texas Christian University Press, 1986.

Thomas, Lewis H. *The Prairie West to 1905: A Canadian Sourcebook*. Toronto: Oxford University Press, 1975.

———, ed. *Essays on Western History in Honour of Lewis Gwynne Thomas*. Edmonton: University of Alberta Press, 1976.

Thomas, Tony. *The West That Never Was*. New York: Citadel Press, 1989.

Thorp, N(athan) Howard ("Jack"), comp. *Songs of the Cowboys*. 1908. Reprint, Lincoln: University of Nebraska Press, 1984.

———. *Pardner of the Wind: Story of the Southwestern Cowboy*. Lincoln: University of Nebraska Press, 1972.

Thrapp, Dan L., ed. *Encyclopedia of Frontier Biography*. 4 vols. Lincoln: University of Nebraska Press, 1988; CD-ROM edition, 1994.

Timmons, William. *Twilight on the Range: Recollections of a Latterday Cowboy*. Austin: University of Texas Press, 1962.

Tinkelman, Murray. *Little Britches Rodeo*. New York: Greenwillow Books, 1985.

Tinker, Edward Larocque. *Centaurs of Many Lands*. London: J. A. Allen, 1964.

———. *The Horsemen of the Americas and the Literature They Inspired*. 1952. Rev. ed. Austin: University of Texas Press, 1967.

Tinsley, Jim Bob. *He Was Singin' This Song*. Orlando: University Presses of Florida, 1981.

———. *For a Cowboy Has to Sing*. Orlando: University of Central Florida Press, 1991.

Torrey, Volta. *Windcatchers*. Brattleboro, Vt.: Stephen Greene Press, 1976.

Towne, Charles W., and Edward N. Wentworth. *Cattle and Men*. Norman: University of Oklahoma Press, 1955.

Tozer, Basil. *The Horse in History*. London: Methuen, 1908.

Tractman, Paul. *The Gunfighters*. New York: Time-Life Books, 1974.

Trimble, Stephen. *The People: Indians of the American Southwest*. Santa Fe: School of American Research Press, 1993.

Truettner, William H., ed. *The West as America: Reinterpreting Images of the Frontier, 1820–1920*. Washington, D.C.: Smithsonian Institution Press, 1991.

Turney-High, Harry. "The Diffusion of the Horse to the Flatheads." *Man* 35 (December 1935): 183–85.

Tuska, Jon. *The Filming of the West.* Garden City: Doubleday, 1976.
———. *The American West in Film: Critical Approaches to the Western.* Westport, Conn.: Greenwood, 1985.
———. *A Variable Harvest: Essays and Reviews of Film and Literature.* Jefferson, N.C.: McFarland, 1990.
Tuska, Jon, and Vicki Piekarski. *Encyclopedia of Frontier and Western Fiction.* New York: McGraw-Hill, 1983.
———, eds. *The Frontier Experience: A Reader's Guide to the Life and Literature of the American West.* Jefferson, N.C.: McFarland, 1984.
Tyler, Ronnie C. *American Frontier Life: Early Western Painting and Prints.* Fort Worth: Amon Carter Museum, 1987.
———. *Prints of the West.* Golden, Colo.: Fulcrum, 1994.
Urbaneja Achelpohl, Luis Manuel. *El gaucho y el llanero.* Caracas: Elite, 1926.
Utley, Robert M. "The Range Cattle Industry in the Big Bend of Texas." *Southwestern Historical Quarterly* 69 (1965): 419–41.
Vallenilla Lanz, Laureano. *Disgregación e integración: Ensayo sobre la formación de la nacionalidad venezolana.* 2 vols. Caracas: Tipografía Universal, 1930.
Van Deventer, M. J. "Chaps: From Batwings to Woolies." *Cowboys & Indians* 1, 3 (winter 1993): 18–22.
———. "The Cowboy Hat." *Cowboys & Indians* 2, 1 (spring 1994): 10–16.
———. "The Story of Wrangler." *Cowboys & Indians* 2, 1 (spring 1994): 56–62.
Vannoy-Rhoades, Cynthia. *Seasons on a Ranch.* Boulder: Pruett, 1986.
Vernam, Glenn R. *Man on Horseback: The Story of the Mounted Man from the Scythians to the American Cowboy.* Lincoln: University of Nebraska Press, 1964.
———. *The Rawhide Years: A History of the Cattlemen and the Cattle Country.* Garden City: Doubleday, 1976.
Vonada, Damaine. "Annie Oakley was More Than 'A Crack Shot' in Petticoats." *Smithsonian* 21, 6 (1990): 131–48.
Wagner, James. "Cowboy: Origin and Early Use of the Term." *West Texas Historical Association Year Book* 63 (1987): 91–100.

Wagoner, Junior Jean. *History of the Cattle Industry in Southern Arizona, 1540–1940.* Tucson: University of Arizona Press, 1952.

Walker, Don D., ed. *Clio's Cowboys: Studies in the Historiography of the Cattle Trade.* Lincoln: University of Nebraska Press, 1981.

Wallace, Ernest. *The Comanches: Lords of the South Plains.* Norman: University of Oklahoma Press, 1952.

Ward, Fay E. *The Cowboy at Work.* Norman: University of Oklahoma Press, 1958.

Watts, Peter. *A Dictionary of the Old West, 1850–1900.* New York: Knopf, 1977.

Webb, Walter Prescott. *The Great Frontier.* Austin: University of Texas Press, 1951.

———. *The Great Plains.* New York: Grosset and Dunlap, 1957.

———. *The Texas Rangers.* Austin: University of Texas Press, 1965.

Weber, David J. "Mexico's Far Northern Frontier, 1821–1854: Historiography Askew." *Western Historical Quarterly* 7, 3 (July 1976): 279–93.

———. *The Mexican Frontier, 1821–1846: The American Southwest Under Mexico.* Albuquerque: University of New Mexico Press, 1982.

———. "Turner, the Boltonians, and the Borderlands," *American Historical Review* 91, 1 (February 1986): 66–81.

———. *The Spanish Frontier in North America.* New Haven: Yale University Press, 1992.

———. "The Spanish Legacy in North America and the Historical Imagination." *Western Historical Quarterly* 23, 1 (February 1992): 5–24.

Weber, David J., and Jane M. Rausch, eds. *Where Cultures Meet: Frontiers in Latin American History.* Wilmington, Del.: Scholarly Resources, 1994.

Weir, Thomas R. *Ranching in the Southern Interior Plateau of British Columbia.* Ottawa: Queen's Printer, 1964.

West, Elliott. *The Saloon of the Rocky Mountain Mining Frontier.* Lincoln: University of Nebraska Press, 1979.

Westermeier, Clifford P., ed. *Trailing the Cowboy: His Life and Lore as Told by Frontier Journalists*. Caldwell, Idaho: Caxton Printers, 1955.

Weston, Jack. *The Real American Cowboy*. New York: Schocken Books, 1985.

White, G. Edward. *The Eastern Establishment and the Western Experience: The West of Frederic Remington, Theodore Roosevelt, and Owen Wister*. New Haven: Yale University Press, 1968.

White, John I. "A Montana Cowboy Poet." *Journal of American Folklore* 80 (July 1967): 113–29.

———. *Git Along, Little Dogies: Songs and Songmakers of the American West*. Urbana: University of Illinois Press, 1975.

White, Richard. *"It's Your Misfortune and None of My Own": A New History of the American West*. Norman: University of Oklahoma Press, 1991.

Widmark, Ann Heath, ed. *Between Earth and Sky: Poets of the Cowboy West*. New York: Norton, 1995.

Wilbur-Cruce, Eva Antonia. "Indian Country." *Journal of Arizona History* 26, 4 (1985): 351–74.

Williams Alzaga, Enrique. *La Pampa en la novela argentina*. Buenos Aires: Estrada Editores, 1955.

Wissler, Clark. "The Riding Gear of the North American Indians." *Anthropological Papers of the American Museum of Natural History* 17 (1911): 1–38.

———. "The Influence of the Horse in the Development of Plains Culture." *American Anthropologist* 16, 1 (1914): 1–25.

Wittliff, William D. *Vaquero: Genesis of the Texas Cowboy*. San Antonio: Institute of Texan Cultures, 1972.

Wolfskill, George, and Stanley Palmer, eds. *Essay on Frontiers in World History*. College Station: Texas A&M University Press for the University of Texas at Arlington, 1983.

Wood-Clark, Sarah. *Women of the Wild West Shows: Beautiful, Daring Western Girls*. Cody, Wyo.: Buffalo Bill Historical Center, 1991.

Woods, Lawrence M. *British Gentlemen in the Wild West: The Era of the Intensely English Cowboy*. New York: Free Press, 1989.

Worcester, Don. "The Spread of Spanish Horses in the Southwest." *New Mexico Historical Review* 19 (1944): 225–32.

———. "Spanish Horses among the Plains Tribes." *Pacific Historical Review* 14 (1945): 409–17.

———. *The Spanish Mustang: From the Plains of Andalusia to the Prairies of Texas.* El Paso: Texas Western Press, 1986.

Work, James C., ed. *Prose and Poetry of the American West.* Lincoln: University of Nebraska Press, 1990.

Worster, Donald E. "The Significance of the Spanish Borderlands to the United States." *Western Historical Quarterly* 7, 1 (January 1976): 5–18.

———. "New West, True West: Interpreting the Region's History." *Western Historical Quarterly* 18, 2 (April 1987): 141–56.

Wrobel, David M. *The End of American Exceptionalism: Frontier Anxiety from the Old West to the New Deal.* Lawrence: University Press of Kansas, 1993.

Wunder, John R., ed. *At Home on the Range: Essays on the History of Western Social and Domestic Life.* Westport, Conn.: Greenwood Press, 1985.

Wylder, Delbert E. *Emerson Hough.* Boston: Twayne, 1981.

Wyman, Walker D. *The Wild Horse of the West.* Caldwell, Idaho: Caxton Printers, 1945.

Wyman, Walker D., and Clifton B. Kroeber, eds. *The Frontier in Perspective.* Madison: University of Wisconsin Press, 1957.

Young, James Albert. *Cattle in the Cold Desert.* Logan: Utah State University Press, 1985.

Young, Mary. "The West and American Cultural Identity: Old Themes and New Variations." *Western Historical Quarterly* 1, 2 (April 1970): 137–60.

Index